Muhammad

the
messenger
of god

Betty Kelen

TAYLOR PRODU

NEW YO

D1115193

MUHAMMAD: The Messenger of God
Copyright © 1975, 1989, 2001 by Betty Kelen
All rights reserved. No part of this publication may be reproduced or trasmitted in any form or
by any means, electronic or mechanical, including photocopy, recording, or any information
storage and retrieval system now known or to be invented, without permission in writing from
the publisher, except by a reviewer who wishes to quote brief passages in connection with a
review written for inclusion in a magazine, newspaper, or broadcast.

Printed in the United States of America
For information, address GRM Associates, Inc., 290 West End Avenue, New York, NY 10023
Telephone 212-874-5964

ISBN 0-929098-12-7

TABLE OF CONTENTS

Foreword

Mecca

The House of God	3
The Orphan	8
Muhammad the Trusty	13
The Call	20
The Mission	28
Opposition	36
Persecution	44
Emigration	52

Medina

The Constitution of Medina	63
The Beginning of the Umma	69
The People of the Book	75
The Battle of Badr	81

After Badr: Ruin to the Qaynuqa   90
The Battle of Uhud   95
After Uhud: Farewell to the An-Nadi   102
Crooked Ribs   106
The Battle of the Ditch: Death to the Qurayza   116
The Pledge Under the Tree   124
Khaybar and the Road North   131
Home to Mecca   141

Islam

The Battle of Hunayn   153
The Pillars of Islam   160
Muhammad and His Flock   174
The Death of Muhammad   180

Appendix:
  Muhammad's Wives   189
  Bibliography   191

Index   193

Foreword

There are patterns in the immense embroideries of history that may seem to bear a resemblance to one another and yet, on examination, are seen to be stitched with quite different threads. We cannot draw a comparison between the ancient arguments of Muhammad and the rabbis of Medina and those that today separate Jews and Arabs. The underlying animosities are not at all the same. Muhammad had a mystical revelation that he believed marked him as a prophet in the line of Moses and the Hebrew prophets. The Jews acted to defend, as they always have, the authority of their revealed Scriptures. They looked at him with the same caution that the Church today employs toward candidates for canonization, and they turned him down.

Muhammad and the rabbis lived in Byzantine times, when an immense Christian civilization was tearing itself to pieces in religious dissensions that seem to us now to be altogether foolish. The word jihad is Arabic, but holy wars and holy massacres were Byzantine. When Muhammad with vigorous dispute, and later with murder and mayhem, pitted himself against Jews, Christians, and pagan Arabs, he was behaving like a man of his time—taking strong measures to correct as speedily as possible people's wrong attitudes about God. He did not know any better than the Hebrew prophets or the Christian fathers that Judgment Day was still a good many centuries off.

Of mankind's greatest religious teachers, Muhammad is the closest to us in time. The traditions that record his life, deeds, and conversations were written by scholars with almost modern historical consciences. The events related in this book are based largely on the account of the "traditionist" Ibn Ishaq, whose information came from the sons and grandsons of people who had known Muhammad or his close associates, and he meticulously recorded the names and genealogy of every informant. Although it is obvious that some fabrications have crept into his account and those of the other traditionists, the mortal shape of the Prophet still arises from them more clearly than we can ever discern Moses, Christ, or Gautama Buddha.

Moreover these traditions reveal to us very accurately the life of Arabia in the seventh century after Christ, and it is here we see a parallel between Muhammad's times and our own that is far more significant than any political accident. It is the psychic crack that strikes now and then between generations, a seismic disturbance in time as it sweeps on. We call it the generation gap. Such a withdrawal between a parent generation and its offspring happened in Buddha's day, when boys of the upper middle class chose to leave their comfortable homes to become monks and beggars. "I thought," says Buddha in a very old account of his life, "oppressive is life in a house, a place of dust . . . while yet a boy, a black-haired lad in the prime of youth, in the first stage of my life, while my unwilling mother and father wept with tear-stained faces, I cut off my hair and beard and went forth from a house to a houseless life."

Except for a reversed ceremony with hair and beard, the scene could have happened today.

Christ also left His home abruptly, and He said, "Think not that I am come to send peace on earth: I came not to send peace, but a sword. For I am come to set a man at variance against his father, and the daughter against her mother, and the daughter-in-law against her mother-in-law" (Matt. 10:34-35).

The gap struck quite recently, some decades before the Russian revolution, when the children of aristocrats and serfs left their homes to become a horde of radical philosophers, even violent assassins and bomb throwers—the Nihilists.

Such breaks with tradition herald profound social change, heady to the young but painful to the old, who feel their lives nullified. Once the spasm has passed, the dry historical record takes hardly any notice of it, as if insensible to the emotions once aroused. Yet, whenever we read of a battle fought by Muhammad and his little band of Muslims against overwhelming odds, we may imagine those small forces composed of youths, runaways, facing older men suddenly faint-hearted and sorry that they had come to slay their own young. Again and again, the story of Muhammad's life shows us evidence of this profound division, of which he was a reflection as well as a leader. When a Meccan hero spanned the ditch at Medina, and Ali, in his twenties, came from the Muslim ranks to meet him in combat, the older man called out, "Stand away, son of my brother, send forth someone older than you, for I don't want to kill you."

Ali said, "But I want to kill you!" And he did.

Muhammad just as ruthlessly cut his folk away from the primitive past and set them on a path that is still well marked and serviceable for modern times. He was not young when he did this but middle-aged. It is unfair to judge him, as Western scholars have often done, against the values of the later world he helped to create instead of the one in which he grew up. Despite what the rabbis of Medina said, he was an Old Testament figure, whether one sees him as prophet or patriarch.

Perhaps now that we have come so far along the road toward Judgment Day, we can look at Muhammad with simple wonder that such a strange thing can happen. That a man can stand in a cave and talk to God—and be answered.

Mecca

Verily, the first house founded for men was that in Bekka, for a blessing and a guidance to the world.

-THE CHAPTER OF IMRAN'S FAMILY

1

The House of God

I f one were a superbeing with a supereye, able to stand above the earth and see at a glance all the activities of man, there would certainly be no sight more astonishing than the endless motion of Islam where the halo of the sun sweeps across the globe. There, on the sickle edge of light, numberless men stand with their faces toward the qibla, Mecca. They kneel and extend themselves on the ground, then rise again and kneel and lie and do it all again and again, folding and unfolding with long elastic shadows, a vast chrysanthemum of men, opening and shutting, while the sun swings on. And when they are obliterated in light or dark as the case may be, there is always another rank of men behind to take up the motion, on roofs and balconies of ancient dwellings or the most modern apartment houses, in mosques, in huts and tents, on mountains, deserts, and green fields. There is never a moment of the day or night when this worldwide ballet of shadows is not in progress, and it has continued without interruption for nearly fourteen centuries.

The perimeters of the great circle are connected with the center by streams of pilgrims flowing back and forth from Mecca, a town in western Arabia—Bekka, the ancients called it, and they believe it stood at the exact center, the very navel of the world. Even today, with some safety of passage guaranteed and a few mod-

3

ern comforts, it is not a place that would appeal to the ordinary tourist trade.

It was a collection of gray, cubicle dwellings rising over narrow cobbled streets, airless and fairly ventless, necessarily closed up against the cruelties of heat, wind, sand, and grit. It lies in a valley clamped hard in the arms of mountains, which are piles of dark, crumbling rocks where the trapped winds heave about with violent intention toward anything not firmly anchored in the ground. Thorn scrub and beaten acacia grow here, the sort of growing things only camels love. It is hard to say why anyone ever remained long enough to build a house here, but according to legend it was none other than our father Adam who did so. It was after the Fall, and probably all places outside Eden looked alike to him. In any case he collected a hollow pile of stones together in this valley and built a thing which he called Beit Allah, the House of God. He made it in a square, not a bad design for a person who had never seen a house. Adam was proud of it. Thereafter he would return every year to walk seven times around this first of man's creations, admiring it with every step he took. However, it had no roof and did not stand long. In the following years, as Adam's seed multiplied, many passersby ignorantly kicked the stones around, and finally the Great Flood came and razed Beit Allah. In the mind of God, though, all things exist in perfect form, no matter what we do to them on earth.

Centuries passed before history, or legend, again brushed the place. That was when Hagar the Egyptian, the beloved handmaid of Abraham, was cast out of his tents with her son Ishmael, because of the jealousy of Sarah, to die in the desert. Muslims do not admit the truth of this familiar Old Testament story. They say that Hagar was a legitimate wife of Abraham and that he had sent her forth alone with the same harsh faith by which he had been willing to sacrifice his son Isaac. He was a man resigned to God's will, and God had promised him that Hagar's child Ishmael was not destined to die but to become the father of princes.

This was not much comfort to Hagar as she dragged about the scorched mountains and dry wadis, where no food or water was possible apart from what she carried in a bundle and a pitcher slung from a belt around her waist. Alone, she had to watch her young child shrivel next to her dwindling breast. Perhaps with a desert woman's knowledge, she made instinctively for the miserable shelter of the valley, or perhaps she came accidentally on a little ruin of stones and used its lonely shelter. For whatever reason she was near the world navel when she pushed her baby under a bush and went off a way to die where she could not hear its wailing. The Angel Gabriel appeared then, God's messenger. Her eyes were opened so that she saw the spring burst from the earth, with a soft noise like zem-zem and sweet as milk and honey. She refreshed herself and retrieved her child. In time she fell in with some Bedouin, who, with that pity desert people bestow on wayfarers, cared for her and made her son their own.

Ishmael grew up very wild, but he turned out to be a champion archer, and generous with his knowledge, teaching the tribesmen of Arabia more than they had ever known about making and shooting bows and arrows. It was his father Abraham who tore him away from this worthy occupation, having kept a possessive eye on the well-loved firstborn all these years. House building was what Abraham had in mind for Ishmael. They were to rebuild Beit Allah together. So they did. Ishmael found the stones and brought them to Abraham, who constructed the walls and shoved all into place. Since neither of them had ever seen a house, God helped by sending down to them His perfect vision in the form of a cloud. Its shadow cast on the ground provided a good blueprint. Because the walls, which were about forty feet in height, presented a formidable problem to builders who knew nothing of ladders, father and son conceived the plan of sinking them below the ground, in trenches. Even so the top ranges of stones were too high for Abraham, who was obliged to find a stone he could conveniently stand on. His footprint never left it, and it can be seen today in Mecca, the Makam Ibrahim.

Was it Abraham who, in the course of building what we now call the Kaaba, pinched in a corner of it, that mysterious object we call the Black Stone? It is said by some to be only a piece of iron, a meteorite, and by others just an ordinary rock from the volcanic mountains round about. Still others believe it to be a shrunken, petrified angel, who once was snowy white but now is black as pitch from the millions of kisses sinful men have pressed on it. The sacred Black Stone is still in its place in one corner of the Kaaba in Mecca. It is in twelve pieces now, held together by cement and a silver band, but nobody knows any more about it than the first man—perhaps Abraham himself—who picked it up and fancied it, and then, reluctant to drop it but annoyed to carry it about, left it in the sacred place to become a puzzle for the ages.

Ishmael married a Bedouin girl and begat his princes, who in turn were the ancestors of all the tribes of Arabia. One of Ishmael's sons begat a tribe that, by the sixth century after Christ, were well in control of the town of Mecca and the Kaaba. They were called, very properly, the "Sharks," or "Quraysh," because they made a good living out of preying on the pilgrims who thronged there annually, to walk in the footsteps of Adam seven times around the sacred house. By that time the Kaaba sheltered a few hundred idols ruled over by a large red agate personage called Hubal. The Quraysh managed to convince everyone that they were the best, most aristocratic tribe in Arabia, selected by Hubal to be keepers of the Kaaba, that Hubal preferred people to walk around him in a special kind of garment, which they might buy from the Quraysh. If they could not afford to do so, they might walk around in ordinary garments, but then they must throw them away afterward. The upshot was that people who could afford neither to throw away their own clothes nor to buy new ones walked around Beit Allah naked.

It was the same with food. Profane food was not to be brought into the city of Mecca but had to be acquired at a suitable price from the Quraysh. And water too. They got away with these petty practices by pretending to be the "sons of Abraham," glossing over the fact that, if they were, so was everyone else in Arabia.

Because of the veneration in which the Kaaba with its god colony was held, all the caravans stopped here as they plied up and down the western spine of Arabia, the Hejaz, between the Byzantine and Persian empires in the north and Yemen and Arabia Felix in the south, mingling the rich goods of half a world away from Mecca. For these strands of caravans did not dwindle before they had crossed the seas to Abyssinia in the west and India in the Far East.

A few decades before Muhammad was born, a new bonanza came the way of the Quraysh. One of the tribesmen—it was Muhammad's own grandfather, in fact, the head of the Clan Hashim, Abd-el-Muttalib—noticed, a small distance from the Kaaba, a magpie pecking in the ground, and he had an impulse to dig for treasure there, thinking perhaps the bird had detected some glitter in the soil. Indeed, he found the grave of an old king with golden ornaments inside. They were obviously too good for anybody to own, so he consigned them to the keeping of Hubal in the Kaaba. Far more important was the spring that came bubbling to the surface with a lovely soft noise like zem-zem. Just as if a spring of any kind was not precious enough in that baked ground, Abd-el-Muttalib was able to turn it into a rich stream of silver dirhems leading into his own pocket, for he said he had heard a voice from Heaven identifying it as that spring that had once saved the life of the Arab All-Father, Ishmael. From that time on the Clan Hashim had the keeping of Well Zem-Zem and of purveying its waters, at a price, to pilgrims. The latter were sorry to find that it had lost its milk-and-honey properties and was bitter and purgative—but, nevertheless, cleansing to the sin-stained soul. Well Zem-Zem is still an active spring in Mecca, as sacred to devout Muslims now as it was before Muslims were ever heard of.

By the time Muhammad was ready to come into the world, in the sixth century A.D., some small measure of sophistication was burgeoning among the Quraysh. Many of them were learning to read and write, and there was curiosity starting up, especially among the young, about the Jewish and Christian holy books, which seemed to them full of fascinating mysteries. Moreover, more distinguished ways were being found of making a living. For example, for a fee the Quraysh would guarantee safe-conduct to caravans posting up and down the coast. They earned their fee by maintaining treaties with nomadic tribes, who then acted as safe-conductors—or else as robbers, according to whether or not the fee had been paid. In the past hundred years the Quraysh had themselves engaged in trade, acting as middlemen for small operators in the Yemen and Hadhramaut, or even forming caravans carrying produce brought out of Yemen or Africa.

6

They had no produce of their own to offer, except the skins and wools they gathered in from the nomads. And so, as they came to understand the workings of trade, they commenced lending money to each other to invest in caravans, and they learned to speculate and to charge interest. They became capitalists, in fact, owners of paper wealth, an occupation that is improving to the arithmetic but not necessarily to qualities of mind and spirit. A great many Meccans took to gambling while waiting for their camels to come home—or to drinking when they failed to do so. Some merchants, finding that power and influence were the rewards of successful speculators, became ambitious. Rifts of rivalry appeared between the clans of Quraysh.

Poor as they were materially, and deep in poverty of spirit also, the Quraysh still shared one marvelous and ancient possession with all the inhabitants of the severe land of Arabia. It was poetry. Poetry had come about because of the Arabs' need to communicate over time and harsh distances, and it flourished where nothing else grew. Like other ancient peoples with the same problem—the Homeric tribes, for example, the Serbs, the Irish, and many more—whenever they had something important to say that they desired to be noticed and remembered, they would say it in verse. Or they might write it down to be affixed to the walls of a shrine for all to see and learn. Or they might personally recite it in long, rambling, clangorous lines that could be rolled about on the tongue like thunder or like a dish of thirst-quenching fruit. If a person had no talent for this sort of thing, he could hire a poet to recite his recent deeds of prowess in battle, throwing in compliments to his ancestors or his true love. So a class of poets sprang up, both men and women, who were press agents as well as poets, very quick minded and good at reciting or extemporizing in arresting word and rhythm.

When the great fairs were held at the various shrines, at Hubal's shrine in Mecca, or those of certain goddesses who lived not too far away and who were considered Hubal's wives, daughters, or both, the tribes would come together under the safe-conduct of "sacred months" and "sacred places," fixed by ancient, unwritten law. And to these would also come the poets, relating with drama and pathos the news of the day and the legends of the past, weaving a culture together with words. Then, as now, poets were not thought by established social opinion to have much solid human quality. They were overemotional and "different." They were popular enough. Some of them could have you rolling on the ground in mirth at their raucous insolence or obscenity, or move you to tears of anger or pride. But many poets seemed quite mad, as if possessed by an evil jinn.

What nobody knew at the time was that, in their tireless inventions of words and phrases, these poets were busy manufacturing one of mankind's greatest artifacts, the Arabic language.

Soon it would be ready to write one of the richest of books.

7

And when kinsmen are gathered together for the division of inheritance, and the orphans and the poor, let these too have a share.

-THE CHAPTER OF WOMEN

2

The Orphan

Abd-el-Muttalib, keeper of Well Zem-Zem, had a son Abdullah who engaged in trade, traveling with Meccan caravans northward to Syria. He was extremely attractive to women, carrying a special blaze in his eyes which enchanted them, but he made a love match with Amina, a woman of Quraysh. After that his other sweethearts wanted nothing to do with him, for they said that the blaze had gone. Abdullah died while on a business trip to Yathrib, a kindly oasis north of Mecca which we call Medina. He was only twenty-five and never saw his son.

Muhammad was born in 570, the Year of the Elephant. His mother, Amina, did not thrive well afterward. Abd-el-Muttalib, who as head of Clan Hashim had charge of her, did not oblige her to marry one of Abdullah's brothers, but allowed her to live alone with her child and an Ethiopian slave. He surprised everyone when he called the orphan baby by the rather pretentious name Muhammad, which means "the Praised." Perhaps he meant it for luck.

So fiercely did the mad Meccan winds blow on infants that most Meccan ladies who could afford it gave out their children for fosterage to Bedouin women of the desert, who would come to town with their breasts full of milk, hawking their wares from door to door. One day such a group of Bedouin of the vast

Hawazin tribe came into town looking for babies, and we have it from Halima, of the Sa'adite nomads, how she came to acquire Muhammad as her foster child. It was a year of drought and famine, and her breasts were quite dry. She hadn't slept a wink the night before because of the moaning of her own child, and in the morning even the she-camel could not make up the lack. Halima lagged behind the others on the journey to town because her starved donkey couldn't keep pace with the rest.

When we reached Mecca, we looked out for foster-children, and the Apostle of God was offered to every one of us. Each woman refused, upon being told he was an orphan, because it was a child's father who usually paid his keep. So we passed him by because of that.

Every woman who was with me got a suckling except me, and when we decided to go, I said to my husband, "By God, I do not like the idea of going back without a suckling. I'll go and take that orphan." He replied, "Do as you please."

So I took him because I couldn't find another. As soon as I put him to my bosom my breasts overflowed with milk which he drank, and so did his foster brother. Then both of them slept. My husband went to the old she-camel, and lo; her udders were full!

That Halima! She probably grew fat in her old age making up interesting stories to tell about Muhammad around the cooking pots of the Hawazin. Perhaps we owe to her the famous story of the day the little foster brother came running and saying, "Two men in white have seized that Qurayshi brother and thrown him down and opened up his belly and stirred up something inside!" Halima and her husband ran to Muhammad and found him standing up, his face livid. They held him close and got out of him what was the matter. He said, "Two men in white raiment came and threw me down and opened up my belly and searched inside for I don't know what."

The foster father said, "The child has had a stroke."

To this day many people think the same—that Muhammad had fits. However, the story is not unlike others told by mediums and psychics of being molested in childhood by supernatural beings. The story could reflect some strange experience of Muhammad's infancy related to his psychic nature that we do not properly understand.

No harm was done to the child. No further "fits" troubled him. He was a sturdy little boy, though reserved and sensitive. When he was five, he was returned to Amina in Mecca. He must have been terrified to be thus given away from one mother to another. He ran away from Amina and not without difficulty was found again and deposited with his grandfather, who happened to be making his evening circumambulation of the Kaaba. Abd-el-Muttalib picked him up, put him

9

on his shoulder, and continued to walk his seven times around.

Muhammad always remembered the days when he ran free with the Bedouin. He used to say, "There is no prophet but has shepherded a flock."

"Even you, Muhammad?" the city folk from the oases asked him.

"Yes," he replied. "I am the most Arab of you all."

When Muhammad was six, his mother Amina took him northward on a two-hundred-mile journey through severe country to Yathrib, where his father had died. We do not know the reasons for this trip. She may have wanted to show him his father's grave or to introduce him to a clan related to her own that had settled there. Perhaps she hoped that her own failing health would improve in the more comfortable climate of the oasis town. It did not, and foolhardily she started home again, attempting the hard trail with only her young Ethiopian slave-girl, Baraka, a camel, some provisions, and Muhammad. The incident is quite mysterious, for she must have been aware of the dangers. Perhaps, realizing at last that her illness was going to be fatal, she was in a hurry to return to Mecca and secure her son's future. She did not survive the journey. The sere weather attacked them with wind and sand, and Amina died. Baraka found some villagers to help her bury Muhammad's mother in their village, Abwa, and then she somehow managed to bring the child to Mecca and turn him over to his grandfather Abd-el-Muttalib, who in spite of numerous progeny and a host of grandchildren had a soft spot for his son's orphan and made a personal pet of him. The good life lasted for Muhammad but two years. Then Abd-el-Muttalib died, leaving him in charge of his uncle Abu Talib, his closest relative by virtue of being his father's brother by the same mother.

Abu Talib was a kindly man, and Muhammad grew up in his house not uncomfortably but unobtrusively. The fortunes of the Hashim family seem to have taken a turn for the worse about this time. Possibly having to divide up Abd-el-Muttalib's property among nine sons and six daughters did not do them much good. One thing is certain: Muhammad's share, if anyone thought he was entitled to the inheritance of his father Abdullah, evaporated like the desert rain. That he might have felt left out is shown by his vehement denunciations in later years of those who despoiled orphans or did not notice a small orphan loitering in the background when family goods were being divided.

He grew up as a boy of no account, and even much later, when all Arabia was talking about him, no one came forward with impressive recollections of his childhood in Mecca. The name of no special friend is recorded, though the household abounded in cousins and even uncles little older than himself. There were no exploits, no games. It looks as if he was as shy and unassuming as he was always to be before God made him bold. He might have learned his arithmetic as well as anyone else in that merchant's town, but he was not taught to read or

10

write. At least he always denied that he could do so, and probably he was semi-literate at best. Even if he had learned his letters, there were few enough books in Mecca to practice on.

When he was fifteen, the Wicked Wars broke out, so called because they had flared up over a murder committed during the sacred days when all the tribes mustered to pay their respects at the shrines of Hubal and his wives. At such times homicide was unlawful. The Quraysh were not involved in the original crime, but they were dragged into the fighting because of alliances with confederate tribes.

One might expect a boy of fifteen, when he belongs to a brawling society and feels right to be on his side, to face a good fight with his manhood rising to the challenge, running about everywhere at once, shooting off arrows and loving his baptism of fire. Instead, we are told that Muhammad went where the enemy's arrows fell thick on the ground, picked them up calmly, and handed them to his uncles.

Muhammad was always to be like this—active and determined when bloody deeds were afoot. Certainly he was able to rouse others to battle like no other man. But he was not bloodthirsty, and he never prolonged a battle.

No early adventures with girls are reported of Muhammad, although the moral climate of Mecca would not have forbidden them. Years later it was noticed of him that in his attitude to women he was shy "as a green virgin," and he said himself he had never so much as touched a woman in the unmarried state.

That is the little we know of Muhammad's childhood and youth. He probably helped to discharge the Hashim family duty, that of purveying the waters of Well Zem-Zem to pilgrims. Whatever he did he might have done rather well, because quite early in life he acquired a nickname: al-Amin, the Trusty.

When he was almost grown, in his late teens, Abu Talib organized a family caravan, and Muhammad hung upon the excitement with such intensity that his uncle had not the heart to leave him behind. He may have gone south to Yemen or north to the Holy Land. These are mysteries, but they are scrutinized carefully by scholars who want to know where Muhammad learned his rather eccentric Biblical lore. Of course, he might have learned much just by staying in Mecca, for the caravans passing through brought exotic wayfarers, men of the Orient and Africa, and Christians of many different sects who held forth in all manner of heresies. Far to the north the intellectual life of the Byzantine Empire was being worn to a frazzle by incessant arguments about the nature of God, which they believed to be very complex.

Muhammad would have heard talk of such burning issues from Christians passing through Mecca. Jews would come his way also, because they traded along with the Arabs. Christian or Jew, a man would not have been human if he did not enjoy telling Bible stories beside a campfire to a curious boy.

Muhammad was curious and humbly envious of the People of the Book who

11

had such tremendous knowledge. He remembered everything, winnowed what sense he could out of it, and stored it all in his mind, which happened to be that of a genius.

Did He not find thee an orphan and shelter thee? Did He not find thee erring and guide thee? Did He not find thee poor and nourish thee?

-THE CHAPTER OF THE MORNING

3

Muhammad the Trusty

When Muhammad was in his early twenties, it is believed that he accompanied a caravan to Syria and there executed commissions on behalf of his family which he acquitted well. When, shortly after, a distant kinswoman of his, Khadija, was left a widow (for the second time) and looked for an overseer to take charge of her caravan, Muhammad's uncle, Abu Talib, told her that she could not do better than engage the young man whom the Quraysh called al-Amin. It was an excellent opportunity for him, because Khadija was a rich woman. She had inherited from her two husbands wealth and a thriving banking business, which she ran with profit and acumen, investing her depositors' money in the caravans—at least one of which she owned and others of which she owned shares.

The fact that a businesswoman like Khadija saw fit to engage Muhammad as her factor might bear witness to his good character and reputation for competence. But we have not one tradition to show what he actually did with Khadija's caravans or where he took them. Presumably he led them to Syria and brought them back laden with goods, grains, and silver dirhems, with his bookkeeping in good order. Khadija realized that she had found a treasure and like a good banker that she had better put it in safe deposit.

13

One tradition has it that her slave Maisara, who had traveled with Muhammad to Syria and become his friend, praised the young man highly to her. She then told him to sound out Muhammad's feelings about marriage. Muhammad said at once that as a poor man, worth only his salary and commissions, he had not thought of adding to his expenses by acquiring a wife and children. Maisara suggested delicately that he might look around for a wealthy widow. Muhammad laughed. He could not imagine that many wealthy widows were looking around for him. He was dumbfounded when Maisara mentioned the name of his employer. As he well knew, there was not a Quraysh in Mecca who was not eager to take over the management of Khadija and her business.

The next step was taken by Khadija, who asked him to call on her and spoke to him very flatteringly, using the name usual between relatives: "O son of my uncle, we are kinsmen, and I like you because of your high reputation, your trustworthiness, good character, and truthfulness." She then made him a proposal of marriage. He said he would consult his uncles.

A stroke of luck like this for a young man without resources was almost beyond belief. Abu Talib was delighted, and he lost no time in going, along with another of Muhammad's uncles, Hamza, to call upon the head of Khadija's clan, her uncle Khuwaylid, to ask for her hand in marriage on Muhammad's behalf. It was not expected that this gentleman would look kindly on the request. We suspect again that Muhammad's family had fallen in fortune and were not considered the best marriage material. Possibly the present head, Abu Talib, was not a strong leader or else had been an unwise investor. Furthermore, it was not common sense to suppose that Khadija's uncle would want to place a young husband with a large family next to Khadija's barrelful of wealth.

Thus it was that trickery was resorted to in order to get Muhammad well married. On that day when Abu Talib and Hamza called on Khadija's uncle, some friendly relatives of her own were present. A party was soon in full swing with wine flowing and merrymaking, in which Khuwaylid's cup was filled again and again. When the racket was at its height, Abu Talib made his request, which was seconded by a cousin of Khadija's, Waraqa ibn Nawfal. The old man burbled agreeably in response. When much later he came to his senses, he was outraged to find that his rich and clever ward had just been married to an insignificant Hashimite orphan. "But, Uncle," said Khadija, "you said I could!"

Khadija's cousin Waraqa had a strange way of being present at crucial moments in Muhammad's life. Years before, when a little child of five, frightened to death of being made to live with his own mother, had slipped away and gotten lost in the narrow streets, it was this same Waraqa who had found him and returned him to his grandfather.

Waraqa was Mecca's official Christian. He could read well and used to collect the books of the New Testament. He is one of those suspected of having instruct-

14

ed Muhammad in the Judaic and Christian Scriptures.

Muhammad married Khadija in 595 A.D., when he was twenty-five years old. She is traditionally stated to have been fifteen years older than he—that is, forty—but since she bore him seven children, some modern students have questioned the tradition. She might have been somewhat younger, perhaps in her thirties. The first three children were boys, all of whom died in infancy. Only the first, Qasim, was remembered, since by custom Muhammad's honorific name—by which people addressed him when they wished to be civil—became Abu'l-Qasim, father of Qasim. The rest of the children were girls, Zaynab, Ruqayya, Umm Kulthum, and Fatima, and they grew to womanhood, sharing Muhammad's unique life.

When Muhammad's life was first studied in Europe, he came in for some historic criticism for having been a penniless young man who married a widow reported to be rich and elderly. Yet history has recorded few happier marriages. Up to his fiftieth year, when Khadija died, no suggestion crept into the record that he was anything but a faithful and devoted husband. Khadija adored him. Their family life, apart from the tragedy of their dead children, could only have been happy and affectionate, since Muhammad loved all his daughters dearly, and they were much attached to him and their mother.

The most convincing account of his attitude comes from a story told by saucy Ayesha, the darling young wife of his later years, who once asked him if he did not think that she herself was an excellent substitute for dear old Khadija, who was then dead. Muhammad grew very serious and told her firmly that no one could take the place in his heart of the lady who had first loved him, believed in him, and sustained him by her belief.

Muhammad is reported, even in those years before divine magic touched him, to have had a very sweet nature, captivating to those who knew him well. While he did not act as a robber toward Khadija's golden hoard on his own account, being modest in his wants, he became known for his generosity to the poor. Khadija indulged him proudly in his charities.

She gave him a slave as a present, Zayd ben Haritha. The boy was a Syrian Christian, kidnapped from his parents and sold into Arabia. Some years later, his father tracked him down and came to Mecca with money to buy his son back, but Zayd had become so attached to his master that he was appalled at the notion and begged to remain Muhammad's slave. Muhammad made both father and son happy by taking Zayd promptly to the Kaaba, where he officially freed him by public pronouncement. Then he adopted him as his son. Zayd became one of the close companions and friends of Muhammad's life.

Another male member joined the inner circle of this household some years after the marriage, when the couple had thrice suffered the tragedy of losing their

15

male children. Uncle Abu Talib, while growing poorer in wealth, found himself too rich by one son, his youngest child Ali, and so Muhammad took over the upbringing of Ali, thus repaying his uncle for his own childhood home. Muhammad loved children. Ali became to him as his own son, an affection which the child was to repay in good measure.

Once married to Khadija and with his financial problems erased, Muhammad seems not to have taken further trips to Syria or anywhere else, preferring to settle down at her side, possibly assisting her in her banking business and managing the investments of stay-at-home clients, without making any mark of his own as a businessman. He did interest himself, however, in a group called the Hilf ul-Fuzul, or the "League of the Virtuous," a confederacy of businessmen, or rather business clans, that had been founded about 580 with a praiseworthy aim. For the members had bound themselves "by solemn agreement that if they found that anyone, either a native of Mecca or an outsider, had been wronged, they would take his part against the aggressor and see that the stolen property was restored to him."

Evidently such transgressions had become frequent during the fairs and pilgrimages when Mecca and the shrines of the Hejaz were crowded with potential troublemakers. Although the restrictions against murder were usually obeyed, pilgrims were frequently preyed on in other ways. The more sophisticated townsfolk, among them the men of Clan Hashim, realized that if they did not enforce strict rules to protect such votaries of Hubal, men would eventually find other, holier shrines, and the goose that laid the golden egg would then be slain.

Some accounts of Muhammad's life emphasize the humanitarian and moral aspects of this League of the Virtuous. But the cold eye of scholarship, scrutinizing this and other business clubs of Mecca—such as the "League of the Scented Ones," who had agreed to look after one another's interests "as long as the sea wetted seaweed"—sees in them something similar to political parties, in which the members support self-serving notions with little regard for the original party platform. As Muhammad was now a man of substance and in a submerged part of his nature a born leader, he became a party man. And since we know for certain of his lifelong regard for weak and helpless people, we can agree with the most devout Muslims that he might have been one member who kept in mind the ideals of the Hilf ul-Fuzul. Yet later, in the years of his trials, it can be discerned that some of his persecutors were not so much God's enemies as Muhammad's party opponents.

It is sometimes said that great teachers of mankind are not so much radical thinkers as reflectors of the best and highest thought of their times. From this standpoint, Muhammad's early behavior sheds light on his people, the Quraysh. Here was a remote tribe of Arabia with one foot in prehistory, and with the other about to step away from semisavagery to a more civilized frame of life.

16

Symptomatic of this were their attempts to organize themselves ethically and morally and their curiosity about the People of the Book. If sometimes their well-meant arguments had to be enforced with dirt-throwing and knifepoint, we cannot blame them for that. Like every one of us, they were creatures of their time and place, and Muhammad himself was quite capable of acting with ruthlessness.

We know something of how he looked in his young manhood. He was of medium height, rather stocky, with a round head set on a very straight spine. He had a headlong way of walking as if he were always going downhill. His complexion was very fair for a member of a sun-blistered race, his hair and beard very black and extremely well tended, the locks falling smoothly over his shoulders. His eyebrows grew across his nose. He was fussy about his clothes, which were always spotless.

His teeth are oddly described—set wide apart in the jaw and pointed like the teeth of a saw. But the poets of Arabia described other handsome young men as being saw-toothed, so this might have been only a poetic compliment. Or perhaps in a fit of youthful vanity he had filed them. He kept them very clean, carrying around with him a supply of toothpicks for this purpose. In later years it was noticed that he did not like to face people with dirty teeth.

While Muslims have never claimed a divine origin for Muhammad, we are given to understand that under his eyebrows, where they met, he had a mole and another between his shoulder blades. These are the legendary marks of bhodisattvas, mystics and saints. We do not know if Muhammad had them or if one of his later biographers thought he should have them.

The retiring habits of his childhood followed him to his manhood. We hardly know a word he said in his early and middle years. We know that he had a singular aversion to falsehood or even exaggerated speech, to such an extent that he could not bear to listen to poets at the fairs.

Summing up Muhammad, gentleman of Mecca, we may see him as a man who loved order in dress, in speech, in business practice, in bookkeeping. He was probably gifted with a precise mind that automatically cut through confusion. The one anecdote told of him supports this view.

When Muhammad was thirty-five years old, a scandalous deed rocked Mecca. Hubal, and his scrubby companions who lived in the Kaaba, had been robbed. The thieves had climbed over the outer walls, which were made of loose stones inexpertly piled up by Abraham and his successors, and since the building itself was roofless, they had gained access to the pit where votaries for ages past had thrown offerings to the gods.

The malefactors had been identified and the treasure discovered in the house of a freed slave. He got his hand cut off for his trouble.

All the same, it was necessary to put a roof on the Kaaba. Probably most houses in Mecca were roofless, no more than stone tents really, partly covered by fab-

17

ric or skins. A short while before, a Greek ship had been washed ashore on the Red Sea coast, and some hefty timbers had been seen lying about on the beach. What was also fortunate, a Coptic carpenter was passing through Mecca at the time. The only other obstacle, a snake which lived in the well and was an object of terror because it used to sit on the stones and make rustling noises at worshipers, had recently been carried off by an eagle. The time seemed perfect for roofing the Kaaba.

However, the walls were ages old, they were crumbling and would never hold the heavy timbers. It was therefore decided to tear them down and build them anew and stoutly.

"Now it is to be hoped that the god will be pleased with what we are doing," said the Quraysh, as they pressed into the sacred enclosure and looked nervously at the Kaaba. An exceedingly brave tribesman named al-Walid walked up to the shrine and said, "O God, do not be afraid. We mean what is best for you!" He then proceeded to demolish some of the wall.

Everyone then went home to bed, wondering if al-Walid would be smitten dead by morning, but as he was not, they fell to tearing down the walls. This work was shared by the leading members of all the clans, so that thunderation when it came would have to be distributed widely among them.

When the walls were down to the foundation, a crowbar was placed between two lower stones. Suddenly there was a tremor of the ground and the whole of Mecca shuddered. It was decided to leave the foundation alone.

In one corner of the structure, the traditionists tell, some interesting stones were found. Some were green and joined together like camels' humps. Others were inscribed in an unknown script. The workers summoned a learned Jew, resident in Mecca, to read it for them. It was in Syriac and offered some early local history: "I am Allah, Lord of Bekka. I created it on the day that I created Heaven and Earth and formed the sun and moon, and I surrounded it with seven pious angels. It will stand while its two mountains stand, a blessing to its people, with milk and water."

Now while this work of demolition was being done by leading men, the rest of the tribe were busily collecting good, smooth stones to bring to the rebuilding of the walls, and these were gradually put in place. Now the famous Black Stone, that mysterious object which is still the most precious stone in the world, had been carefully removed from the old wall and laid reverently aside. When it was time to replace it, a dispute arose between the clans, each of which wanted the honor of putting it into its prepared niche. It is only a small stone, seven inches across. Which chief should have the honor of handling it?

There were some angry voices raised over this before all agreed to abide by the suggestion of an elder. Whoever would next enter the courtyard should be asked to judge the matter.

The story goes that Muhammad was the next person to enter the sacred ground. The workers said, "It is Muhammad the Trusty. We are satisfied."

Muhammad heard the problem and studied the stone. He said, "Give me a cloak."

It was brought to him, and he spread it flat on the ground. He took up the Black Stone and laid it on the cloak. He then directed the leaders of all clans of Quraysh to take up the cloak around the edges and by this means lift the stone into its position. The tradition says he gave it the final push himself with his own hand.

Some of Muhammad's relatives were good at poetry, and it was his Uncle al-Zubayr who immortalized in verse the rebuilding of the Kaaba:

> I was amazed when the bird
> Went straight for the snake
> Which would rustle and threaten,
> And sometimes dart out.
> When we wanted to build,
> We were stricken with fear,
> But down came the eagle,
> In a deadly straight fall,
> And bore it away!
> We got on with our work . . .

The actual rebuilding is dismissed in a few lines. It was the eagle-snake miracle that Uncle al-Zubayr wanted us to remember.

One mighty in power taught him, one endowed with complete understanding! And he appeared, a Being of the loftiest plane.

-THE CHAPTER OF THE STAR

4

The Call

According to the speech recorded in old poems and traditions, the Arabs before Muhammad believed in God. They swore by Him "By God!" they said with every breath. They did not, however, have any clear conception of a One God, indivisible and yet personal to every man, or of men united in God. They felt united to their clans, tribes, and confederate tribes. Everyone else was a fair enemy, especially if he owned flocks worth raiding.

When they wished to make some important demand on supernatural powers, they did not bother with "By God!" at all, but with any number of queer objects, including the stone images that jammed the Kaaba. There were also the goddesses of the neighboring shrines where fairs were held: al-Lat at at-Taif; al-Uzza at Nakhla; and Manat at a shrine near Medina. These ladies, consorts of Hubal, may have been much older than he. Herodotus, a thousand years before, had known about a mighty goddess worshiped in Arabia, and perhaps she was one of these known to Muhammad.

If there was no shrine handy, simple stones might be worshiped as gods. Stones have always held a peculiar fascination for Arabs, possibly because in their arid, featureless land, a stone, or a pattern of stones, might be a thing of singularity or beauty, or a landmark of life-and-death significance. In any case, the nomadic Arabs used to carry favorite stones around with them to use for fireplaces, or handy workbenches, or in a religious mood for worshiping. If in the confusion of travel these stones got mixed up, it did not really matter if today's god was yesterday's fireplace. Arabs loved stones.

Moral and ethical notions had come to the surface of their minds, as we may glean from the existence of groups in Mecca like the League of the Virtuous, but these feelings were connected with personal or tribal honor, or even clan politics, not with a sense of responsibility to a power beyond the self. Loyalty to the group, fidelity to one's word, courage in battle, hospitality to guests—these were moral ideals, and they were clan nurtured.

The gods brought life or death, bestowed riches or poverty, gave sons or daughters. If the gods hated a man or were dissatisfied with his offerings, they humiliated him by giving him daughters. He cast his bad luck back in their teeth by burying his surplus female babies alive. He said he did it because women were weak headed and immoral, and had best be prevented from growing up to bring disgrace upon their families. Actually the horrid custom had lingered on because the hard climate, the lack of food supply, the nomadic existence, and the general violence of manners made women a dangerous luxury. But the very fact that pious excuses are on record shows that civilization was creeping up on the Arabs unawares.

The enormous inspiration brought by the teachings of Christ to the Byzantine world and the air of authority that clung to Jewish communities had not gone unnoticed or unenvied. In the decades before Muhammad was born, some whole tribes, especially in the north where the Byzantine influence was felt, had embraced Christianity. They might have turned in similar numbers to Judaism, except that the Jews had a fancy that those who wished to join the People of the Book should be willing to submit to a certain amount of book learning in their Torah schools. This was a hurdle, but in spite of it, many Arabs were becoming Jews.

A crooked line separates a high "culture" from a "civilization." The Aztecs of Mexico were in many ways a more enlightened people than the "civilized" Christians who conquered them. But there is one aspect of a civilization that makes it distinct from even the highest culture. It is founded on abstract principles that are transferable from one people and one race to another. The Aztecs could understand Christianity, but those aspects of the Aztec religion which were interwoven with primitive totemism, animism, and local magic were meaningless to Christians.

21

The abstract principles on which civilizations flourish always derive from a clear conviction that man has an intimate personal correlation with the godhead (by whatever name this may be called); that an unbreakable unity exists between the human and the divine; that Heaven and Earth are interrelated in an orderly universe; that disciplined, moral human behavior reflects this order. This knowledge winds like the wise Serpent around the roots of all the great universal religions, which, growing away from the roots, branch and flower in all diversity, so that they seem to become different plants. Yet they are the same, and the wise Serpent keeps the roots together.

While knowledge of God's unity with His creation lies dormant in every man, it is so densely impacted by the pressures of everyday life that it does not easily come to his consciousness unless some inspired teacher sounds a response in him. There must have been many such teachers to prod us out of the caves and along the path marked out for us. We know a little of the lives of the spectacular few: Moses and a succession of Hebrew prophets; Lao-tse and the Old Masters of China; Krishna and some sages of Vedic times; Confucius, Zoroaster, Gautama Buddha, Christ, Saint Paul. All these seem to have spoken to hordes of people in different parts of the world. All of them lived in times of great confusion of spirit when the collective mind of their societies seemed to waver and tremble on the instant of a new direction. We see this in an incident that happened when Muhammad was a boy. Four men circumambulating the Kaaba suddenly felt foolish doing it and secretly withdrew from their devotions. Afterward they confided their feelings to each other, and all of them subsequently looked for different faiths. One of them was Khadija's Christian cousin Waraqa.

The prevalent mood of anxiety and expectation was evident in all of the various groups of the Hejaz for some time before Muhammad's mission. The Jews were especially aroused, because their seers and astrologers sensed that a supernatural event was at hand, and they talked with excitement about the Messiah who was going to arise at last and lead them back to the Holy Land. Several interesting prophecies are recorded which bear the stamp of legend. Others, such as the following story related by a man of Medina who later became a Muslim, sound rather convincing.

We had a Jewish neighbor who came to see us one day. At that time I was the youngest person in my house, and I was wearing a light robe and lying in the courtyard. He spoke to us of the resurrection, the reckoning, the scales, and Heaven and Hell. My parents said, "Good gracious, man, you don't mean to say you believe this rubbish about people rising up from the dead and being judged? And going to places where there are gardens or hellfire, according to

22

their sins?"

"Yes," said the Jew, "and by Him whose name men swear by, I'd rather be in the largest oven in my house than in that fire!"

And when they asked him for a sign that this was true, he pointed southward in the direction of Mecca and the Yemen: "A Prophet will be sent from that direction." When they asked when he would appear, the Jew looked at me, the youngest, and said, "If this boy lives his natural term of life, he will see him!"

It was actually quite soon after this incident that Muhammad came on the scene, and the Arab family could not understand why the Jew did not immediately become a Muslim. "Weren't you the very man who foretold all this?" they asked their neighbor, but he shook his head, very irritated, saying, "Yes, but this is not the man."

The mountains around Mecca held many caves, and thoughtful citizens formed the habit of retiring to these secluded places for solitary meditation and prayer. This custom, called tahannuth, was a religious exercise, and it had originated, like the word which is related to the Hebrew word for certain special prayers, with the Jews of the Old Testament. But the early Christians adopted the habit during the Byzantine centuries, and now it had traveled southward to Arabia.

Muhammad had a favorite cave on a barren mountain called Hira, where he would retreat for days or weeks, or as long as a month, especially the month of Ramadan, fasting and meditating in complete seclusion except for straggling groups of poor who came to beg some food from him. He always brought an extra supply along to give away. When he had finished his month, he would return to Mecca, walk seven times around the Kaaba, and then go home.

By the time he reached the age of forty, he was known to be a man who kept tahannuth faithfully. Sometimes his family accompanied him to the mountains, either to practice this form of retreat themselves, or simply for the pleasure of camping out like their desert forefathers, at the same time remaining close to the head of their family.

In the year 610, Muhammad was troubled by strange dreams. They concerned nothing in particular, but in his sleep he would have the impression of a burst of brilliance, like a daybreak. He grew even more retiring as these dreams recurred. "God made him love solitude, so that he liked nothing better than to be alone," said his third wife Ayesha, relating what he had told her of those days.

We know so little of Muhammad personally up to this stage in his life that

23

we cannot guess what direction his thoughts took while he was alone. But he was about to step out of obscurity into fantastic light.

He went in the month of Ramadan, 610, to Hira. He was standing one night at the mouth of his cave when suddenly his mind lurched, and he felt himself seized by a mighty force and flung to his knees, while from nowhere an oppression closed on his senses. He knew he was caught in a vision, like his dream vision, but it was not one that could be described in terms of sight. Not even a light was present, just the presence of a Being could be sensed, but its nature was not to be guessed. At first Muhammad thought surely it was God Himself. The Being spoke one word:

READ!

Muhammad became conscious that there was writing before his mind's eye, magnificent calligraphy, and as he marveled, he thought it must be woven into a cloth of rich brocade. He said humbly, "I cannot read."

READ!

The visitant's command bore down on him, and Muhammad felt the oppression smothering him about, caressing and yet cruel, so that his breath was being squeezed from him. "He pressed me again," said Muhammad much later, "so that I thought I should die; then he let me go and said, 'READ!' I said, 'I cannot read.' He pressed me, and I thought surely I should die. He said, 'READ!' I said, 'What shall I read?' I said this only to get free of him so that he would stop what he was doing."

Then the Being said:

READ! IN THE NAME OF THE LORD WHO CREATED,
WHO CREATED MAN FROM A CLOT OF BLOOD:
READ IN THE NAME OF A MERCIFUL LORD,
WHO TAUGHT BY THE PEN,
TAUGHT MEN WHAT THEY KNEW NOT.

The thunder of the words died, and the Being departed. Muhammad said, "It was as though the words were written on my heart."

As soon as Muhammad recovered from stunned amazement, he was terror struck. His first thought was that he had lost his mind. The words he had just heard had the same intangible significance as those of the half-mad ecstatic poets who infested the fairs, and whom he could not abide at any price, for he had a dread of the insane. "I could not even look at them," he said. Now with this bonfire of words consuming his senses, and not at all in command of himself, he rushed out of his cave and began to climb to the top of the mountain where there was a cliff from which he proposed to fling himself, for he thought, "Woe, alas! poet or possessed, whatever I am, The Quraysh shall not say it of me!"

Then, as he was midway up the mountain, suddenly the vision appeared again, and this time he saw it, an immense, dazzling man with his feet astride the horizon and his head in the sky, a sight so shattering to the mind that Muhammad began to dodge from side to side to avoid looking at it. But wherever he looked the vision was there, all the time diminishing until it was quite close.

Now he drew near and hovered over
Until he was but two bow-lengths off or nearer,
And then he told his servant what he told him.
The heart knows what it saw! What?
Will you dispute what he saw?

The vision spoke: "O Muhammad! Thou art the Messenger of God, and I am Gabriel."

The apparition dissolved, and Muhammad fled the place. He ran three miles to Mecca without visiting the Kaaba as he usually did, flung himself into his house, shivering with terror and fever and calling like a child to Khadija: "Cover me, cover me!" She knelt by him, covered him, held him crouching next to her until his shuddering grew less.

In due course she learned what had happened, and although she could not make head nor tail of it, her words were loving. She not think that his senses had been snatched from him. "God would not treat you so, father of my son, since He knows that you are truthful and honest, that you are good to your family and generous to the guests who enter this house."

She saw that he was well wrapped in a cloak, and when he fell asleep, she took her own cloak on her shoulders and went to look for her Christian cousin Waraqa in his house. Waraqa, an old man now and going blind, listened as she related to him her husband's experience. He said wonderingly, "Holy! Holy! By Him who holds my soul in His hand, that was Gabriel, the same that came to Moses in ancient times. Muhammad will be a prophet of this people."

Different accounts of the Call, which cannot be logically fitted together, appear in the traditions and are suggested in the Holy Quran. It is not certain how many of these visions Muhammad had, or whether the two main apparitions that have just been described came to him on the same day or at differ-

25

ent times. Or if there were more. One tradition records another incident, in the words of Muhammad: "I heard a voice calling my name. I looked all around and saw no one. Then I looked up and there He was, sitting on His throne." But who "He" was is not made clear.

Another, rather engaging narrative, suggests that Gabriel several times appeared to Muhammad in his bedchamber when Khadija was present, although Khadija could not see him. And he stood there in such brilliance that the mind could burst looking at him. The pair wondered whether he was an angel or a devil. Khadija applied an acid test by making Muhammad sit on her knee. "Do you still see him?" she asked. Muhammad said, "Yes." She held him closer: "Do you still see him?" Muhammad replied that he did.

Khadija then made Muhammad pretend to make love to her, and Gabriel took his leave abruptly. "Rejoice, my husband, be comforted, for by God that is an angel and no shaitan," said Khadija with confidence.

Ordinary people know nothing whatever of such spiritual experiences, only that they are reported to have happened to some mystics and saints and to have transformed their lives. Some medical men have pointed out the similarity of such experiences to epilepsy, and it cannot be denied that in some cases, like Muhammad's, the symptoms of that illness were present: the heavy fall to the ground, the voices, the bursting light, and then the terror and the rushing madly about. On the other hand, neither can the differences be denied between the mystical experience and the epileptic attack. One is filled with splendor, the other with horror. An epileptic, even one like the Russian novelist Dostoevski, whose attacks had mystical elements, knows that he is gravely ill. He flees his attack and tries to avoid it by any means he can. A mystic, on the other hand, once he has overcome his terror, can hardly wait for the next visitation. He provokes it by religious exercises such as meditation and incantation, even knowing that it might cause him physical distress, as was often the case with Muhammad. As for their personal health, there are numerous examples of mystics, such as Socrates, Saint Paul, Buddha, Saint Joan, Saint Ignatius Loyola, and Muhammad, who were gifted with abundant vigor of mind and body with which they pursued their sometimes strenuous lives.

The truth is we do not know the physiology of these strange mental adventures or how mysticism connects in the brain with epilepsy or with ordinary hallucinations, natural or drug-induced. We do not know whose voice spoke to Paul on the road to Damascus, or to Christ at his baptism, or to Moses from the burning bush; or by what means Gautama Buddha received

26

complete instruction as he sat meditating under a Bo-tree. Because such messages have reached into our highest consciousness, we call them divine and say that they came from God.

As for the mystic himself, his Call lifts him forever from the path of an ordinary man. His previous interests fail, and one compulsion fills his mind—to communicate his message to his fellowman in the face of ridicule, calumny, or even abominable persecution.

By the falling star your comrade lies not, nor is he deluded, nor does he speak in self-interest. He speaks by inspiration, something inspired!
                                                           -THE CHAPTER OF THE STAR

5

The Mission

How little Muhammad understood at first the notions Gabriel was planting in the churned-up soil of his mind is shown by the fact that his first deed when he had recovered sufficiently from his fright was to visit the Kaaba with its hundreds of gods. He stopped at Waraqa's house to hear with his own ears his learned relative's opinion. "This is the same visitation that came to Moses," repeated Waraqa, "but nobody will believe you. They'll call you a liar."

He drew Muhammad's head close and kissed him on the forehead. "I hope I may live to see the day you'll be expelled from the tribe," he said.

Muhammad was aghast. "Are you saying the Quraysh will expel me?" he exclaimed.

"No one has ever brought to his people what you bring without being treated as an enemy," replied Waraqa. "It is the fate of prophets."

Waraqa died before Muhammad's mission actively began. After the Call there followed a period known in Muslim history books as the Cessation of Revelation, during which God was silent and no further communication from a divine source was revealed to His Messenger. When that period ended, or even when it started, is not clear. There is an indication that after the first visions, they continued for a while, and that while wandering alone in the mountains Muhammad received further instruction through the divine ambassador Gabriel. On one occasion, Gabriel is believed to have dug a hole in the sand with his heel, causing a fresh spring to bubble to the surface. With this, he taught Muhammad how to perform the ritual ablutions which always precede Muslim prayers, and he instructed him in the prostrations that accompany them. Thereafter Muhammad spent much time practicing these exercises.

The Cessation of Revelation lasted for perhaps two or three years and served Muhammad as a period of quiet reflection and preparation for the task before him. God, Who knows all, knew that he needed time to ponder all that had happened to him and examine the knowledge that had come pounding into his head beyond anything that had actually transpired: the consciousness that he, the angel, Khadija, their children, and the tribe of Quraysh were but shadows in a shadow play behind which stood the one reality, that there is no God but God. God had permitted them all to play like children for ages past, and they had fallen into the error of thinking that He did not care or notice when they grubbed money, cheated orphans, swindled pilgrims, buried girl babies, and worshiped foolish stones. Now He had selected a Messenger to call Himself to their attention and make them understand that He and He alone was the Creator, first, last, and always; that He was a vigilant watcher, a wide-awake observer, and what is more, a ready reckoner. There would come a Day, a dismal Judgment Day, when rewards and punishments were going to be doled out for deeds, measure for measure.

So the first message that formed in Muhammad's mind to communicate to his fellowman was one of the unity of God. Stemming from that was the conviction of the One God as the initiator of man and his world, who had an intimate interest in His creation. Finally, God wanted it to be known that having invented a puppet with a knowledge of right and wrong, He had every intention of calling him to account.

At first Muhammad spoke of his revelations only to members of his immediate family. Khadija is reckoned his first disciple. The first male convert is usually said to be Ali, although he was only about nine or ten at the time. The second was his former slave, Zayd ben Haritha, now a young man grown. We might expect that these persons who were closest to him, along with his daughters, should have heard his message sympathetically, but the next male convert was a different matter. It was his friend, Abu Bekr. He was a moderately prosperous businessman of Mecca, well liked and respected, "sociable and experienced." Probably the two had become comrades through the League of the Virtuous, since this body used to meet in a house of Abu Bekr's clan, the Taym. He heard Muhammad's messages and immediately accepted them as the truth.

It meant the world to the shy Muhammad that his friend showed such trust in

29

him, and he said long after, "Of all the men to whom I have offered Islam, all asked questions except Abu Bekr. He simply believed me." It is revealing to us that Muhammad could evoke such confidence in a hardheaded businessman.

Abu Bekr was not the kind of man to have a hole-in-corner religion, and while Muhammad himself was silent about his adventure in the cave, Abu Bekr began to talk. He said that Muhammad had been informed by divine revelation that he was the Messenger of God, and he, Abu Bekr, believed him. In his forthright way, which always took the shortest means of getting things done, he commanded all his business employees and household slaves to submit themselves to Muhammad's instruction. The confession of faith might have been formulated in these early days:

There Is No God but God
And Muhammad Is His Messenger

Every day and all day the Quraysh used to gather in the holy enclosure of the Kaaba, and when they had finished their prayers and walk-around, they would linger to do business, invest in caravans or worry about the investments made yesterday, or read the public notices hanging on the walls, or eat a bite of food or doze. The enclosure of the Kaaba was the center of the town's activities. There went Abu Bekr and told them the news. Most people smiled, but others were curious enough to go and ask Muhammad what these mysterious revelations were about. "The Messenger of God (God bless and preserve him)," an ancient source records, "summoned people to Islam secretly and openly; and there responded to God whom He would of young people and weak people."

There it is in a nutshell: the famous partnership that comes together in times of enormous social change. Young people were finding that some of the notions believed in by their honored ancestors did not hold water and that they were about to inherit a world seriously flawed. And weak people—that is, the poor and the clanless—were finding that there was no good reason why they should not be strong. These people listened to Abu Bekr with both ears, and his efforts drew a number of discontented teenage apprentices and the disgruntled sons of rich fathers to join the little group that met around Muhammad.

There were a few men of greater substance too—the sort of thoughtful people who might previously have toyed with the notion of becoming Christians or Jews. But on the whole early Islam was a youth movement, which was at first thought of as a harmless club. There were in those days about forty members, and as the house of Muhammad appears to have had no room to hold this number comfortably, they took to meeting in a larger house on the outskirts of town belonging to a rich young man named Arqam of Clan Makhzum. The House of Arqam is remembered by Muslims as Islam's first meeting place.

Muhammad must have been a rather stumbling teacher at first. He was far from an aggressive man, and his instinct when he entered a group was to sit himself down in any handy empty place, even though everyone present had come to hear him speak. Probably he had a poor vocabulary with which to expound the ideas that in an instant had made infinity plain to him. And God was silent, unhelpful, month after month, stretching to years. In vain Muhammad prayed for a new revelation, yearned for the pain and the suffocating attack that attended the longed-for Voice. But nothing happened. He felt like a wrong instrument, picked up and then cast aside as useless.

As a sounding board for his lonely thoughts, he took Ali about with him, taught the child the importance of prayer and how to wash himself and perform the prostrations. One day, as Ali told it later, his proper father, Abu Talib, came upon them as they practiced these rather strenuous exercises and asked them what they were doing, kneeling and knocking their heads on the ground. Muhammad explained, "Uncle, this is the religion of God, His angels, His prophets. It is the religion of our father Abraham." He begged his uncle to allow him to teach him. But Abu Talib replied with the voice of the old world, "I cannot give up the religion of my fathers." Then he thought a moment, and as if sensing the troubles in store for Muhammad, he said, "But, by God, I'll not forsake you as long as I live."

This was an important assurance coming from the head of Clan Hashim. It meant that no one could offer insult or harm to Muhammad without being accountable to his clan.

To Ali, Abu Talib said, "Your cousin would not call on you to do anything that is not good, so stick with him."

Then he left them, and for the rest of his life Ali would tell of his father's parting shot: "Anyway, I wouldn't want to belong to a religion that made me put my head lower than my backside!"

Then one day God's ambassador tore into Muhammad's mind again. He fell down shivering, in pain from the forces clamoring at his frail understanding. The Voice came like the reverberation of an enormous bell with no beginning and no end, and he huddled fearfully under his close-wrapped cloak and sweated. Yet, when moments later he came to his senses, the words were already fixed in his mind, clear in beauty and even in a certain note of mockery:

O thou who hidest under a cloak!
Arise and warn!
Thy Lord magnify,
Thy garments purify,
Put all uncleanliness away from thee,

31

All selfish deeds behind thee,
And await thy Lord!

Muhammad waited, and this time not in vain. The messages came, ranging from firm commands to words profoundly comforting to the worried Messenger.

In the name of God, the compassionate and merciful,
By the morning!
By the evening!
Thy Lord has not abandoned thee nor hated thee—
The latter would be better for thee than the first!

The last, rather hectoring statement is typical of a tone that God often used toward His Messenger, as if He thought that Muhammad stood just as much in need of correction as any other member of the Quraysh tribe.

Then, one day came the ultimatum that put an end forever to Muhammad's peaceful existence as the well-loved mentor of a young people's club:

So call not on another god but God,
Or you will be punished!
But warn your clan and all of your near kin!
To those of them who follow you, be gentle,
To those who do not, say, "Not on my head be what you do!"
Trust in the One, the mighty and the merciful,
He sees you clear when you stand up.

It was an urgent matter, it seemed, according to God, that Muhammad lose no time in making known the message He was putting into the world to the Hashim. Yet surely God knew, just as Muhammad knew, that hardly anyone would listen to Muhammad. Ali, who was thirteen at the time, recollected, "The Apostle of God said to me, 'God has commanded me to warn my family and near relatives, but I knew I should never be able to do such a thing, I would only arouse a lot of unpleasantness. So I kept quiet. Then Gabriel came and told me that if I did not do as I was told, I would be punished.'"

Certainly he quailed at the thought of making an announcement of this nature to a gathering of his distinguished uncles. Anyone would. Moses had been no less timid when ordered to go before Pharaoh, but he had at least the courage to ask God for a helper. Muhammad did not think of this, so he had to make do with small Ali. "Get mutton and milk," he said to Ali, "and call the sons of Abd-el-Muttalib."

They came, a tide of uncles and cousins, large and small, straggling over the golden ground toward the hill called Safa, where Ali had arranged a sort of picnic. "Tell them I am one who talks plainly," God admonished. Instead of doing this, Muhammad signaled for the food to be brought on and led the feast himself, tearing into some meat with his saw teeth. By the time all had finished eating, it was getting late. One of the uncles, Abu Lahab, forestalled speeches by jumping to his feet and leaving. The rest followed.

This fiasco is probably embroidered by the traditionists in order to bring down early blame on the head of Abu Lahab, who was Muhammad's most hostile uncle. The truth of what happened on the hill of Safa is better reflected in the straightforward account given of the second occasion when Muhammad managed to muster all his relatives in one place. Quick and bold he arose, before Abu Lahab could say a word, and after reciting for his family some significant revelations, spoke: "O children of Hashim, I know of no Arab who has come to his people with a nobler message than mine. I bring you the best of this world and the next. For God has ordered me to call you to him. So which of you will join me to be my helper in this matter?"

This untempting invitation met with no response. Uncles and cousins sat in silence like desert stones, and time stretched out like time read by the stars. At length Ali could bear it no longer, and he said shrilly, "O Prophet of God! I will be your helper in this matter!"

At the sound of his young voice, laughter broke over the Clan Hashim. They slapped their thighs and hung on one another's shoulders. Pale and taut, Muhammad drew the boy close to him and placed his hand on his head. He said, "Then this is my helper, my brother, and my executor. Hear him and obey him in all things."

The Hashim were beside themselves. They yelled at Abu Talib, "Hi! Did you hear what he said? He said you have got to obey your own son!"

They went rolling merrily down the hill of Safa to the Kaaba and told the other clans of Quraysh that Muhammad was going mad. Battle lines began to be drawn then. Although, out of loyalty to Abu Talib, the individual members of his own clan did not act against his wishes, still they were not solidly behind him. Clans Makhzum and Abd Shams took the lead in opposition. Clan Makhzum might well have been watching with annoyance the use to which their rich young relative Arqam was putting his good house in the suburbs. It has been remarked too that the clans most hostile to Muhammad's ministry were those who previously had been most opposed to his activities in the League of the Virtuous. Possibly they thought it was devilishly clever of Muhammad to bring the support of a divine voice to that group's pious platform of protecting the poor and the weak. From this point of view, the struggles of early Islam might have been entwined in the familiar conflicts of capitalism: self-interest and survival-of-the-fittest principle at war with more humanitarian aims.

33

Two men in particular were ringleaders of Muhammad's detractors: the red-headed and fiery-tempered Abu Jahl of Makhzum and Abu Sufyan of Abd Shams, the carrier of the Quraysh battle flag, commander of their military strength, in fact. At first they contented themselves with grumbling and jeering, but in the course of time they became bitter and dangerous enemies, spreading it about that Muhammad was a liar, a poet, and a sorcerer, possessed by an evil jinn, and in any case a first-class troublemaker who went about calling the Quraysh way of life foolish, insulting their forefathers, reviling their religion, and cursing their gods. Indignation was worked up not only on behalf of Hubal but of his wives in the other shrines, since the business interests of the Quraysh extended to these other temples.

There is no need, however, to diminish the fact that some of Muhammad's opponents, such as his Uncle Abu Talib, were genuinely jealous of the honor of their tribal forefathers and their religion. It was beyond them to discern that Muhammad's comprehension, forcibly stretched by Gabriel, went beyond tribal tradition to embrace those of the whole Semitic subrace of Arabs. If Ali's recollection is reliable, Muhammad had told Abu Talib that his was the "religion of Abraham." This was before the concept of Islam, a word which means "submission" or "surrendering" to God's will, as Abraham surrendered when he prepared to sacrifice his son. In those early days Muhammad spoke of himself and his followers, as hanif, monotheists—as, he supposed, Abraham was a monotheist, even before anyone had ever heard of Jewry.

The first victim of the criticism that was coming his way was his young daughter Ruqayya, who was betrothed to a son of Uncle Abu Lahab and according to the custom was living at the home of her future husband. Abu Lahab and his wife (who was Abu Sufyan's sister) now decided that they did not want the daughter of a madman as a member of their family, and they sent Ruqayya home in disgrace. Another daughter, Zaynab, was already married. A deputation of well-meaning businessmen called on her husband, Abu'l-As, urging him to put her away. He told them he wanted no other girl in Mecca than Zaynab and that they had better drop the subject.

Another daughter, Umm Kulthum, may have been repudiated by her betrothed husband at this time. It is not clear in the traditions. Fatima, the youngest, was a child living at home. She probably spent her time trotting after her cousin Ali, whom she was later to marry.

For a time Muhammad and the others remained aloof from the Kaaba. Not that Muhammad had given up his reverence for the sacred house founded by Adam and Abraham, but in the early days of his ministry, wishing to distinguish his teaching from Hubal worship, he looked to Jerusalem as the spiritual center of the new faith that was taking shape in his mind. When his little flock met to say their prayers, it was to Jerusalem they turned and touched their foreheads to the ground.

By and by he began to make his appearance again at the shrine. He had no choice really. God had commanded him to preach to the Quraysh, not to a group of friends in Arqam's house, and so he must face them, even though Abu Jahl had been heard to say loudly that he would crack open the head of any follower of Muhammad who got in the way of his circumambulation.

God was in the meantime doing His part by sending down revelations which intruded on the Prophet at any hour of the day or night, gradually building his edifice of thought. Those early communications of Mecca repeated with vigor the initial message of God's unique and all-seeing nature, and how eventually everyone would be raised from the dead to face judgment and answer for their sins of greed and dishonesty.

When the earth shall quake, quaking,
And the mountains shall crumble, crumbling,
And become like dust before the wind,
Ye shall be of three sorts:
The ones of the right hand—what lucky ones they are!
And the ones of the left hand—what unlucky ones they are!
And the first ones in the forefront . . .

The "first ones" who were not going to be kept waiting in suspense were the first Muslims. Those on the right were the ordinary run of good Muslims, who were to be transported to the gardens of Paradise where their houris, "like hidden pearls," awaited them with trays of their favorite fruits. But those unlucky ones on the left! Hot blasts, boiling water, and clouds of pitchy smoke were in store for them.

These revelations fell from the lips of Muhammad, but devout Muslims believe them to be the veritable speech of God to man, through Muhammad. Many of the revelations begin with the word "Say!" exactly as an efficient executive might tell his secretary: "Take this down!"

Eventually they were compiled into the Holy Quran.

35

I take refuge in the Lord of the worlds, the King of men, the God of men, from the evil of the whispering devil who whispers into the hearts of men and jinns, and then slinks off.

-THE CHAPTER OF MEN

6

Opposition

Hostility to Muhammad began gently enough, not overstepping the bounds of decent behavior due to a member of Clan Hashim. It would have been extremely dangerous for the Quraysh to lay violent hands on Muhammad, for he was not a slave or clanless person, and by tribal law any harm or insult offered to him would have to be returned in kind by his clan. For ages past, the strict accounting of the lex talionis—"the law of retaliation," an eye for an eye, a tooth for a tooth—had kept the passions of Arabia in check. In recent decades, to be sure, gentler ways were gaining headway. It was becoming possible, for example, to kill a man, and if his kinsmen did not too seriously lament his passing, they might consent to receive a blood price for him. A hundred camels was becoming fixed as a proper price for one man.

On the other hand, in a country with a sparse food supply, a cessation in murderous habits was bound to bring about an increase in population, which in turn provoked changes in the social order. It was these very forces, working with and against each other, that created a mood of contentiousness among the poor, the weak, the clanless, and the young. Beyond the understanding of all of them, it had created the need for the philosophical change of which Muhammad was the herald.

Forces were at work within him too, transforming a gentle man into a formidable leader with fires of anger burning on his tongue, a man who was "jealous for the Lord." Not the closest scrutiny of the traditions or the Quran itself can disclose in Muhammad the slightest suspicion of desire for personal fame. An urgent task had been laid on him. That in fulfilling it he would bring a world to an end and set up a new one with himself as leader did not occur to him.

So, with a persistence matched only by the vehement prophets of Israel—whom he resembled—he preached to the Quraysh about their misdeeds. Besides their natural objections to his remarks, they became seriously alarmed at the effect they might have on the pilgrim traffic. Considerations of personal rivalry were also present. Abu Jahl had no doubt seen himself growing old in a position of leadership. Now here was this hitherto passive Hashimite, whom he had known all his life and hardly given a thought to, making authoritative statements about what was going to happen to them all on Judgment Day. So he fought back, and when Muhammad rose to preach in the sacred enclosure, he would fling out a lewd name. He was a substantial citizen. Under his prodding, other citizens ceased to listen to Muhammad and formed an opposition, which was eventually to become virulent.

Still, there was a lot of secret listening. Even his enemies, including Abu Jahl, went secretly to the Prophet's house by night to stand about in the shadows and hear the recitations coming through the air vents. Then, coming and going, they would bump into each other and angry words would ensue: "What are you doing here? You ought not to be hanging about here. Don't come again—suppose some silly fool should see you and chatter?"

Somebody did see them and did chatter.

Never did the Quraysh openly acknowledge interest in Muhammad's opinions, and when he would recite by day at the Kaaba, they would say, "Oh, our hearts are veiled, we don't understand such talk." Or, "Sorry, there seems to be a lump in my ears." The politer ones might say, "A curtain divides us, you must go your way, and we shall go ours . . ."

Some of God's revelations in these days show that He was becoming exceeding wroth: "Verily," He commanded Muhammad to tell the Quraysh:

What you have been threatened shall surely happen!
And when the stars shall be erased
And the Heavens rive
And the mountains blow like chaff . . .
Woe on that day for those who say it is a lie!

God might menace and speak ill-humoredly, but Muhammad was finding within himself huge powers of tolerance for abuse. All his life he was to forgive easily and readily the most extraordinarily insults, even murderous attempts on his person. But mockery of his miraculous Quran, the very word of God, was stored up vengefully in his memory, and he harbored a curious hatred of all who used words eloquently against his words, as if words themselves were sacred instruments that must never be basely used.

There was a man in Mecca who had traveled far into Persia and had learned some of the scintillating legends and folktales about the kings and heroes of that land. Until Muhammad came, he had enjoyed a reputation as an entertainer at the Kaaba. Once, after Muhammad had finished telling people about God and a silence fell, this man broke it, saying, "By God, I can tell a better story than that!" And he told it.

It was a story that, years later, he wished he had never heard.

This storyteller, unsympathetic and jealous, was one of those the Quraysh sent as an emissary northward to the oasis Yathrib, which we call Medina, to consult the learned rabbis who lived there, and ask them what they thought of this Muhammad setting himself up as the Voice of God on the same level as Abraham and Moses. It can be imagined that the rabbis didn't think well of it, and they sent back some rather foolish folk riddles for Muhammad to answer, pretending in this way to test whether he was a genuine prophet or not. Only one question seemed to have much relevance, and perhaps it contained the nugget of the Jewish test. It was, "What is the spirit?"

And God, who cared not a jot for the impression He or His Messenger was making on the rabbis of Yathrib, replied, "'Tell them the spirit is your Lord's business and that you don't know anything about it."

The Quraysh were getting bored with this insolent poet who kept telling them scraps of old fables from the Jewish and Christian Scriptures. "Old fables, are they?" said God. "Tell them that He who knows the secrets of heaven and earth is sending down to them these old fables. Yet," He added, as if to soften His words, "God is merciful and forgiving."

A man picked up an old bone, crumbled it in his hand, and blew the dust in the Apostle's face: "Are you trying to tell me that God can raise life in this after it has decayed?"

"Yes I am," snapped Muhammad. "God will raise it and you, and then he'll send you to Hell!"

God did not like this crude response, and as He quite often did, obliged Muhammad to go over the same ground in more godlike tones:

Has man not seen that He created him from a clot?
Man creates likenesses of Us, and forgets that he is but Our creation,
And asks: "Who will put life into these rotten bones?"
Tell them: "He who gave life will put it back!

38

He who knows about all creation,
Who can strike flame from a green tree if He chooses, and set you on fire
with it!"

Now God, who well knows how to strengthen our duty to Him, by putting temptation in our path, does the same for His prophets. One day a certain chieftain came and sat by Muhammad, and speaking tactfully, said, "O son of my brother, you are one of us, one of the noblest of the Quraysh, sharing our great ancestry. You have come to us with a message that is difficult to hear patiently, for who can listen to his gods reviled and his ancestors insulted? So listen to me and I shall make some suggestions.

"If what you want is to be rich, we will gather part of our property, each and every one, and give it to you. You will be the richest of us all. If you want honor, we'll make you a chief. Indeed, we'll crown you king like the king of Byzantium if you like.

"And if this ghost who comes and mumbles in your ear can't be gotten rid of in any other way, we'll call an exorcist. It is not too unusual that a familiar spirit takes possession of a man, but he can be cured of it."

Muhammad heard this silently. Then he said, "Now listen to me." For a long time afterward he held his listener transfixed as he recited how God, in His love for the Arabs, had decided to reveal to them their own Book as a guidance and a healing for their sin-beset souls, and how he, Muhammad, a plain man, as insignificant as any Arab born, had been chosen to bring them the truth of things, from beginning to end, in God's own words. "What?" said Muhammad,

Are you going to deny Him who created the Earth in two days?
And set up your gods as equals to the Lord of the Worlds?
Worlds on which He placed firm mountains and blessed them,
And apportioned food—in four days, if anyone should ask—
And made Heaven, formed it of clouds of smoke,
And said to Heaven and Earth, "Come together, you two, whether you want to or not!
And they said to Him, 'We are coming . . .'"

He went on enumerating wonders, how God had bedecked the lower Heavens with lamps and populated the skies with guardian angels. The elder listened spellbound. Later he advised the Quraysh leaders: "I think we ought to leave this man severely alone. Somebody will probably come along and kill him one day, and then we'll be rid of him. If they don't, he'll be famous, and we'll share in his glory."

They replied, "He has bewitched you with his tongue."

"I've told you my opinion," said the elder. "Do as you please."

39

The Quraysh said to Muhammad, "Very well. You have refused our reasonable proposals, even though they were generous. So let us just see what your God can do. We don't live such an easy life here in Mecca compared to life in some other countries. Why don't you ask your omnipotent Lord to take away these mountains that smother us in? Make Him cause rivers to spring up in the desert like the one in Syria and Iraq. And give us castles with treasure, and gardens full of flowers and dates. And since He can raise people up from the dead, let's see Him raise up our wise ancestors so that they can tell us whether you are a liar or not."

Muhammad replied calmly that no such dramatic events were likely to take place. He was empowered only to bring them God's Word, which was miraculous enough, it seemed to him. They might accept it and be glad, or reject it and be sorry.

"Then why does He speak to us through you? Why not through one of the chieftains? Better still, why doesn't He send an angel to teach us directly?"

Since God had not seen fit to explain His actions, Muhammad had no good answer for this.

"We believe in angels," said the Quraysh, "but how does He expect us to believe in you? Didn't your God realize we would sit here and raise these very arguments? Didn't He give you the power with which to convince us?"

Muhammad said that he could only deliver the message as it was revealed to him.

"Well, our conscience is clear," said the Quraysh. "We have given you every chance. Now, by God, we'll destroy you—otherwise you will destroy us."

Muhammad went away from this conference leaving the Quraysh morose and vindictive. Abu Jahl said, "By God, I'll wait for him tomorrow with a stone I can hardly lift, and when he puts his head down on the ground, I'll split his skull with it."

He did no such thing. He didn't dare.

God often reminded Muhammad that he was only a lowly mortal like everyone else, and so it is not surprising to find the Prophet behaving as anyone would in his position. He courted public favor. The traditionists excuse him: "He was anxious for the welfare of his people, wishing to attract them." Probably at first he saw himself as something like a Jewish rabbi, a respected teacher toward whom the community leaders would gravitate for good advice by day, while by night he consulted expert opinion, not the Torah but the Angel Gabriel.

Whatever he may have thought, there are some incidents on record showing Muhammad trying hard to ingratiate himself with the leaders of Quraysh. Once when he was in deep discussion with them, a blind man came on the scene and, unable to see that Muhammad was occupied with important company, loudly demanded to hear the Quran. The Apostle did not rebuke him, but he turned his back with annoyance showing on his face. God was not slow with His rebuke. The oppression and the pain closed down on him, and the Voice with its dry humor chastised him:

You frowned and turned your back when the blind man spoke!
But how did you know that man might not have been purified?
Or at least heard a little, and remembered a little?
Oh no! You preferred to deal with aristocrats!

The lesson burned, but it did not sink in all at once. There was in store a far more horrifying fall from virtue, for Muhammad, who could not be tempted by money or power, was open to that most insidious bribe, the love and acceptance of his own kin. Indeed, he may have hungered for that very thing all his life, never realizing that being an orphan had primed him for the ordeal of standing alone and apart from the organism of the tribe.

The traditionist Ibn Ishaq says, "When Muhammad saw that his people had turned their backs on him, he was pained, and he longed for a message that would reconcile them to him."

He longed so hard that it finally blossomed in his mind. One day, when he was preaching at the Kaaba—his listeners perhaps somnolent or resigned to his persistent voice—suddenly and surprisingly there fell from his tongue the following verse:

You remember al-Lat and al-Uzza?
And Manat, the third, the other?
These are swans, high-soaring ones!
Surely you may ask for their favors?
Surely you will not be ignored!

The Quraysh were electrified, as well they might be. These goddesses, Hubal's harem, swelled the pockets of all who had invested in their shrines. Besides they were older than the world and mischievous. The buzz sped around the holy enclosure: "This is the first time he has had a good word to say about the old gods!" Their goodwill and relief that he had at last come to his senses was immediate and ungrudging. They joined him in prayers and, wonderful to behold, knelt and knocked their heads on the ground. For the first time in his life Muhammad tasted the wine of popular success.

We do not know how long he continued to bask in this friendly atmosphere before what God called his "self-accusing soul" rescued him from error. We may imagine his spiritual struggle when he admitted to himself the hugeness of his betrayal of the One God, and if he did not squirm on his own accord, there was

41

Gabriel in his ear: "What have you done, Muhammad? You have told these people something I did not bring to you from God!"

The hour of expiation came some days, or perhaps weeks, later, when a new revelation brought a correction:

> You know al-Lat and al-Uzza,
> And Manat, the third, the other . . .
> They are but names you have named, you and your fathers before you.
> God has given no power to such as them.

Thus did Muhammad find, as many politicians do, that sudden popularity may come to a sudden end. At a still later date, another revelation came from God, placing blame for the incident squarely on the Prophet's shoulders. It was Muhammad's vain ambition that had caused the lying whisperers to take possession of his tongue.

> We have never sent an apostle or a prophet,
> But when he has cherished some selfish ambition,
> Satan has not thrown something into it,
> But God throws out what Satan throws in
> And makes all perfect.
> God is knowing, wise.

Never again do we see Muhammad personally giving God cause to correct His Quran, although later on, when He came to reveal laws for the regulation of the growing Muslim community, He sometimes corrected Himself of His own accord.

It was after the repudiation of the "satanic verses" that the Quraysh lost all patience with Muhammad and began to throw the respect due to Hashim to the four winds. A deputation was sent to Abu Talib, the patriarch, to persuade him to forsake his protection of his nephew, cast him out of Hashim. Once removed from the shelter of his clan, he could be kicked or killed. No one would be entitled to call the account, even to the value of a hundred camels. They put it to the elder: "O Abu Talib, he has cursed our gods and mocked our fathers, and either you must stop him or let us at him. Don't you understand that this is your problem as well as ours?"

Abu Talib gave them a tactful reply and sent them away. And he did nothing. Again they approached him: "You have a lofty position among us, but we have asked you to curb the activities of your nephew, and you have not done it. Now you are leaving us no choice except to fight Hashim."

Abu Talib was distressed, but he returned no satisfactory answer. After they

42

had gone, he sent for Muhammad and expostulated with him. "Spare me and spare yourself," he said, "and do not give me a heavier burden than I can bear."

Muhammad knew that his uncle, as patriarch, really had no sensible alternative to abandoning him. He said in despair, "Oh, my uncle, by God, if they put the sun in my right hand and the moon in my left on condition that I give up this cause, I would not give it up until God made it victorious or I died for it." Then he broke into tears, covering his face with his mantle. He rose and fled from his uncle's house.

But Abu Talib was just as swift to rise and call him back. "Go, say what you like," he told Muhammad, "for I will never abandon you."

Hashim paid a high price for their chieftain's loyalty. The Quraysh placed a boycott against Muhammad's clan, refusing to do business with them or to permit their clients or confederates to deal with them even to the point of selling them food. Marriage with Hashim was forbidden and betrothals broken off. Since no one was allowed to bring food to them in the city, the Hashim had to pick up their households bodily and remove them to the outskirts of town.

The boycott was not totally effective, principally because there were sober and softhearted citizens left in Mecca who were not really eager to see Hashim die of starvation. Once Abu Jahl caught Khadija's nephew taking food to his aunt. He hung on to his cloak and said, "By God, before you and your food move from here, I'll denounce you at the Kaaba!" Another tribesman came along and said, "What is going on here? Are you trying to stop the boy from taking food to his aunt? Let him go."

Abu Jahl refused, and a fight ensued, in which his adversary seized a camel's jaw and knocked him down with it. Then he trod on him and gave him some instructive kicks.

"Meanwhile," the traditionist records, "Muhammad was exhorting his people day and night, openly proclaiming God's command, without fear of anyone."

One day, someone noticed that the document of boycott, which had been posted on the walls of the Kaaba, had been eaten by ants—a sure sign, it was argued, that the gods did not support the boycott. So it was allowed to dwindle into nothingness, and the Hashim picked up their households and moved themselves back into their old homes.

43

When it is said to them, "Follow what God has revealed," they say, "Nay, we will follow what our fathers agreed on." What? Even though their fathers are doomed to the blaze?

-THE CHAPTER OF LUQMAN

7

Persecution

Muhammad continued to preach—he had no choice with Gabriel continually prodding him with God's own Voice. But as the years passed, few listened to him except for the fun of hooting him down. He became one of the curiosities of Mecca. Visitors to the holy city were curious about him and would have been glad to hear him speak, but not wishing to draw the ridicule of the Quraysh, they had to content themselves with edging closer to the faithful while they prayed in their mysterious and spectacular manner at the Kaaba. God, wishing to encourage such stealthily interested parties and at the same time spare them the embarrassment of being noticed, sent down a command to Muhammad that is observed in Muslim prayers to this day: "Do not say your prayers too loudly, nor yet whisper them, but seek a way between."

The first man to get tired of this state of affairs was a slave named Abdullah. He did not see why the very word of God should not be proclaimed aloud. His comrades among the faithful tried to dissuade him, fearing for his safety since he had no clan protection, but Abdullah was bent on becoming famous in history. He went to the sanctuary and raised his voice above the crowd, the first man in Islam apart from the Prophet to recite the holy book in public, and he chose a passage wherein God celebrates, as He loved to do, the glory of His creation.

In the name of God, the compassionate and merciful—
He taught the Quran,
He created man, taught him plain speech,
Gave to the sun and moon their appointed time,
Set out the grasses and the trees to adore,
And the heavens . . .

Abdullah did not get much farther than this before the Quraysh came swirling around him, yelling, "What is the son of a slave saying?" When they realized it was the Quran, they began to punch him in the face. His friends pulled him free eventually and got him to safety, but he returned to the bosom of the flock a badly battered man.

It was "weak people" like Abdullah who bore the full brunt of the persecutions and harassment now visited on Muslims, who become the butt of every poor humorist and petty sadist. Slaves especially were beaten, starved, and occasionally subjected to atrocities such as being dragged by camels or obliged to watch their mothers being whipped. Abu Bekr made a point of buying the freedom of slaves who confessed Islam. His fortune began to dwindle as he did so, but his commitment to Muhammad was total, and Muhammad's opinion of worldly wealth was low. One day, passing a desert spot, Abu Bekr heard a man's voice groaning, "One . . . one . . . one . . . one God, by God!" It was a great black Abyssinian named Bilal, staked out under the blistering sun with a huge rock on his chest. Abu Bekr arranged to buy his freedom. Bilal was to become one of the most famous of the early Muslims.

It was in order to remove such unprotected followers from danger that in 615, about five years after the Call, Muhammad organized the first emigration to Abyssinia. The Abyssinians were Coptic Christians, People of the Book who generally practiced tolerance toward other sects. About eleven families departed from Mecca. Others followed later, eighty-three people in all, traveling southward along the coast of the Red Sea to the cape near Aden, where only a short ride by the efficient sailboats the Arabs call dhows separates Arabia from the coast of Africa. It was a brave adventure for the pioneer group, among whom were the Prophet's daughter Ruqayya and her new husband Uthman. They had no idea, outside their trust in Muhammad's word, how they would be treated. The Quraysh sent fast on their heels a delegation to the Abyssinian emperor—the Negus, he was called, then as in modern times—requesting him not to shelter the Muslims and instead to hand them over as captives to the Meccans. It is not quite clear why the Quraysh pursued the little group so vindictively, instead of thank-

45

ing Hubal for having got rid of them. Abyssinia was a central distribution point for the riches of Africa—"ivory and apes and peacocks," metals and gems—which were then siphoned through Mecca to the luxury-loving Byzantines and Persians. Possibly the Quraysh were terrified that Muhammad's followers might contrive to seize the golden thread in their own hands, and they therefore tried to persuade the Negus that Muhammad's teachings were antagonistic to Christianity, and blasphemous.

The Negus had the fairness to summon the Muslims to a hearing in the presence of his bishops. They came in trepidation, asking one another, "What are we going to say?" Their leader Jafar replied, "There is only one thing we can say—what the Prophet has taught us."

So, standing before the Negus and speaking through an interpreter, Jafar told as simply as he could how Muhammad had brought a message to them and what changes his words had brought into their lives. The Negus listened with interest and asked if they would recite to him from the Quran. Jafar chose to recite from the Chapter of Mary, which tells Muhammad's version of the Annunciation and subsequent birth of Jesus, how He was born under a palm tree, which his mother seized and shook, and how He could speak the instant He was born.

Whatever questions this tale evoked in the mind of the Negus, it arouses our immense curiosity, for it is strangely similar to the story of the birth of Gautama Buddha, and we wonder what exotic quirk of the Divine Mind poured it into the Holy Quran.

The Negus saw no harm in the Muslims, and he granted them refuge.

At home, Muhammad's long tussle with the Quraysh continued, becoming ever more embittered. For it soon became clear that the new doctrines had the power, as a slender plant splits stones, to crack the tough family lines, dividing the clans against each other, particularly the young from the old. "By God, his speech is sweet," an elder is reported to have said, "his root is a palm tree whose branches are fruitful . . . He is a sorcerer who has brought a message by which he separates a man from his father, or from his brother, or from his wife, or from his family."

Abu Jahl found to his rage that his own young brother confessed the faith. Abu Sufyan, having forced his nephew to repudiate Ruqayya, now saw her married and off to Abyssinia with his cousin Uthman. Abu Lahab found himself at loggerheads with his brother, Abu Talib, on Muhammad's account. He appeased his rage by following the Prophet about at pilgrimage time, warning all who stopped to listen to the recitations, that it was only his insane nephew speaking, a known liar whose mind wandered. His wife assisted him by gathering thorns and scattering them outside Muhammad's house, a menace to all good Muslims, especially to those with bare feet.

46

We hear of one acrimonious incident described in the words of an eyewitness who overheard some of the Meccan notables complaining, saying that they had never known anything like the trouble they had endured from this fellow, who was dividing the community against itself and disrupting the customary worship of the gods.

While they were talking, the Apostle came and kissed the Black Stone. He passed them as he walked around the temple, and they flung some insults at him. I could see this from his expression. He went on and passed them a second time, and the same thing happened; then a third time and he did the same. He stopped then and said, "Will you listen to me, O Quraysh? By Him who holds my life in His hand, I bring you death!"

The mocking men froze in their laughter and stood dismayed. This was their lifelong companion, Khadija's shy husband, the gentle man who in spite of great provocation over several years had never raised his hand or even spoken with much asperity except when repeating the threats of that rude jinn of his who whispered in his ear. The tribesmen stopped their tongues and even the rudest of them spoke kindly to Muhammad, using his honorific name: "Go home, Abu l'Qasim, for by God you are not a violent man."

Muhammad went home then, but when he returned to the Kaaba the next day, he found that passions were again high against him. They had heard the menace in Muhammad's voice, sensed a purpose that had not been there before. They began to circle around him, saying, "Are you the one who has cursed our gods and our religion?" The Apostle said, "I am."

One seized his robe and began to pull him about, but Abu Bekr rushed up to defend him, crying out, "Are you going to kill a man for saying God is my God?" So they turned on Abu Bekr and began to pull him about by the hair and beard.

This incident is said to have been the worst of the persecutions visited on Muhammad—harder than the lot of Gautama Buddha, but nothing like the fate of Christ and Zoroaster. Muhammad's torments lay in the mental realm, in the distress of being cast out by his tribe, a cell cut from the body, in his pain at the stubbornness of his tribesmen and his fear for their spiritual safety.

Abu Jahl deserved his greatest anxiety. This gentleman gave himself the extraordinary trouble of obtaining the fetus from a she-camel to place on Muhammad's neck when he performed his prostrations in the Kaaba, no doubt encouraged by happy sniggering from the mob.

One day, passing Muhammad as he sat quietly in meditation, he flung him an insult to which the Prophet did not reply. A woman who had overheard this thought she might drum up a little interesting mischief. It happened that Muhammad's uncle Hamza, a man of his own age, was reputed to be the strongest and most active of the Quraysh, their champion in war and sports. He spent most

47

of his time hunting in the hills. On that day, as he returned from the chase with his bow swinging from his shoulder and went toward the Kaaba for his evening walk-around, the woman ran after him and asked him if he had heard how Abu Jahl had heaped abuse on his nephew's head.

Hamza found himself at the end of all patience. He liked Muhammad, although he did not understand him. He went on the run to the mosque, where he saw Abu Jahl sitting among his friends. He lifted his heavy bow and gave him a great bang on the head with it. "Will you insult him when I join his religion?" he shouted, flexing his great muscles under the noses of the Quraysh. "What will you do when I recite the Quran, eh? Anybody want to hit me back?"

Several of the Beni Makhzum arose to bang Hamza's head, as they were bound to do by tribal custom, but Abu Jahl wisely put a stop to an incipient feud. He said, "Let him alone. I was really rude to his nephew."

But Hamza became a Muslim, and this put teeth into the faith. Some of the Quraysh became more careful about calling Muhammad a poet.

Yet somebody was a poet. The marvel of the Quran itself, the drama of the lines and their power to shift the insubstantial soils of the spirit, made converts, sometimes from among the most influential clans. One of the great early Muslims was Umar, a member of the prestigious Abd Shams. A man of combustible temper, he was one day seized with rage that such a person as Muhammad could be allowed to exist to attack the gods of the Kaaba, and he took up his sword and rushed out into the street toward Muhammad's house with the idea of slicing off the Prophet's head. A friend waylaid him: "What on earth is the matter with you?"

Umar told him, and the friend, wishing to save him from a deed he would regret, said, "Before you kill Muhammad, you had better look to your own family. Your sister Fatima and her husband have declared the faith."

Fuming all the more, Umar changed direction and without sheathing his trusty sword made for his sister's house. There, as it happened, she was listening, with her husband, to a fellow Muslim reciting from some manuscripts containing recent revelations. As they heard Fatima's brother enter the house, they hurriedly stuffed the sheets out of sight. But Umar had calmed down sufficiently to have paused at the door with his ear alert. "What is that rubbish I heard?" he bellowed.

"You heard nothing," said Fatima.

"By God, I did," said Umar, and began to set about him with wrathful sword. The reciter took cover. The brother-in-law cleverly protected himself behind his wife, while she interposed between husband and death. Covered with blood, she faced her brother: "Do as you will, we have professed the faith."

Umar stared at his sister, offering her life for a poem. His wrath left him as quickly as it had swept his reason away. He let fall his sword and humbly asked to hear again the lines he had heard before. The reciter allowed himself to be coaxed out of hiding, and when they had all washed and bound up their wounds, he repeated from the chapter mysteriously entitled "T.H.":

In the name of God, the compassionate and merciful—
We have not sent down this Quran to torment thee,
Only as a reminder to the God-fearing,
That a message has come down from the One who created
the earth and the high heavens,
From the merciful on His throne!
His are what is in the heavens,
His are what is on the earth,
And His whatever is betwixt them or beneath the ground.
And the thoughts you may speak publicly belong to Him,
And those you hold in your secret mind,
Yes, and those that are more hidden still . . .

Umar was enthralled. He wanted to be made a Muslim then and there. With his triumphant relatives escorting him, he strode off to Muhammad's house to make his confession of faith. Next to Ali and Abu Bekr, he was Muhammad's closest companion and a great general of Islam. He became the second caliph, and the Mosque of Omar in Jerusalem is named after him.

God, or the Being speaking with His Voice, was wont to describe himself with wondrous ornamental names—the Ninety-nine Names of God as they are called by those devout persons who have counted them in the Quran. Mostly He was the Compassionate and Merciful One. Every chapter introduces the Speaker in those terms. Yet they were the very qualities He did not exhibit to His chief servant, who continued to receive commands by means of painful, exacerbating attacks.

God used Muhammad mercilessly, and Muhammad labored ignominiously for nine years without a single doubt or faltering or reproach to Heaven. Then God rewarded him with a magnificent adventure of the spirit.

One night, as the Prophet lay asleep, he felt himself prodded by a foot. It was Gabriel's. Muhammad rose and followed the angel through the night streets to the entranceway of the enclosure of the Kaaba. There he saw standing, waiting, stamping its foot, a glorious milk-white steed—a magical animal, half mule and half donkey, with jeweled eyes, silken flanks, and wings neat against them. It shied as Muhammad approached. Gabriel said, "Shame on you, Buraq, to shy away from this honest man!"

Buraq stood, sweating and trembling, as Muhammad mounted him. Then Prophet, horse, and angel rose from the ground in a mighty clatter and sweep of wings and soared into the upper air, close to the lamps of the sky, and every stride

49

that Buraq took carried them to the next horizon. Muhammad clung for his life, but he was terribly interested in the trek of caravans beneath, making their way to Mecca.

They sped northward and eventually reached Jerusalem, the qibla to which Muhammad and his congregation turned as they prayed. There Buraq came to rest atop a hill beside a temple. The Prophet dismounted and entered. Around him he recognized a company of important persons. Surely, all the prophets of the Book were gathered there, the ancient preachers who had gone before him and had been persecuted and reviled for their pains. And there stood our father Abraham, and Moses—tall, thin, ruddy-faced and curly-haired, with a fierce nose—and Jesus, a man of medium height, reddish in complexion and freckled, with hair straight, even lank, having a wet look, as if He had just come from a bath.

It was Abraham whose looks most arrested Muhammad, because he said afterward, "I never saw a man who looked more like myself!"

He was offered both wine and milk to drink. He chose milk, and Gabriel said he was wise: "You have been rightly guided to this natural drink, Muhammad, and so will your people be. Wine will be forbidden you."

Muhammad left the temple and found Jacob's ladder erected before his feet, populated by angels, and he climbed it through seven heavens to the very throne of God. And on the way the gloomy angel Malik, the one who keeps Hell, lifted up the lid of that crimson pit so that he was able to see the poisonous fumes leaping high and greedy into the air. "I saw men with lips like camels," related Muhammad. "In their hands were lumps of fiery stone which they thrust into their mouths, and they would come out of their posteriors. I was told that these were once men who had sinfully devoured the wealth of orphans."

On the other hand he had glimpses of quite a different sort of furniture of the worlds beyond the world—the charming maidens who attended the couches of the virtuous, unforgettable for their dark red lips and luminous eyes. There was one especially adorable damsel. The Prophet asked her to whom she belonged, and she said the name of his adopted son, Zayd ben Haritha.

Awakening the next morning, Muhammad delivered this excellent news to Zayd, and to the faithful the rest of it. When the story became known in Mecca, far from attracting converts, it called forth ridicule, and many new converts left the faith. Even Abu Bekr, when he first heard about the Night Journey, said it was rubbish, though later, after learning that Muhammad himself was telling the tale, he said, "If he says it happened, then it is true."

In fact there is no reason to disbelieve in Muhammad's complete sincerity in relating this or any other vision of his. He was an illuminé, subject to queer adventures of the mind. We cannot know if these visions, or those of other mystics such as Swedenborg, or imaginative geniuses such as Dante, reflect some kind of objective reality. That they have symbolic veracity we do know, because we live by the pattern they prescribe, like so many dancers in a ballet conceived by a master choreographer.

In later years the Prophet's wife Ayesha gave his version of the experience, as he had told it to her: "The Apostle's body remained where it was, but God removed his spirit by night." Modern psychic research would call this an "out-of-the-body experience," and it is not unknown that such astral travelers have seen events at a distance which were later verified. It is recorded that the caravans that Muhammad had seen from Buraq's back meandering toward Mecca presently arrived there and convinced some doubters. Clairvoyant incidents are quite common in the traditions of Muhammad's life.

Truth or legend, the Night Journey carried the Prophet across farther horizons than even he could have imagined at the time, for the story, living in Muslim minds, connected his ideas to the roots that entwine them with those of Moses and Christ.

51

And when the misbelievers plotted to keep thee prisoner, or kill thee, or drive thee forth, they plotted well; but God plotted too. And God is the best of plotters.

-THE CHAPTER OF THE SPOILS

8

Emigration

Ten years after the Call, Muhammad was a failure with a handful of followers, many of them far off in Abyssinia. Only his faith and the loyalty of his immediate following sustained him. Occasionally direct words of encouragement came his way from the Voice, which assured him: "Long before you, people have mocked at the message of prophets; yet in the end, they were overwhelmed by that which they mocked."

In 619 Abu Talib lay dying. A delegation of the Quraysh visited him and prevailed on him to express a last wish to his nephew: If Muhammad would cease to preach in public, they would cease to persecute him. Muhammad was sent for, and the dying man did his best to bring him to compromise. Muhammad said, "Let them but say these few words: 'There is no God but God, and Muhammad is His Messenger,' and I will make peace with them."

So Abu Talib closed his eyes, leaving his nephew with a hard row to hoe. He did not himself accept the faith, and Muhammad did not attend his uncle's funeral.

Another blow fell when Khadija died, his loved wife, disciple, and close friend—furthermore, his financial support. The bulk of her fortune had long been dissipated in charitable gifts. Muhammad was a poor man once more.

Abu Lahab, the most hostile of his uncles, was now the leader of Hashim, and he made it clear that Muhammad no longer enjoyed clan protection. This amputation must have cost Muhammad great grief, wedded as he was, in love and fury to his clan and tribe. It was, however, urgently necessary for him to find protection, no matter whose. How little support he expected from among the clans of Quraysh is shown by the fact that he looked for it in at-Taif, the mountain home of the Thaqif. Perhaps in former days he himself or Khadija had had pleasant dealings with this tribe, which was noted for wit and intelligence, and this gave him hope to count on their understanding. Still, it is curious to find him traveling to at-Taif, which was also the shrine of the goddess al-Lat, whom he had denounced as a superstition, "only a name."

The Thaqif were not only not friendly, they were insulting. "Couldn't God find anyone better than you?" they wanted to know.

One of the clever ones said, "If you are God's Messenger, you are too important for me to speak to. And if you aren't, you are too big a liar for me to listen to."

Muhammad left the town, requesting them only to keep his visit a secret. But they did not, and a rabble of slaves and louts caught up with him, jeering and throwing clods of earth. He took refuge in a vineyard, whose owners took pity on him to the extent of giving him refreshment—grapes decently laid on a platter. But they did not offer him shelter or protection. Muhammad reentered Mecca secretly and sought the protection of various clans. All refused him on one pretext or another, until one chieftain was found who accepted him. Thereafter, this man, or his sons and nephews, bristling with weapons, would follow Muhammad as he walked about Mecca and to the fairs—a pale-faced Prophet, with long black hair and a red cloak falling over his white tunic. They did this out of a sense of fair play and because of old treaties. They must have agreed to observe a certain hands-off policy with hecklers such as Abu Lahab—"that sleek fellow with two locks of hair"—who would also follow the Prophet to throw stones when he prayed, or drown out his voice by jeering as he preached.

He continued to occupy his house, along with Ali, now a young man, and Zayd. A few weeks after the death of Khadija, Muhammad married a widow named Sawda, the first of many wives of his later years. These late remarryings have drawn upon his head the criticism and animosity of Western scholars of a monogamous turn of mind, even though he was fifty before he began wife collecting and was heir to an entirely different moral climate from their own. He should certainly be forgiven Sawda, who was not young and charming but the widow of a Muslim. She may well have been disowned by her clan, since her brothers later fought against Muhammad. It was customary for clan patriarchs to wed spare and unprotected widows, and this was probably the spirit in which Muhammad married Sawda. At any rate, she was a good housekeeper.

53

The following year he betrothed himself to Ayesha, a child of seven, at the request of her father, Abu Bekr. This too was not unusual in his society. Abu Bekr wanted to place his daughter firmly and legally in the care of the best man he knew. The Prophet adored children, and there is no doubt that Ayesha was a good friend, extremely intelligent and mischievous. Ali did not like her, but then Ali was influenced by the opinions of Fatima, who did not care for this invasion of her father's affections by the charming little girl. Muhammad brought Ayesha up carefully as a good Muslim, though rather a spoiled one. She became the delight of his old age and would also have been the agony of it if God had not by that time steeled Muhammad against all the naughtiness in Arabia.

At this low point, Muhammad seems to have become to the Quraysh more of a butt and a joke than a threat to their way of life. Yet the winds of change were blowing, and the year 620 brought a little success. Some important members of several tribes, who had heard Muhammad preaching at the fairs, had been unable to get the splendid cadences of the Quran out of their heads. They came back to him and confessed that God was One. Certain nomads, coming to pilgrimage, began to wonder why they were throwing their slight worldly goods into the pit of the Kaaba. Muhammad's group was a tight-knit community whose members owed alms to one another and prayers to God. It seemed a more practical arrangement.

As his following grew, Muhammad's capacities as a leader kept pace with his responsibilities. God could hardly afford to keep him bedazzled. He had to deal with the everyday problems of men and women. He was becoming wise with the wisdom of the serpent—and shrewd and also tough. It was no longer sufficient for Muslims to recognize One God. They also had to avoid stealing, fornication, slander, murder, and the burying alive of baby daughters. In other words, Muhammad, along with his Collaborator, was beginning to frame social codes which conformed to the behavior Muslims would have to answer for on Judgment Day, and this good conduct had to be enforced by the strength of his authority. A decade after the vision of the cave, Muhammad was a different man from the one who had run like a child from the visitation, calling to his wife to cover him.

Reports of Muhammad's steady mind and character traveled to Yathrib. In 621, at the time of the Great Pilgrimage, a delegation from that town arranged a meeting with him and put forward an interesting proposal—that he transfer the scene of his operations to their pleasant oasis. The reason behind this was that Yathrib contained two Arab tribes who were continually at each other's throats and had been so for generations. Certain leaders felt that Islam, which appeared to have unifying power, might serve as a balance, putting an end to their perpetual, tiresome feuding.

They might have heard that Muhammad was looking about for a place to

54

establish an Islamic community. If so, it is an indication that even at this time Muhammad had begun to see himself in the light of a political leader, but we do not know the scope of his foresight. He probably just wanted somewhere to settle down and cultivate the social reforms that were taking shape in his mind, beyond the reach of jeers and clods of earth.

The meeting with the men of Yathrib took place at their encampment at Aqaba, a little valley outside Mecca, the Quraysh being told nothing about it. Here the men of Yathrib made certain promises: They would embrace Islam, admit that God was One and Muhammad His Messenger, and avoid all the sins he told them to avoid. In return he would be a sort of good-conduct guide for them, a mediator something like a Jewish rabbi. There were many such in Yathrib, serving the large Jewish community.

Muhammad asked the men of Yathrib if they would be willing to defend him by force of arms against the Quraysh, should their wrath pursue him. They were taken aback by this. They were not sure, they would have to think about it. The first Pledge of Aqaba is known in history as the Pledge of Women, because it had no muscle in it. The men of Yathrib went home without a prophet.

The year 622 brought them again, and it is obvious that much vigorous planning had been in progress because the deputation now had seventy-three men, comprising members of all the clans and groups of Yathrib. There were even two women. They met again at Aqaba by night, coming "as softly as sand grouse" so as to frustrate any opposition that might have been in the air. Muhammad was accompanied by one of his friendlier uncles, Abbas, a very practical man who never put down a false step in his life. He it was who made certain that the second Pledge of Aqaba was a Pledge of War—that is, an understanding that the clans of Yathrib accepted full responsibility for Muhammad's personal safety.

"And if we die in the cause of God, what then?" the Yathribites wanted to know.

"Happiness in Paradise" was the reply.

"And when you feel safe enough, will you leave us and return to the Quraysh?"

"No, never," said Muhammad. "Your blood is my blood. I am yours, you are mine."

"Your hand then!"

In this way Yathrib took over custody of Abbas' hot potato of a nephew. With a good heart and exhilarated by new challenges, Muhammad gave orders for all of his people to emigrate from Mecca, in small bands, with as little noise as possible so as not to arouse the Quraysh. The Hijra, or Emigration, began in June 622. From this time, Yathrib was to acquire a new name: Medinat un-Nabi, which means the City of the Prophet, or simply Medina, the City.

There were horrid squabbles when the Quraysh realized what the Muslims were about, and tussles developed wherever Muslim camels were seen being loaded. Some Muslims were kidnapped, hidden, locked up in fetters by their relatives to prevent them from emigrating. One loving family group, in struggling to keep a man's wife and son from joining him, tugged the child about so that his arms were dislocated. None of this was done in spite but in heartbreak. The Emigrants were beloved children now breaking ties with their parents and tribe, cutting loose from an established way of life. Muhammad was thought of in exactly the same terms as a modern guru or a revolutionary leader, who is accused of "brainwashing" the children of respectable families. Many Quraysh were convinced that, if only they could remove their young from his clutches, hold them away from his charming tongue, keep them close, force them to apostatize, then these bent lives could be straightened out, got back on the proper rails. They did not understand that their children were not in Muhammad's clutches, but in those of time, which sweeps with a cruel broom.

At length all who were going had gone. Only Muhammad, Abu Bekr, and Ali remained, waiting for God to give permission for His Apostle to leave Mecca. By this time the Pledge of War was common knowledge among the chieftains of Quraysh, and they were enraged against the Prophet, with good reason. He had put something over on them. Medina was not far from the coastal caravan route, and the Medinans had treaties with local nomads on whom depended the safe-conduct of caravans proceeding to and from Mecca. It needed no clairvoyant eye on the future to realize that a strong Muhammad in Medina could be an endless nuisance to the Quraysh. They therefore held agitated discussions to determine how to handle the situation, while keeping strict watch on Muhammad lest he should slip through their fingers.

One day as they conferred, a venerable man, enswathed in a fine mantle, joined them, introducing himself as a sheikh of the mountains and wanting to participate in these critical talks. Historians of later generations have identified the stranger as Satan himself.

He listened courteously while the Quraysh recounted their favorite ideas. One man said that Muhammad had best be put behind bars and in chains. The sheikh of the mountains objected, saying that the plan would only drive further the wedge into the Quraysh, arousing a fever of sympathy for Muhammad and drawing on their heads the wrath of his friends in Medina. Another man suggested that Muhammad ought to be forced to emigrate instead of being hindered from doing so, and in whatsoever direction he chose so long as it was far enough away. Once again the sheikh, who happened to be gifted with the authority of perfect diction and compelling delivery, found fault. He said that Muhammad would be sure to win over the most distant peoples and eventually lead them back to destroy the Quraysh.

Then Abu Jahl spoke up with the plan of plans: Each clan would choose a young, powerful warrior, equip him with a sharp sword, and together these men would go to Muhammad's house to pierce him through in unison, so that no blame or blood price could be attached to a single clan. The sheikh of the mountains applauded this scheme. We cannot help but suspect that he was not Satan at all, but just an irresponsible sheikh, because the plan was ill-conceived from beginning to end.

First of all, Muhammad learned the secret almost as soon as it was breathed. Perhaps one of his ubiquitous aunts or uncles was at the meeting, or perhaps the sheikh of the mountains was really a Muslim spy. Certainly Gabriel was present, because God remarked on the business to Muhammad in the famous revelation that heads this chapter.

Whatever was the case, Muhammad was quickly aware of the game afoot. As darkness fell, peering out of the narrow windows of his house, he could see his executioners slinking about the alleyways or pretending to doze next to the neighboring houses. Muhammad instructed Ali to wrap himself up in his own green cloak and lie down on his mat.

According to legend, Muhammad then sneaked out of his house without being noticed by the assassins, on whom God cast a temporary blindness. They spent the night outside the house, occasionally putting their heads in the window to peer at their victim under the green cloak. It is not explained why they simply did not enter the house and slay the man on the mat. An unconvincing explanation is given that the current code of honor forbade entering houses to commit murder for fear of embarrassing women caught in immodest situations. Some inhibition against housebreaking there must have been, or it is inconceivable that Muhammad would have told Ali to lie down on the mat in his place.

For one reason or another, the assassins prowled the night through, certain that their green-mantled prey had not left his house. Ali was safe until dawn. Then he sat up and wished them all good morning.

In the meantime Muhammad had made his way to hiding, although we do not know where. He might have spent the night praying, for during that time he received from God the hoped-for permission to migrate. At noon the following day he appeared at Abu Bekr's house to forewarn him. His friend said, "Are we to go together?" and when Muhammad assented, he burst into tears of joy. It had been the greatest desire of his loyal heart to make this journey with the Prophet, and he now eagerly confessed that he had been holding two camels and a driver in readiness for some days.

First, some business affairs had to be wound up. It seems that even after he became a Prophet, Muhammad's reputation for reliable business dealings had not deserted him, and people, probably from among the poor and weaker clans, were in the habit of depositing their valuables and records of investment with him. These now had to be turned over to Ali with instructions for returning them to their owners. Then, in the dark of night, the Prophet and Abu Bekr climbed out of a back window of Abu Bekr's house and, closely enswathed, stole through the silent streets to the outskirts of town, whence they dodged about dunes and scrub until they gained the overhanging mountains. There, on Mount Thor, they settled themselves in a cave where they remained in hiding for three days. A freedman of Abu Bekr's had kept his flock nearby, and he supplied them with milk and good mutton. Abu Bekr's fifteen-year-old daughter, Asma, also brought them provisions from Mecca, and his son Abdullah came with news of the town, particularly of the fury of the Quraysh at Muhammad's escape. They had offered a reward of one hundred she-camels to anyone who would return to them the Prophet, or merely his head.

Hopeful pursuers searched Mount Thor quite thoroughly in those three days and would have searched the cave also, except that a certain spider—who is believed to have been miraculously inspired—contrived to build a large and established-looking web over the mouth, mute evidence that no one could possibly have entered there for some time past. Abu Bekr's freedman also performed unusual exertions, driving his flock back and forth over the ground to cover up the signs of the lively traffic of Asma and Abdullah.

At last Abdullah reported that interest in the chase was waning. It was deemed safe to continue the journey. The camels were prepared. Asma had brought a large bundle of provisions for their journey but had not included a rope, so she tied it on the camel with her girdle—"she-of-the-girdle," Muslim tradition calls her. Abu Bekr did not know it, but he carried on his person all that remained of his fortune. Asma, who was remaining behind with Abdullah and Ali, had padded the household moneybox with stones to make their father believe he was leaving them well provided for. There are no end to the stories told—and probably they have foundation—of the loyalty of ordinary people, particularly the young, toward Muhammad, and the sacrifices they willingly made for him.

At the last minute Muhammad was seized with a feeling that he should not make the Hijra on a borrowed camel or one that he had not bought. A short haggle ensued before Abu Bekr consented to pocket some money in return for history's most famous she-camel, a creature named al-Kaswa.

They turned their steeds northward for the nine-day journey to Medina, guided by the camel driver and the shepherd, Abu Bekr's freedman. There was an incident of danger at the outset, when a puff of dust behind them was rapidly punctuated by the figure of a horseman approaching at a fast clip. The robber, intent upon adding one hundred she-camels to his worldly goods, came within bowshot, and Muhammad turned calmly to face death. But just as the man was about to let fly, his horse's forelegs sank into some soft sand, and he was pitched onto the ground. He knelt there and apologized, asking for his life, which was granted. Not believing his good luck, he asked Muhammad for a written contract that no revenge would ever be taken on him for his deed that day. A piece of bone was found and the contract written on it by Abu Bekr.

Then suddenly, as he contemplated the sorry spectacle of this man, Suraqa, Muhammad had a revelation. "Cheer up," he said to him, "because one of these days, you'll wear the bangles of the king of Persia."

And so it came to pass.

In the meantime, the Muslims who had previously emigrated had settled in an oasis south of Medina which belonged to the Qayla, one of the Medinan clans, and the whole town was keeping a constant watch from a lookout point on top of a lava flow. As it happened, a sharp-eyed Jew, who had become interested in what the Arabs were doing, was the first to spot the approaching Prophet. He rather spoiled the drama of the occasion by shouting out raffishly, "Ho there, Qayla! Your luck has come!"

An Arab gave this account of the scene:

We went to greet the Apostle who was waiting in the shade of a palm tree with Abu Bekr, a man of the same age. Now most of us had never seen him, and the people crowding around did not know who was the Apostle and who was Abu Bekr. But then the shade shifted away from him and Abu Bekr got up with his mantle and shielded him from the sun. Then we knew.

They found lodgings in Quba while waiting for Ali. Aside from Abu Bekr's family and the womenfolk of many families who had stayed behind until settled living conditions could be arranged, the Hijra was now complete. It was June 28, 622. From the beginning of the next lunar month, which fell on July 15, the Muslims reckon their calendar—A.H., as we note it in English, AFTER THE HIJRA.

Medina

Every nation has its apostle; and when the apostle comes, he deals out justice between them. And no one is wronged.

-THE CHAPTER OF JONAH

9

The Constitution of Medina

The first day he spent in Quba, the Prophet laid the foundation stone of Islam's first mosque or place of public prayer. Then, until Ali came, he received deputations from the tribes and groups of Medina, all curious to inspect this magic-tinged man who had come to lead them. And like any electorate jumping on the bandwagon—and wanting a return for their enthusiasm—they embraced Islam.

On the Thursday following his arrival, Muhammad left this oasis, which lay about three miles south of Medina proper, and began to travel toward the central town. The route was lined with multitudes of merry Medinans, wearing their best clothes and shouting a welcome, while the women sang songs from the rooftops. And the rich ones stopped him on his way, eager to offer him wealth and protection if only he would consent to make their homes his own. For a Prophet starved of honor in his own country, it must have been a shining day.

Yet he would not stop. Muhammad had developed a special feeling about this she-camel he was riding, al-Kaswa, which had brought him safely on the track of the Hijra. He was convinced she was under the drivership of God. Therefore he gave her a slack rein, and whenever someone wanted to stop or guide her, he would say, "Let her go her way." From oasis to oasis, from one chieftain's house to another they progressed, until, reaching the main settlement, they came to a wide yard where dates were drying. There al-Kaswa stopped, knelt, and waited to be relieved of Muhammad. When he did not alight, the camel arose and wandered for a little, turned, and came to rest again in the same place. Muhammad knew then that he had come home.

There was a modest house by the yard, and one of the Medinans carried his baggage into it. A prosperous Medinan wanted to provide him with better lodgings, but he smilingly refused, saying, "A man should always stay with his baggage."

The Prophet hardly rested before making plans to build his mosque. He pitched into the work himself, slogging away with mud and bricks, sawing and hauling the trunks of palm trees, learning the art of thatching a roof with palm fronds—and learning it none too well. The hospitable Medinans came to help him. From this time, his followers in Medina were termed Ansar, "Helpers," to distinguish them from the Meccans who were the Muhajerin, or "Emigrants." The traditionists have faithfully collected for us eyewitness accounts of these historic labors, the jokes and rows and the songs the workmen sang:

"While the Prophet works, who dares to loaf,
May rightfully be called an oaf!"

One woman noticed the Prophet's habit of running his hand through his thick long hair and how he merrily stopped work to tell a man's fortune. When the structure was finished and the palm-leaf roof fixed on somehow, it was far from elegant. At certain seasons the rain poured in, and gravel was put on the floor to avoid having to make prostrations in a bog. The Apostle preached leaning against a palm trunk that held up the roof, but the message he brought, like this one recorded by the traditionist Ibn Ishaq, did not differ from those one might hear today from the most elaborate pulpit:

Love what God loves. Love God with all your hearts and weary not of the Word of God and its mention. Harden not your hearts from it.

Out of everything God creates, He chooses and selects. The actions He chooses, He calls khira; the people He chooses He calls mustafa; and the speech He chooses He calls salih. From everything that is given to man there is a choice between the lawful and the unlawful.

Worship God and place nothing beside Him. Fear Him as He ought to be feared. Carry out loyally towards God what you say with your mouths. Love one another in the spirit of God. Verily God is angry when His covenant is broken.

Peace be on you.

The Emigrants, few of whom had ever taken a breath unchoked by dust, were

64

enchanted with Medina. It must have seemed to them that Muhammad had transported them to Paradise even before the promised time. The town was not one large oasis, but a cluster of small ones scattered over a wide area, each being mainly occupied by a separate clan together with its weaker allies, freedmen, slaves, and other hangers-on. Each oasis had its tall stronghold, a structure of several stories where meetings were held, grain and wealth kept, and dates set to dry. Every flat-topped house wore a lovely headdress of fronds, flowers, and women, and the settlements were set about with irrigated fields for grain and date growing, unbelievable sweeps of dazzling, shimmering greenery from which came much of the food supply of the Hejaz. It is not surprising to find that in Islam the sacred color is green.

The streets of the town were filled with the excitement of bazaars, where trade was brisk in bits of treasure that had straggled down the caravan routes from the Byzantine and Persian lands to the north, or hides and woolens from the hinterlands, and the fine bronze armor made by local Jews, beaten and burnished, with helmets to match and gleaming swords whose swift cut could make the very air whistle.

The town smiled at the Meccans. Yet Medina was in truth a town in trouble, a chopped-up, torn, lawless, and murderous place, a test tube of the decadence besetting ancient Arabia as the old tribal system with its codes and curbs broke down and turned to nonsense.

The many clans of Medina were embraced by eleven main groups, three of them Jewish, and all were bound together by age-old complex alliances, or else held apart by blood feuds of similar antiquity. The intricacies of their relationships cannot be understood today. The clans for years had been in a constant state of simmer and boil, now and again erupting into uncontrolled violence, with riots, sieges, rapine, pillage, assassination, and an inevitable aftermath of dragged-out, dreary, enervating blood feud—the eye-for-an-eye accounting of tribal life. Roughly, the battle lines fell between the two main Arab tribes, the Aws and the Khazraj. They cherished a rivalry so self-destructive that they themselves had begun to realize it. During the latest blood bath, which had taken place in 618, just a few years before Muhammad's arrival, there had been a helter-skelter war so hopelessly ensnarled in oaths and grudges that no man knew his friend from his enemy. Out of this fracas there had emerged a leader, Abdullah ibn Ubayy, a practical politician who by tact, wheedling, blackmail, bullying, bribery, sound common sense, and all other recognized forms of politicking, had coerced not only his own tribe, Khazraj, but Aws too, back to a sort of explosive quiescence.

Ibn Ubayy might have become a great long-forgotten pacificator, but just about this time certain citizens were seized with the notion of putting their political affairs into the hands of a Prophet, in the hope that his spiritual and moral weight would anchor their passions permanently. Jewish talk had fortified them

65

in their hope, perhaps instigated it. The rabbis of Medina were forever promising that soon a Messiah would appear to restore to Jews their Temple, bring peace on earth, and distribute favors all around. It was a time when religious help was not only needed but expected.

The Jews were to play a curious and tragic role in this drama of Muhammad. There were three main Jewish tribes in Medina: the Qaynuqa, the an-Nadir, and the Qurayza. There were others, but we hear little of them in the traditions. These great tribes were the ones Muhammad had to reckon with.

The Jews were prosperous, so far as settled and industrious lives can enjoy prosperity in a land where food is measured by the bite, and where the energies of the population went to maintaining the food supply, either by growing it or else by killing people who would otherwise consume it. The Jews were mainly in the business of food growing. By hard work and perseverance, they had been pioneers in inducing wide stretches of Arabian sand and dust to burst into dates and grain. The Arabs, with their historic feuds leading back into prehistory, had done their share for centuries by keeping down the number of mouths that had to be fed. The moment this happy balance was altered—and in the seventh century it was altering year by year—the economy faltered, and rivalry began.

These Jewish settlements of Medina, and of other thriving Jewish oases such as Khaybar to the north, are believed to have originated with the Diaspora, when the later Roman emperors and other persecutors drove Jews from their homeland and set them wandering across the earth. For hundreds of years, wherever Jews went, they agreed to accept alien peoples into their religious communities so long as they would take instruction and observe the laws proper to Jews. The promise of a Messiah was certainly not the least of the advantages they held out to possible converts. Early Jewish communities, far from practicing the exclusivity attributed to modern, established groups, were not set apart or aloof or remote from the life about them except in one important respect: They had a Book.

Because they had a Book, the Torah, and maintained schools wherein to teach their young the significance of this mighty heritage, the Jews Muhammad knew had a great reputation for scholarship, legal brains, Solomonic wisdom, astrological lore, even magical powers, when called for. Certainly, because of their schools, they had more disciplined minds. However, they were generous with their advantages, not objecting if Arabs, young or old, attended their schools, and such Arabs often joined the Jewish community and faith. Even if they did not, the two groups intermingled and intermarried, the children being usually packed off to school by the Jewish parent and hence considered to be Jews for the rest of their lives, even though they lived, breathed, ate, and slept with the Arabs.

This process, starting with a few immigrants from the Holy Land, had continued for generations. By the time Muhammad came, the Jews had long since ceased to be a race distinct from the Arabs, with whom they shared names, lan-

guage, traditions, treaties, business and commercial interests. Although possessing the sophistication which is the reward of those who stick to their books in
youth, they shared with the Arabs certain historic follies, being caught up in the
same unholy ballet of feuds, blood money, retaliation, and assassination, even
though their various alliances pitted one Jew against another, clan against clan,
tribe against tribe, and interfered with the solidarity of their religious community.

In 622, they were heartily tired of it. They were making a great nuisance of
themselves when mayhem was in progress by refusing to kill anybody on Sabbath
and holy days. The an-Nadir and Qaynuqa were on excellent terms with the
Khazraj leader, Ibn Ubayy, and would have supported him politically if
Muhammad had not stolen the scene. The Qurayza leaned toward Aws, with
whose leaders they had treaties.

At first, when Muhammad came, the Jews were friendly and receptive. To
them he might have seemed quaint and untaught, but a good man and possibly a
strong leader, so they ran with the rest in the streets applauding him. Even as they
watched the Arabs embracing Islam, they felt no twinge of alarm. Why should a
Jew object to hearing a man say, "There is no God but God"?

Muhammad was equally friendly toward the Jews, because he needed the
backing of their authority. A document is preserved, fascinating, for it is probably
the brainchild of the Prophet and his chief collaborators, in which an attempt is
made to set forth correct and proper relationships among three main groups of
Medinans: Muhammad's Emigrants, the Medinan Helpers, and the Jews. The
Constitution of Medina, as it has been dubbed, while making use of rather gory
tribal jargon, is obviously the work of benign and forbearing minds. The articles
concerning Jews have a unifying spirit. The Jews were to be considered as followers of Muhammad in a political sense, without embracing Islam. "Jews have
their religion, and the Muslims have theirs," said Muhammad. Yet, they were to
be "one community" with the believers, entitled to Muhammad's help and protection. They, on their side, would be obliged to the larger community in matters
of blood price and the defense of Medina under siege by the Quraysh or any
other enemy.

As in all Arab compacts of those days, the terms covered confederates, clients,
and hangers-on of the main parties, so that the Constitution of Medina was an
umbrella to much of the population of Medina. "Yathrib," it was stated, "shall be
a sanctuary for the people of this document."

Such was Muhammad's hope and obvious intent—to unify, pacify, and provide a haven of security for Aws, Khazraj, Muslims, Ansars, Jews, with himself as
the cushion for all hard words that might be spoken between them. The
Constitution informed all citizens "when you differ, it is to be referred to God and
to Muhammad."

As a guidance to himself, he kept an eye on Jewish customs and borrowed many of them. He instructed Muslims to observe the Jewish Sabbath and fasting on the Day of Atonement.

Yet in that document of peace, probably without design, Muhammad firmly planted the sword of Islam, which once drawn was to cut away worlds from each other, not only Arabs from Jewish traditions, but from their own traditions before the Hijra, and eventually carve out the shape of Islam in history. The critical article set forth that no Muslim might go to war with another Muslim for the sake of a non-Muslim. A logical statute, yet with this one statement Muhammad created a new kind of tribe, distinct from all others and with immense growing power, because it was bound not by blood but by ideas, which have no boundaries in time or space.

The first twinge—and it could have been no harsher than a smile—was felt by the Jewish communities when they became aware that, so far as their Arab brothers were concerned, the Messiah had come. And he was no Jew but one of their own kind.

*Remember when ye were few in number and weak in the land, fearing lest people
should snatch you away: then He sheltered you and aided you . . .*
-THE CHAPTER OF THE SPOILS

10

The Beginning of
the Umma

While the mosque was being built, Muhammad, Zayd, and Ali did
not move from the house that had first sheltered them. It belonged
to a member of a clan related to Muhammad on the maternal side.
The Prophet, not wishing to rob the family of their living quarters,
which were on the upper level, insisted on occupying the less elegant ground
floor—a kind of stable, normally—saying that it was more convenient to him for
the reception of guests. His consideration did not please his host's family, who,
living above his head, were in terror of spilling any undignified substance on it
through the floor slats. Once when a jar of water broke, the whole family, having
no cloth handy, leaped to make mops of themselves, soaking it up with their
clothes.

The womenfolk arrived: Abu Bekr's daughters, including little Ayesha and her
mother; Muhammad's younger daughters, Fatima and Umm Kulthum; and his
wife Sawda. Huts were built for them next to the mosque and quarters for Abu
Bekr's family nearby. There was a raised platform at one corner of the enclosure,
which from that time was occupied by the poor and homeless. Later it accom-
modated those who wished to devote their lives to religious exercises.

All this construction work, at Muhammad's insistence, was being paid for

69

meticulously, and money was getting low. After a while Abu Bekr had to stop building and go to work in the date gardens to feed his dependents, and he was no worse off than many Meccans, poorer than he, who had arrived in Medina penniless, only to fall victim to the fevers prevalent there. This was probably malaria, brought about by mosquitoes breeding in stagnant spots. We hear also of diphtheria among the faithful. Ill and semistarved, these followers came to the mosque, but having not the energy to stand upright for prayer, lay about the floor, so that Muhammad spent much effort coaxing them to their feet with the dictum (which devout Muslims still attend to) that God listens more closely to prayers addressed to Him standing up.

Meanwhile, people coming to inspect the Prophet and judge the new religion thought that the congregation must be possessed of evil spirits, and they went away again.

To God Muhammad said: "O God, make Medina dear to us as Mecca was, and even dearer; and bless its food; and carry the fever away."

He did not catch the fever, but his belt was knotted tight; he would sometimes tie a stone on it at night. He married Ayesha soon after her arrival, when she was nine, probably to relieve her father of the mouth to feed. Certainly she had a slender wedding feast. She remembered always the hardship of those days: "We used to go forty nights on end and never light a fire," she said. They lived on water and dates.

We need not dwell on the abuse to the child of such a marriage. It was the custom of young brides to be brought up in their husbands' homes, though usually under the instruction of a mother-in-law. In Ayesha's case, Sawda filled the bill. To the end of his life, Ayesha was dear to Muhammad, and she loved her Prophet. We can conclude that the relationship between the two was free from outrage.

A hut was built for Ayesha close to that of Sawda, and she brought to it her dolls and toys. Muhammad's compound was for some years filled with the shouts of little girls running in and out, delighting him and winning him from moods of despondency that sometimes attacked him, for he loved children. Once he saw them playing with funny bags lined up.

"What are those?" he asked.

"Dolls," said his wife.

"Ah, but what is that one over there?"

"A horse."

"But it looks as if it had wings."

"Well, didn't you know? King Solomon's horses have wings."

"He laughed," Ayesha recollected long after Muhammad was dead, "until I saw his back teeth."

He married his cherished youngest daughter, Fatima, to Ali, along with a dowry of some clothes, some furniture, and a basket of dates. The newlyweds starved along with him. Once Fatima fainted with hunger before his eyes. However, when times improved, they presented him with his beloved grandsons, Hasan and Husein, and visitors to the mosque might see the Prophet galloping around the courtyard on all fours with a child on his neck. "What a great horse!" a man called out.

"A great horseman, too!" laugh Muhammad.

Once God's Apostle was seen with a child, playing at "spit."

We may picture Muhammad as he was then in the fifty-second year of his life, a short, strong, sturdy man, still walking in a rush that made it hard for more imposing men to keep up with him. Rough hands, rough feet, from work and hard going. His round, bumptious forehead made the straight, joined eyebrows beetle over the black eyes. His beard grew thick, and the curly hair flowed long around his pale face, sometimes being caught in a plait. The hair on his chest came to a point down to the navel in a line "as if drawn with a fine pen," from which we may infer that the quality of the hair was fine, though abundant.

His personal habits were clean and abstemious. He liked meat, which he believed to be good for the hearing, but he never gave up the disciplined habits formed during the days of starvation, and lived chiefly on dates, honey, butter, and milk. He would not eat onions or garlic, because he said that he did not wish to offend the people to whom he spoke confidentially.

His manners were naturally considerate. When he called on a man, he never posted himself in the middle of the doorway, but always stood at the side of the door asking if he might enter. He never interrupted anyone speaking. He did not willingly give commands, but preferred to find ways of making his wishes known indirectly.

He had a ready wit and loved to poke fun, but only Ayesha often saw his back teeth. He usually smiled, with a most charming smile. He disliked lewd talk or coarse language, and was quite prudish. He never touched the hand of a woman other than his wife, even in oath taking. When a woman confessed Islam, a bowl of water would be brought, and Prophet and votary would put their hands in it.

There is a tale, hard to believe, that he was terribly shocked to learn in Medina that date palms were male and female, and that in cultivating them the fertilization had to be done with the human hand. He is said to have forbidden Muslims to participate in this indecent practice. Then, realizing that such a prejudice might result in acute famine throughout western Arabia, he reversed himself, giving a famous command which his followers did not hesitate to obey: "I am only a mortal. If I give you an order about religion, receive it. But if I give you an order out of my own head, remember that I am mortal."

Muhammad never reproached anyone's personal fault except one which he considered insulting to God or His Quran. He disliked hearing criticism of any-

71

one and could be counted on to cover up or minimize other people's faults. If, as pastor of his flock, he felt obliged to chase sin out of a man, he did it by gentle, gradual prodding, often wittily—yet relentlessly.

Humility, patience, love of man and all creation—these qualities invade the spirit when the membrane of egoism breaks, flaring into a light that guides others. And they are characteristic of the people we call saints or prophets or bhodisattvas.

But God had said to Muhammad, "Verily this is a heavy command we have laid on thee." The command was "to succeed"—to get the message across victoriously, not only as a spiritual guide, but as a political leader. And this prodding insistence of the Voice forced him to words and deeds that cannot be judged in the courts of the spirit, but only in those of the ordinary world of action.

Revelations came on him plentifully during the early days in Medina. The form in which they came is not clear, either from the Quran or from the traditions. They have been the subject of discussion among learned Muslim for centuries. God Himself informed us without satisfying our full curiosity: "God does not speak to mortal except by inspiration, or from behind a veil, or by sending an Apostle inspired by what He pleases. Thus, We have inspired thee by means of a spirit doing our work."

The "spirit" is the being generally called the Archangel Gabriel.

Next to God's explanation, we have Ayesha's memory of a conversation between Muhammad and a friend who asked him how revelation came. Muhammad replied, "Sometimes it comes to me like the reverberation of a bell, and that is the hardest on me; then it leaves me, and I have understood what He said. And sometimes the angel takes the form of a man for me and addresses me, and I understand what he says."

Ayesha said that she had sometimes seen Muhammad, when a revelation came, even on the coldest days, with his forehead running with sweat. Yet in many traditions, we read of Muhammad receiving God's dictation without the slightest signs being visible to his companions.

We may conclude that, however many kinds of revelation scholars may define, there were two main ones: The first was almost like a friendly chat with Gabriel—not in words actually "heard," but nevertheless reaching the immediate understanding. At other times, there was the terrible, shattering sound of the absolute Bell, the cosmic sound perhaps of which the Far Eastern mystics tell us, the Bell revered by Tibetan lamas and Irish saints. This sound bore Muhammad to his knees in pain and sweat, or knocked him to the ground. He did not try to stave off such visitations. Indeed, he induced them if he could, through fasting and prayer, spending hours of the day in meditation or standing upright throughout the night.

While the Bell spoke no human speech, yet he understood what it said. He never forgot any revelation. He could always recite reams of the Quran, a word which means "reading" or "recitation." Yet the revelations would have been forgotten by others if, as they spilled from his lips, there had not been secretaries at hand to take them down in "plain Arabic" (as God called it). Paper, skin, bone, rag, wood, any handy material offered by that sparse culture was used to record the holy words. After they had been committed to memory, they were preserved in a fine jumble in a box.

The general tone of the Quran is rather chastising, ranging from mild rebuke through heavy scolding to furious invective—the wrath of God, vibrant and alive. There are also passages of high philosophy and poetry of surpassing loveliness, exhortations to virtue, reminders of God's compassion, and here and there some rather witty comments on the human scene.

The grand poetry of the Quran belongs mostly to the early years of the Call when in urgent and arresting terms he described—or rather God described—the might of God, the magnificence of His works, and the fear that ought to be entertained by sinners bound for Hell. Quite suddenly after the Hijra, the revelations change their tone, as if both Muhammad and his Master realized that their pressing task was now to deal with practical, everyday matters, personal and family relationships, beliefs and customs, even such trivial details as whether garments were to be considered unclean when a baby wet on them.

As day by day, with every revelation, the Quran increased, the community was being given a code of conduct distinct from tribal custom and reflecting novel ethical attitudes as well as practical needs. Many people who do not care to give God credit for practicality suspect that Muhammad made these rules up out of his head and announced them as coming from God. Even if it were credible that Muhammad acted out painful fits and sweats, there is really no ground for doubting his complete sincerity. He felt himself divinely commissioned, his every decision divinely inspired from first to last.

One very practical revelation of the early Medina days instituted the custom of taking "brothers in God." This was a means of caring for the immediate needs of the starving and ailing Emigrants. The Helpers, that is, the Medinan converts of settled livelihoods, were asked to bind themselves to Emigrants in a bond of brotherhood, sheltering them in their homes, caring for their needs, and actually offering them half their substance. For poor farmers such as the Medinans mostly were, this was a stiff demand. One Meccan absolutely refused to accept the help offered, saying, "Just lead me to the bazaar." There, this Quraysh merchant began to buy and sell with such acumen that he soon had the money to buy himself a bride.

Others were not so clever, and they remained a charge on their brothers until they found their feet.

The custom of alms, the giving away of goods to the needy, which later was

73

to become a characteristic feature of the Muslim umma, the community, was firmly implanted at this time. The most generous of men himself, Muhammad left no
room for doubt in the minds of his followers that one of the main reasons for getting rich was to be able to give riches away.

He learned to be judge and arbiter in these early days, devised laws for conduct and punishment. He kept an eye on Jewish social customs and borrowed
many of them, including the dietary laws.

From his position of authority, for the first time he insisted on the practice of
daily prayer as obligatory for Muslims. It is believed that he might have required
only three prayer sessions a day at first, a number later raised to five, and the time
of prayer was fixed at inconvenient hours so that the faithful would have to stop
and remember God even when they were very busy. No aspect of his teaching
aroused more opposition among the early followers than this one, which many
considered to be arbitrary, humiliating, meaningless, and a general nuisance.
Muhammad was obdurate. It was something of a stroke of public relations, setting
his umma—which is believed to have numbered about one thousand to fifteen
hundred people—apart from all other Medinans.

Noting that the Jews were accustomed to calling their people to prayer with
a horn and Christians with a bell, and not wishing to imitate them, he ordered a
clapper to be fashioned and beaten when Muslims were to pray. For some reason
God did not express Himself directly against this clapper, but He caused one of
the faithful to be visited repeatedly by a dream which he duly related to the
Prophet:

*A phantom visited me in the night: there passed by me a man dressed in green carrying a clap-
per which I asked him to sell to me in order that I might beat it and call people to prayer. But he
offered to show me a better way: it was to say three times loudly, "God is great! I bear witness that
there is no God but God! I bear witness that Muhammad is the Prophet of God. Come to prayer!
Come to prayer! Come to salvation!"*

Muhammad was more than pleased. He said the dream could only be a revelation. Since Bilal, the huge Abyssinian whom Abu Bekr had rescued from torture
under the desert sun, had the loudest voice in Arabia, he was ordered to learn by
heart the call to prayer. Thus, he became Islam's first muezzin, and though he had
no graceful minaret to climb to, he made do with the flat roof of the tallest house.

The woman who owned the house used to hear him climbing the roof at
dawn. She said he never started the call to prayer without first stretching out his
arms and saying, "O God, I praise Thee and ask Thy help for the Quraysh, and
let them accept Thy religion."

Was this Bilal's wish, or was he only relaying a message to God from
Muhammad?

"God and yours . . . there is no argument between us and you . . . God will call us together, and to Him the journey is."

—THE CHAPTER OF COUNSEL

11

The People of the Book

The trouble with the Jews boiled up gradually, starting with religious arguments and ending in fear and chagrin. The chagrin was Muhammad's when he realized that the Jews were not going to hail him as the Messiah. In fact, they were not going to admit that he was a true prophet in the line of prophets or accept his revelations as genuinely coming from God like those of Moses.

He desperately needed this Jewish authority. There were still those, too many of them, who believed that he communicated with a jinn or other demonic being. Of the enthusiastic Medinans who had embraced Islam on his arrival, many had fallen back into paganism, or else they were only pretending to be Muslims. They clustered around Abdullah ibn Ubayy, who had confessed Islam only for the sake of solidarity with the other tribal leaders but who made no secret of his boredom with Muhammad's preaching. The discontented group were called munafiqin, usually translated as "Hypocrites." Muhammad had no doubt that they were afflicted by a "sickness of the mind" in this world and bound for Hell in the next. Far from expostulating with these doomed souls, the Jews encouraged their sin and provided them with arguments against Muhammad that they would not have thought up for themselves.

Before matters reached the point of open hostility, there were some interesting encounters in Muhammad's mosque, where the rabbis came in curiosity, and in the Jewish schools, where Muhammad went to preach. Religious disputation was a favorite pastime of those days, in Medina no less than in the great cultural centers like Alexandria and Byzantium. It was the sport of intellectuals and the entertainment of the masses. But it was an explosive and dangerous game which sometimes led to riots, massacre, and holy war.

Muhammad need by no means be thought of as a mere country preacher facing sophisticated scholars. The shoe is really on the other foot. He was a world genius facing backwater rabbis, and his charmed tongue made converts even among them. Nevertheless, as long as he stood in an Arab's complete awe of Jewish learning, they had him at a disadvantage.

When he arrived in Medina, the rabbis lost no time in pouncing on him about a matter that must have been rankling for some time: the insolent answer he had returned to them from Mecca in reply to their testing question: "What is the spirit?"

God had replied, "Tell them the spirit is God's business and you know little about it."

"Now," the rabbis wanted to know, confronting him, "did He mean that only Arabs like you knew little about it, or Jews too?"

"He meant both," said Muhammad.

"But don't you know, Muhammad, that we have the Book, the Torah, in which is explained everything in the world?"

Muhammad retorted that compared to God's knowledge the Torah was minuscule, though quite sufficient for Jews if only they would carry it out.

Later, God confirmed this opinion by a famous revelation: "If all the trees were pens and all the ocean ink with seven seas more to swell it, still God's word would not be exhausted!"

God was an interested observer, and indeed a participant in all these discussions, ever ready to prompt His Messenger even before the event. "If you are a prophet as you say," said the rabbis, "tell us when will be the Hour of Judgment."

"They will ask you about the Hour," God had forewarned. "Tell them, 'None but my Lord knows it.' They will ask you as if they expected you to know it. Tell them only God knows."

In time Muhammad became most astute in dealing with rabbis. God, of course, was a past master at it.

The other people of the Book, the Christians, had no consistent policy toward the Muslims, perhaps because they were divided among themselves, being in the same doubt about the nature of the Trinity that had all Byzantium by its ears. We read of whole Christian villages becoming Muslims, just to put an end to the wearisome Christian arguments. Others stuck bravely to their guns. One important Christian living in Medina had been in such a huff, when Muhammad was appointed leader, that he went to live in Mecca among the Quraysh.

Once, an entire Christian village, which boasted that all the heresies in Christendom were represented among its population, came to call on Muhammad dressed in their best Yemeni linen, to argue with him about the divinity of Jesus son of Mary. On this point Muhammad had found himself in double trouble— with the Christians for teaching that Jesus was a man like other men, and with the Jews for teaching that Jesus was a prophet of the line of prophets, including himself and Moses. It happened that rabbis were present when the Christians arrived, and Muhammad warily kept silence while the two groups threshed the matter out. The Jews made mincemeat of the Christian argument. "You haven't a leg to stand on," they said. The Christians retorted that neither did the Jews have a leg to stand on, since if Jesus was not divine, then neither was the Torah, nor was Moses a true prophet.

"Just listen to them!" said God to Muhammad. "Don't they ever read the Scriptures? They neither of them know what they are talking about, but wait! They'll know it when God judges them on Resurrection Day!"

It was on this same occasion that God revealed to Muhammad the true nature of his religion. Muhammad had been telling people for years that Islam was the religion of Abraham, but the Jews were not open to this suggestion. They said Abraham was another Jew like themselves. Some Christians had also come from out of town to state that Abraham was a Christian. God now sent down a revelation, through Muhammad, to all of them: "O Scripture folk! Why do you argue this matter, knowing very well that the Torah and the Gospels did not appear on earth until long after Abraham? Don't you understand? Why don't you argue about things of which you know a little, not about things of which you know nothing and God alone knows? Abraham was neither a Jew nor a Christian. He was a Muslim hanif!"

By hanif, God meant a man who refused to worship idols, but who lived at a time before the major religions had been created. In making this point, Muhammad placed Islam, along with the whole race of Arabs, on a direct line of authority from the spiritual father of both Jews and Christians. From this position, it was easy to develop the notion that the Jews had somehow gone astray; that going astray was the result of wrong thinking; that wrong thinking generated wrong behavior. God thoroughly agreed with this train of thought, and in the Quran we may read at length of his dissatisfaction with the Jews, particularly regarding their poor treatment of His prophets.

Thus the rift between Muhammad and the Jews widened. Even those rabbis who had treated him seriously at first began to smile at his curious interpretations of their Scriptures, which he was studying hard under the tutelage of a converted rabbi. It was a grief to him tantamount to his rejection by the Quraysh when they said to him bluntly, "O Muhammad, you have not brought us any proof we recognize that you are a true prophet, and nothing God has revealed to you persuades us to follow you." In a kindly spirit they exhorted him to forget his Mission and lead his followers into Jewry. They said to the Medinan Arabs: "We simply do not recognize anything he says."

The Christians were equally concerned. They advised him to become a Christian.

God commented mildly at first: "Many of the Scripture folk want to make unbelievers out of believers, being envious, since the truth is plain. But forgive them, be indulgent, and obey God's commands. God can do anything."

Later on the encounters became acrimonious, or what was worse, mocking on the part of the Jews who took to jeering at Muslims in the street. And this only reflected the attitude of some rabbis who had become carelessly cruel and insolent in their treatment of Muhammad, playing upon his lack of learning and delighting to muddle his mind with complicated numerological riddles such as Kabalists love to extract from their holy books. Or they would ask foolish questions whose answers were known only to rabbinical folklorists, such as "What was Isaac's favorite food?"

They had a trick, far from kind, of pretending to believe in Muhammad even to the extent of pronouncing the Confession of Faith, then reversing themselves with incoherent excuses. "Tell us about the spirit who talks to you," they would ask.

"The spirit is Gabriel."

"Oh, what a pity! As you know, Muhammad, that angel is our enemy, coming only with violence and bloodshed. If it weren't for this, we would all surely become Muslims."

On one occasion, during the period of hunger and extremity, Abu Bekr went to ask alms from the scholars of a Jewish school. One of the rabbis said, "We are not poor compared to your God, but He is poor compared to us. We do not humble ourselves to Him as He humbles Himself to us, asking alms. We are independent of Him, but He needs us."

Abu Bekr hit him very hard in the face.

The news of these deteriorating relations traveled to Mecca, spreading deep satisfaction among the Quraysh who sent to their commercial allies, the Jewish tribe of Beni an-Nadir, suggesting that Muhammad be assassinated without delay.

Because of the terrible unwinding of events in the years that followed, Muslim historians like to dilate on the street insults and obscenities offered by Jews to Muslims in those early days, the practical jokes and way of twisting the normal greeting, "Peace be unto you!" into similar-sounding words which meant, "May death overtake you!" Even if these are not exaggerations or inventions of a later date—as they may well be—it is not likely that they cut deeply into Muhammad.

78

For he was used to the coarse treatment of the vulgar, and he knew how to defend himself with wounding words against the Jews, especially as these same words seemed to him to come from God Himself.

The Jews sealed their doom when they began to play tricks with the Scriptures, misquoting or misrepresenting. "God has spoken to no man after Moses," they told him.

"God has spoken to prophets He has told you of," replied Muhammad, "and to prophets He has not told you of."

"How can you claim that your words come from God," they wanted to know, "since they have no resemblance whatsoever to the Torah?"

"My words come from God! You could find them in the Torah if you looked! Could man or jinn together produce the like of the Quran?"

But the Jews rejected the divinity of the Quran as staunchly as they had once rejected the divinity of Baal. They may have been only backwater rabbis, but they knew their duty to their Holy Book. Still, in pitting themselves stubbornly against a powerful current of history, they would have to pay a terrible price.

As if these religious disputes were not trouble enough, business interests clashed, further dividing the two groups, for it dawned on at least one of the Jewish tribes, the Qaynuqa, that the Meccans were not going to settle down in Medina as farmers like the other Arabs, but, merchants to the bone, would want a corner of the bazaar, hitherto largely their own domain. With commercial jealousy reinforcing religious dissension, the Jews began to work not only openly, but secretly, against Muhammad, subverting the minds of the faithful, dissuading them from contributing to the public expenses as every Muslim was obliged to do. "We are only thinking of your good," they said.

Relations became so painful that Muhammad took measures. He forbade his followers to admit either Jews or Christians to their friendship, because, he said, "They will spare no pains to corrupt you, longing for your ruin. Behold! You love them, but they love you not!"

This sad observation, which is in the Quran and therefore can be taken as having fallen from the lips of Muhammad, reflects his bitter disappointment in the Jewish rejection of his Mission, which he had counted on to support him, not only in the eyes of the Medinans, but in the eyes of his beloved Quraysh. At some time, about a year and a half after the Hijra, he steeled himself against them, put them out of his head like a strong-willed lover determined to chase a faulty loved one out of his heart. He no longer sought Jewish converts. He changed the Muslim Sabbath from Saturday to Friday. He did not celebrate the Day of Atonement in his second year in Medina, as he had done in 622. Instead, he substituted the fast of Ramadan, honoring the month in which he had received the Call. This is still the central event in the Muslim religious calendar. He relaxed many dietary laws.

79

Most pervasive of all, he changed the qibla, the "niche" whence God emanates, from Jerusalem to Mecca. Once again, when the men of the desert prayed, they turned not to an alien temple, but to the heart of their own land, to the Beit Allah in which is set the ancient Black Stone.

When you asked your Lord for succour, He answered, "I will assist you with a thousand angels, and a thousand more behind them."
                                                    -THE CHAPTER OF THE SPOILS

12

The Battle of Badr

The oasis of Medina may be imagined as situated at the apex of a long, narrow triangle stretching along the edge of Arabia, the lower extremity being at Mecca, and the third on the main caravan route to Syria running along the Red Sea. At these points, and in the surrounding area, a series of battles were to be fought involving a very few desert heroes, whose main weapons were bows, arrows, javelins, and yells. Yet it would be hard to name more scientific fracases that had a greater impact on world history.

The first battle was at Badr on the caravan route. It took place in March of 624, a little less than two years after the Hijra. Muhammad had realized for some time that drastic measures would have to be taken to fill out the flesh of his hungry Emigrants. They could not depend forever on the charity of their brothers-in-God who were for the most part poor farmers. Yet, with a few exceptions, they did not fit into the unfamiliar agricultural occupations open to them in Medina. They had brown thumbs. The answer came to Muhammad in an important revelation, which announced a change of policy. In Mecca God had authorized him only to preach, exhort, and accept insults. Now He announced:

Permission is given to fight

81

To those who have been wronged;
And verily, God has the might to help them.
For they have been driven forth without cause from their homes,
Only because they said, "God is God!" ...
But God will help him who helps Him—
Verily, He is mighty, powerful!

In other words, not friends but enemies would have to feed the Emigrants through these hard times—none other than their fellow tribesmen the Quraysh, whose healthy caravan trade pounded to and fro between Mecca and Syria. This scheme of Muhammad has branded him a robber in the eyes of people who frown thoughtlessly on caravan raiding as a means of making a living. Yet in his day, particularly among the nomads, the razzia on camps and caravans was considered gainful employment—indeed, one of the few means of livelihood available. Nomad tribes raided or took bribes to refrain from raiding. By this means not only was wealth distributed more evenly, but new blood was injected into the tribes in the form of captive wives or labor in the form of captured children, and the general population was kept in check by death in battle.

Above all, razzia was a sport, involving deeds of heroism and enhanced prestige.

Settled people tried to avoid raids by sending their caravans forth bristling with fierce outriders or by concluding treaties with nomads. No desert pirate would dream of raiding anyone with whom he had a treaty, and it was certainly unusual to find related clans preying on each other. Muhammad, however, was in the curious position of having been expelled from his tribe so that the Quraysh were his legal game. Besides, he could argue that his Emigrants were only wanting to be compensated for their lost property and livelihood. Of seven initial forays, six were launched against Meccan caravans, showing the fairly honest direction of their thoughts, and the fact that only Emigrants took part, leaving the Medinans out of it, fortifies this point of view.

Still, the Emigrants were by upbringing bribe payers, not bribe takers, and they had to retrain themselves in the noble and ancient art of razzia. As amateurs they flubbed all the initial attempts. The first was launched by the Prophet himself, who took one look at his helpless prey and silently led the way home again.

The next sally forth was led by one of his loyal uncles, Ubayda, with about eighty men. They encountered a Quraysh caravan by a water hole, conducted by their chief enemy Abu Jahl, and shot an arrow at it. Nothing else happened, except that two of the Meccans, probably youthful in years, took this splendid opportunity to desert and join the Muslims. Two more mouths to feed.

Nevertheless, the arrow was the first to be shot in Islam, and Muhammad was so pleased that he gave his Uncle Ubayda Islam's first flag.

Again an expedition went out under Muhammad's largest and most belliger-
ent uncle, Hamza, also with a flag about which Hamza has left us a poem to say
that it was Islam's first flag rather than Ubayda's. God, as Muslim historians
always say in a tight spot, knows the truth of this. In any case, Hamza deserved
no flag at all, because when his band intercepted a Quraysh caravan, even though
Abu Jahl was again leading and at their mercy, Hamza did not murder that enemy
of God, but sat down and had a chat with him. Very likely both warriors were
glad to have news of their respective relatives.

The Prophet thought he had better lead the next raid. Again he came within
sight of his victims, turned, and returned to Medina.

After meditation and strengthening of spirit, he led out a new party. They succeeded in picnicking in a date grove, where on a full stomach they concluded a
treaty of friendship with some nomads. Then they went home.

These martial adventures could be recounted at length and serve only to
absolve the Emigrants of expertise in razzia. However, timorous as the first raids
were, they fulfilled an important purpose in Islam by teaching Muhammad's
young Muslims the art of weaving invisibly among desert dunes and winning the
friendship of an assortment of nomad clans. In this way were laid the foundations
of a crack spy service that was to serve Muhammad well in the future, catching
for him every whisper blown about by the jinns of the desert.

It was one such espionage team that brought home the first booty in Islam. A
group went out to spy on the Quraysh and at Nakhla came upon a small caravan
rather well laden with grains and leather, traveling without precaution because it
was a sacred month and they were headed for the sacred ground of the goddess
shrine at at-Taif. They caught sight of Muhammad's young men but felt no suspicion when they saw that one had his head shaved like a pilgrim.

The Muslim band knew that, under the old laws, to raid this caravan would be
a crime, a desecration of sacred times and territories, and they debated what they
should do. They might have been very hungry or aware of the vast need in
Medina. Or perhaps the laws of Islam were crowding the old laws out of their
minds. In any case, they decided upon razzia, and they came down on the caravan like a storm of young men. An arrow was loosed, a Quraysh fell dead. Goods
were taken, prisoners bound. In willful spirit, like so many Bedouin, they divided
the loot among them, proudly setting aside a fifth for Muhammad. They returned
with joy to Medina.

But Muhammad received them in silence. An icy cold seized their limbs as
they watched while he, disdaining their gift to himself, appropriated all of it and
put it into escrow until God pronounced judgment in the matter. Through the
town of Medina and up and down the coast of Arabia people were shocked and
shaken by the scandal of shedding blood in the sacred month. The last time it had
happened, when Muhammad was a boy, it had brought about the Wicked Wars.

83

The Jews told everyone that it was a terrible omen against the Prophet, the sort of thing they had warned against all along.

But God, who knows best, said to Muhammad: "They will accuse you of killing in the sacred month. Say: 'Killing in the sacred month is indeed a serious matter; but it is more serious to keep people from following in the ways of God, and persuade them to disbelief, and seduce them from visiting His sacred mosque!'"

So, Muhammad vindicated the young men of Medina, and they did not mind when he distributed all their ill-gotten gains to the poor, including the ransom of one of their prisoners. The other prisoner decided to stay in Medina and become a Muslim.

The affair at Nakhla was the first blood shed in Islam. Later, God confirmed by revelation that Muhammad was to receive a one-fifth share in the spoils of war—this was rather less than the usual sheikh's share of one quarter. Furthermore, God specified that such spoils were to be used for kindred and orphans, the poor and the wayfarer.

The Helpers were watching the efforts of their brothers-in-God in some anxiety. They were still bearing the brunt of the Emigrants' support, and they realized that, if greater bellicosity was not brought to bear on these raids, they would have it forever. They decided to take a hand in them. To be sure, they were also a settled folk, but because of their frequent civil strife they considered themselves experienced warriors. This, and the hope of loot, may have been the reason that, when the great expedition to Badr took place, the force of eighty-six Emigrants was strengthened by 238 Helpers.

It was a splendid caravan they were after—Quraysh owned, plowing down the coastal road from Syria with a large slice of Meccan wealth in money and goods worth fifty thousand gold pieces laden on the backs of one thousand pack camels. It was led by one of the great Meccan chieftains, an old enemy of Islam, Abu Sufyan of Abd Shams. Seventy men had taken the caravan north. Now, homeward bound along the Arabian routes, Abu Sufyan decided to send to Mecca for an escort. To impress his fellow citizens with a sense of urgency his messenger had orders to descend on the town making the traditional signals for dire distress in the desert. Accordingly, he appeared in Mecca like bloodstained doom, his camel's nose cut, his clothes rent, and shouting at the top of his voice that Muhammad was on them with rage and ruin.

Almost the entire town rose to the call except Abu Lahab, Muhammad's base uncle, who said he was not feeling well and sent in his place a man who owed him money. Fat Umayya, the onetime owner of the Abyssinian muezzin Bilal, also decided to stay at home, but a kindly friend gave him a piece of scented wood, telling him to wear it around his neck like a pretty woman. Umayya took the hint, found a horse agreeable to carrying him, and rode off with the rest. He should have preferred the scented wood.

The enterprise gathered excitement when it became known that a woman of Hashim, Muhammad's aunt in fact, had had an alarming dream the night before, portending disaster for Mecca. Abu Jahl, commander of this force, was furious when he heard about it and grumbled to Muhammad's Uncle Abbas: "Isn't it enough for the men in your family to be prophets, without the women starting in?"

With all speed, 950 warriors thundered northward with 700 camels and 100 horses to intercept Muhammad, who was traveling east from Medina at the head of 324 men, with Ali and one of the Helpers carrying his flags before him to the right and left. The martial effect was perhaps dimmed, because there were only 70 camels and 2 horses, and they had to take turns riding, the Prophet along with the rest, sharing a camel with Ali and Zayd, and walking when need be. Eighty miles were traversed in this tiresome way, and they had to put up with the attentions of nomad groups who crunched around wanting to look at God's Apostle. "If you are he," one of them cried, "tell me what is in the belly of my she-camel?"

"If it was you who jumped her, she's carrying an old goat!" cried one of the Muslims. The Prophet turned on him in rare anger: "Enough of that! You spoke obscenely to the man!" He could not bear salacious talk. Later, on this same expedition he refused to ride between two mountains lewdly named.

Upon getting word of the mighty force approaching from Mecca, he called his captains around him and asked for their advice. The Emigrants replied as he expected. "If you led us to Yemen we would fight with you and God," said one of them.

The Helpers were another matter. Under the Pledge of Aqaba they were obliged to defend him in Medina but not to participate in provoked battles on the shores of the Red Sea. Their reply to Muhammad now, spoken by the Aws chieftain Sa'd ben Muadh, amounted to a revision of this pledge, setting a precedent for the future: "By God, if you led us to plunge into this sea, we would plunge into it behind you!"

He added a few pointed words about their experience in warfare and their anxiety to show the Prophet how to get into a fight.

"Forward then," said Muhammad, "for God has promised me one of two triumphs." By this he meant that victory over the army, or else over the caravan, would be theirs by the will of God.

They gained the wells of Badr, and Muhammad gave orders to make camp a distance away, out of sight. After dark, they took some captives—slaves of the Quraysh, stealthily drawing water by the wells, who upon being questioned revealed that the Quraysh were not far away among the hills and were about one thousand strong. This news caused some beard chewing among those Helpers who had previously spoken bravely, because sad to say, up to this very hour, all

85

had heartily hoped that God would award them triumph over the rich caravan and loot, rather than over God's enemies, the Quraysh.

In the meantime Abu Sufyan's caravan was plowing southward, but that wily leader was not with it. He was ranging far and wide on a fast steed, pointing his nose to wind and ground like a good bird dog, and finally he found what he was seeking. Next to the wells of Badr were lumps of camel dung bristling with date stones. "There lies the fodder of Yathrib," he told his companions, pointing to it, and swiftly they posted back to the caravan to lead it doubling away from Badr, by devious routes circumventing the place. In this way Abu Sufyan saved his caravan which, throughout the historic day that followed, wended safely home.

The Quraysh learned during the night that Abu Sufyan had eluded Muhammad, and many of them now hoped that they might fold their tents and follow him to Mecca. But Abu Jahl, the redhead, was one of those thin, fanatical men with sharp features, sharp tongues, and no doubt razor-filed teeth, which, once he got them fixed into an idea, would not let it go. He had come so far to scare the daylights out of the Muslims. He did not wish anyone to think that they had frightened him away. He said, "By God, we'll not go back before we've watered at Badr. We'll slaughter some camels there, have a feast, break the wineskins, and get some girls to play for us. That way certain people will see how we came together for a fight, and perhaps they'll be more careful in future."

That night another of Muhammad's relatives had a bad dream, and some Meccans, hearing about it, slipped off home. They were not cowards, but they had no heart for taking up arms against their own kinsmen.

Abu Jahl approached Badr with about six hundred men. He found that of twelve water holes, eleven had been stopped up, and the remaining one was in the possession of Muhammad's men. Muhammad was indeed exhibiting a flare for good generalship. He had managed to choose his battleground and position himself in a way that the rising sun was against the enemy's eyes. These good ideas were not invented by him, but he knew sound advice when he heard it.

The next step, the idea of Sa'd ben Muadh, was to make a little shelter for their Prophet out of sticks camouflaged by palm fronds from which he could watch the fighting. He thanked them and promised to stay in it quietly, praying for victory, and to make for Medina should the battle turn against them.

In the evening the Quraysh topped the hill and came down into the valley of Badr. Muhammad dodged out of his hut, stood in the sunset, and cried, "O God! Here come the Quraysh in their vanity and pride, contending with Thee and calling Thy Apostle a liar! O God, grant the help which Thou didst promise me!"

He caught sight of the Quraysh chieftain Utba, whose son was a Muslim in his own army, and he had one of his clairvoyant flashes: "If they listen to that man, they'll not fight us."

He gave orders not to molest the enemy when some of them came to the cistern to drink.

The Quraysh pitched camp, night fell and silence, except for the gentle chiming of armor being oiled and polished and the velvet tread of scouts about their business of inspecting the enemy. Utba made a speech that night, urging his tribesmen to melt away home. He sent to Abu Jahl proposing that they not join battle. But Abu Jahl said, "Utba does not believe his own words, but he knows his son is among them, and he is afraid someone will kill him."

At sunrise of Friday morning, the sixteenth of Ramadan, 2 A.H.—or as we should say it, March 15, 624—the battle started. As from time immemorial it began with feats of individual valor, one or more champions of either side stepping out between the hosts and after a bit of bragging, challenging the enemy to send out opponents fit to cross swords with them. Such combats provided the stuff of gossip and poetry for years to come.

Utba was first forward, smarting under the accusations of faintheartedness, flanked by his brother and nephew. Three eager Helpers leaped into the field, but they were beaten back by shouts of displeasure from Mecca: "Who are you? We have nothing to do with you! O Muhammad, send forth to us our own!"

So Muhammad sent out the Emigrant champions, Uncle Hamza, Great-Uncle Ubayda, and son-in-law Ali. Ubayda went against Utba, who promptly cut his leg off. Hamza and Ali made short work of Utba's relatives, then turned and dispatched Utba. They carried Ubayda back to Muhammad's palm hut, where he was pronounced a martyr of Islam, and he bled to death happily, reciting poetry to the Prophet.

The two hosts, now properly angered by the death of heroes, and with all the banked-up annoyances of the past boiling in their brains, clashed. In spite of their unequal numbers, the victory was grasped by the Muslims from the first. The determination to stake their lives for God and Muhammad, and the expectation of the Paradise populated by doe-eyed damsels he had told them was reserved for martyrs, spurred their battle rage. The Quraysh, on the other hand, were sadly hampered by a man who kept riding around their host reminding them that their sons and nephews were on the other side and that already several of the younger Meccans had deserted to Muhammad and were fighting with him. Moreover, they were not eager to stir up blood feuds with the Helpers, with whom they really had no quarrel.

Yet some hot tempers were at work, and Abu Jahl was busy howling about old grudges, magnifying Hubal and their noble ancestors, and on all sides swords sang with no hope of stopping them.

Muhammad was in his hut praying, in his excitement speaking rather bossily to God: "If You let us be killed, there'll be no one to worship you!"

Abu Bekr said to him, "Be careful you don't annoy God with all that praying. He has already given you His promise, after all."

87

Presently Muhammad fell into a sleep. He arose and said to Abu Bekr: "Be of good cheer: Gabriel is among us, leading his horse." He ran outside his hut, picked up a handful of pebbles and flung it at the enemy, crying, "Foul be thy faces, O Quraysh!" It may be, as some say, that the few pebbles became a wild storm of dust that flew in the faces of the Quraysh and sent them back with their shrieking camels, scrambling for the clean hills. God knows the truth about that.

Abu Jahl met death bravely. When his slayer put his foot on his neck and crowed, "Has God put you to shame, you enemy of God?" he replied, "How am I shamed? I am only another man you have killed. How is the battle going?"

Something up to seventy Quraysh lay dead at Badr, many of them chieftains. Fourteen Muslims were lost. That night a great pit was dug for the burying of the dead, and Utba's son, white-faced, saw his father thrown into it. Muhammad spoke to him kindly. "I do not grieve for my father or his death," said the boy, but he added, "it is just that he was a good man, and I'd hoped he would come to Islam one day."

That night Muhammad went to the pit and addressed the dead. "O people of the pit!" He called them by name, one by one, those well-known names of men he had grown up with and had once thought his friends, but from among whom he had been caught up by a Power no one understood and bent into the shape of an enemy: "O people of the pit! Do you know now the truth of God's message to you? Do you know now the truth of God's message to me?"

"What are you doing? Talking to dead bodies?" asked those who were with him.

"You don't understand me any better than they do," Muhammad told them. "But they cannot answer me back."

His men spent that evening stripping the dead and binding up their living captives. Fighting broke out over spoils, and Muhammad ordered all loot to be thrown onto a common pile. Later, on the way home to Medina, when tempers had cooled, he divided it with scrupulous fairness among those who had taken part in the fighting, reserving for himself the fifth.

The taking of prisoners was rather in the nature of a family reunion, as old friends and relatives found each other, embracing with cries of joy before the unpleasant formalities with shackles were carried out. Umayya, the fat man, was unlucky. He had just given himself up to an Emigrant, a friend of his youth who was delightedly greeting him, when he was seen by Bilal, his former slave whom he had staked out in the scorching desert under a stone. The black man rushed him, flailing with his sword and shouting, "The idolator! The enemy of God." Umayya was hewn in several pieces over the protests of his captor.

The Prophet's Uncle Abbas also appeared with a rope around his ankles, and the Prophet could not sleep that night for worrying whether his uncle's bonds were chafing him. Nevertheless, when the ransoms were set, he did not let his uncle go free, though Abbas, the wiliest man in the Hejaz, protested that for some time since he had been a secret Muslim. Muhammad replied, "God knows best about that. So far as I can see, you fought against us, so you owe us your ransom."

"O Apostle of God, I have no money," cried Abbas, forgetting that he was speaking to a man who not only had second sight but knew him down to the ground. Muhammad said, "Oh? Then where is the money you left with your wife, telling her exactly how to divide it among your children?"

Uncle Abbas paid up.

In this, the first of his victories, the Prophet committed an act of cruelty. Among the captives was the man who, long ago at the Kaaba, had maintained that his Persian folktales were better worth listening to than the Quran. Muhammad ordered him executed. The man begged for his life: "O Muhammad, if you kill me, who will care for my children?"

"Hell's fire," replied Muhammad.

Muslims have disputed the truth of this famous story, yet it is hard to explain why the traditionists should insert it without good authority. The fact is, Muhammad was a grim enemy to those who diminished the holy Word.

Among those we have created is a nation guided in truth and behaving justly. But there are others who say our signs are lies and them we will cut down one by one, they won't know how. So let them do as they please—verily my plan will turn the trick.

-THE CHAPTER OF AL-AARAF

13

After Badr:
Ruin to the Qaynuqa

Although the Prophet's callousness to the enemy of his Quran did not go unremembered, his humane treatment of many prisoners made a greater impression. Many were let off without ransom, simply for being the fathers of large families. Others who knew how to read and write were freed upon their oath that they would teach others to do the same.

His son-in-law, Abu'l-As, husband of his daughter Zaynab, was also taken prisoner. This was the young man whom the Quraysh had urged to put his wife away, but he refused. In due time his ransom arrived from Zaynab in Mecca. It was a necklace her mother Khadija had given her for a wedding present. The Prophet was terribly shaken in looking at it. He asked permission of the others to allow Abu'l-As to return to Mecca, ransom and all, and they gave it. Nevertheless, he may have imposed on Abu'l-As a ransom harder still—that is, his wife. Because shortly afterward Zaynab left her husband and joined her father in Medina. She did not make the journey without trouble. The Quraysh, smarting from defeat, saw the Prophet's daughter making northward in her camel howdah under the protection of Abu'l-As's brother and came after her with arrows, which they pointed at her menacingly, ignoring the threats of her brother-in-law. Zaynab, who was pregnant, had a miscarriage then and there. Abu Sufyan, the new chief now that Abu Jahl was slain, had a talk with her menfolk. He said he didn't care about Zaynab herself, but he couldn't bear her leaving Mecca in that provocative manner in broad daylight. She therefore remained awhile in Mecca and later was allowed to steal out secretly at night and rejoin her father. Her loving husband, a very prosperous man, remained in Mecca to nurse his fortune, but his riches were like ashes in his mouth, and he eventually embraced Islam, and his wife again, in Medina.

Muhammad needed the comfort of this daughter, for while the Battle of Badr was in progress, his eldest daughter, Ruqayya, had died. She was married to one of his principal captains, Uthman, a cousin of Abu Sufyan.

The Prophet's elder wife, Sawda, had given him some trouble after Badr, where her father and brothers were among the Meccan dead. Unable to bear the sight of living captives in their bonds as they were brought into the mosque enclosure to await their ransom, she burst out at some of them, "Why did you surrender? Why didn't you die like heroes on the field?"

To her horror, the Prophet overheard these remarks, and he was terribly displeased. "What are you trying to do?" he demanded coldly. "Make enemies for God and His Apostle?"

Poor Sawda! She had no understanding of the strange role history had cut out for her husband. She was only a tearful fat lady, anxious for his digestion, who tried to be a good mother to little Ayesha. After her disloyal outburst, fearful that she would be divorced, she apologized with tears, and Ayesha joined her tears lest Sawda should have to go away.

It was perhaps at this time that by agreement Sawda became more housekeeper than wife. Umar, who was one of Muhammad's most useful captains, had a daughter Hafsa, who had been widowed at Badr, and her father, as was his duty, anxiously offered her about among his friends. Unfortunately, although Hafsa was a beauty of eighteen years, she had inherited the fiery disposition of her father, which all the world admired in a warrior but was not eager to find in a wife. Uthman, recently widowed, refused her. So did Abu Bekr. With the Sawda trouble afflicting his compound, Muhammad married Hafsa, much to the annoyance of Ayesha who, now eleven years old, considered herself to be the central figure of the household. However, she found Hafsa's strong and defiant disposition a perfect match for her subtle and willful one, and these two became friends.

The Battle of Badr was a landmark in the history of Islam, a turning point with a touch of mysticism, as if it were a sign to confirm Muhammad's statement that he was God's chosen Apostle. His prestige increased, poems were written about him, and his mosque began to fill up with visitors. As his knowledge of the Scriptures increased and his skill in telling stories became more polished, he became something of a fabulist, enlarging upon the familiar tales, retelling them in his singing style and conveying to us a sense of the drama and dash of the

91

desert poets. The Quran tales have an exotic charm absent from the austerer versions in the Old Testament.

The Jews of Medina remained uncharmed, and so did the unconvinced or defected Muslims called Hypocrites, who formed a treacherous opposition to Muhammad's growing popularity. Assembling in the mosque to hear him, they would put their heads together and snicker. Or they made up witticisms about Muslims behind their backs. Their poets satirized him. A woman poet, Asma, from a tribe that had not honored the Pledge of Aqaba, fashioned such hurtful rhymes that to silence her a group of Muslims crept into her house by night and slew her in bed next to her seven children. Muhammad expressed no reproach or pity for this or similar assassinations. He praised them.

The Jews saw early that Muhammad was far from a figure of fun. One day a Jewish businessman passed by a group of young Muslims laughing together and could hardly believe his eyes. They were Aws and Khazraj, behaving like friends! Such a short time back they had been at one another's throats, dragging all Medina, Jews and Arabs alike, into a frenzy of killing. It gave this man to wonder if something much worse might not happen to Jews if Arabs should cease to squabble. He sent out young Jews into the streets to remind Aws and Khazraj of their old bitterness, wherever they were seen consorting, and to start whatever other trouble they could. To Mecca was dispatched a famous poet, Ka'b, to sing songs of sad anger against Muhammad, which would have made the stones of the desert damp with tears. This man was the son of an Arab father and a Jewish mother of the an-Nadir tribe, and he had been brought up as a Jew. Muhammad counteracted Ka'b's effective propaganda in two ways. First, he hired the services of an equally talented poet named Hassan ben Thabit to sing his praises, chronicle his deeds, and generally act in the same capacity as would a modern press officer. Second, he let it be known that he would not be sorry to hear the last of Ka'b.

Presently some Muslims tricked Ka'b into meeting them at a lonely place at night, and there they killed him.

Muslims have never worshiped Muhammad as a god or even claimed him as a saint. Still less did Muhammad claim to be more than a faulty man, and if he ever got too far above himself, God soon brought him low again.

He was now embarking on a tide of fortune when, in order to keep his balance, he had to reach out and without compunction destroy all who might have pulled him down. We do not have the historical evidence to judge whether he did this coolly or in anguish, or as part of a calculated strategy that would presently send his God's Word arrowing in all directions. Possibly his acts were only intuitive, and ruthless because ruthlessness happened to be the shortest distance between two limited objectives. We must also take into consideration that he acted under the command of supernatural influences, whose origin we do not understand but which he felt compelled to obey at all costs.

Thus it is that bloody deeds are to be recorded of a man who, according to every reliable account, was personally gentle, loving to his wives, loyal to his friends, as a leader tolerant and just, and as an army commander courageous, compassionate, and so considerate that he would share his camel with any raggle-taggle camp follower, or make his army detour around a bitch giving birth on the road.

Yet the Voice that guided him made it plain: Success was imperative, and bloodshed or any cruel action for the faith was to be condoned. He thus became responsible in the eye of history for jihad, holy war, for deeds of savage butchery and schemes that resulted in the ruin of many.

He made up his mind after Badr that the Jews were his enemies and had to be disposed of.

A good number of the Quraysh had fallen at Badr, and Muhammad's least favorite uncle, Abu Lahab, who had stayed at home, died of the pox as if the very hand of God had turned aside to smite him down on the Prophet's behalf. This did not harm Muhammad's prestige among the younger folk and slaves, who secretly rejoiced at the Muslim victory. But Abu Sufyan, who had brought the rich caravan safely home, was now the chief man of the tribe, the one to whom all others turned for counsel, and he was only the more stiff-necked in his resolve to exact revenge. He forbade the Meccans to mourn their dead and vowed that, for his part, he would not oil himself or approach his wives until he had raided Medina.

Accordingly, ten weeks after Badr he launched a razzia. It was only a token foray, permitting him to resume his usual domestic habits and at the same time warning Medina of fiercer trouble to come. It resulted in no more than the burning of a few houses and the scattering of some bags of barley meal, from which it got its historic name, the "barley-meal raid." But Abu Sufyan used, as the base of his operations in Medina, the house of a Jewish business associate from whom he got dinner and information.

This gave Muhammad the justification he needed to accuse the Jews of treachery. Some clashes had been taking place in the streets between younger Muslims and Jews. One of these, involving the Qaynuqa tribe, was now whipped up into a battle, and instead of getting off with a few bruised heads, the Jews found it necessary to retreat in haste to their stronghold while Muhammad and his Muslims laid siege without. The Jews were amazed by this extreme reaction and quite unprepared for it, so after fifteen days they surrendered.

The traditional records of these happenings contain inferences that Muhammad planned severe punishment for the Qaynuqa, even condemning the entire tribe to death. But the Hypocrite leader, Abdullah ibn Ubayy, interposed on their behalf, not without danger to himself. In seeking audience with

93

Muhammad he was flung rudely against a wall by a guard, so that his face bled. Still, courageously, he pushed ahead to a place where the Prophet was about to pass by, and he said, "O Muhammad, deal kindly with my confederates!" Muhammad pretended not to have heard. Then Ubayy caught hard hold of the collar of Muhammad's robe so that the Prophet was brought to a stop. He turned around, so angry that his face turned dark and said, "Confound you, let me go!"

Ibn Ubayy's life was not worth a date stone at that moment, but like a good Arab, he did not forget his debt to past friendship.

"No, by God, I'll not let you go. Four hundred of the Qaynuqa without mail on their backs and three hundred with mail protected me from my enemies. Do you think I am going to let you cut them all down in a day?"

The Apostle considered for a minute and then relented. The lives of the Qaynuqa were saved. They were given three days to collect the money owing to them in debts and then banished from Arabia. They are said to have moved northward into Syria.

Of the three main Jewish tribes in Medina, the other two being the an-Nadir and the Qurayza, these Qaynuqa were the most mercantile. They were merchants in a small way, trading in the bazaars. But chiefly they were metalworkers, having learned the art of beating out the splendid shining armor, the moon-curved swords and sun-catching helmets that glorified warfare in the desert. After their expulsion there must have been a serious lag in armaments manufacture for a long time.

The bazaar trade, however, did not suffer. It was operated by the Emigrants— the ones with brown thumbs.

Verily, those who turned their backs on that day when the two armies met—it was Satan who made them slip because of something they had done. But God has forgiven them now. Verily, God is forgiving and clement.
                                         -THE CHAPTER OF IMRAN'S FAMILY

14

The Battle of Uhud

In Mecca it was decided that the entire wealth of the caravan Abu Sufyan had brought safely back in the year of Badr would be devoted to the next large-scale attempt against Muhammad. Revenge for Badr was not the sole motivation. That summer, a Meccan caravan, winding northward in great silence by a route rarely taken, through trackless wilderness and well to the east of Medina, was set upon by a Muslim force commanded by Zayd, which routed it utterly and brought back to Medina spoils worth one hundred thousand gold pieces. The episode shows how well Muhammad's intelligence network was working for him.

Abu Sufyan sent no further caravans northward that year. Trade with Syria came to a stop. But he applied himself with passion to the destruction of Muhammad, borrowing money right and left, sending off embassies to strike treaties with all possible nomads, and calling on old confederacies to render him their sworn duty. The women of Quraysh, cheated of their year's wealth, were thoroughly on his side, their emotions wound to the sticking point by the eloquence of his wife, Hind, a beautiful woman with a wild nature, whose father Utba had been the first to fall at Badr. Between the two of them they scraped together an army of Napoleonic proportions for those times—three thousand men composed of Quraysh, their confederates from among lesser tribes and

Bedouin, slaves, and black mercenary troops from Abyssinia. To all these men, seven hundred of whom wore mail, there were added a like number of camels and two hundred horses. Moreover, perched on the summits of many camels were little huts, or howdahs, in which rode a squadron of women well trained by Hind to sing warlike ballads that would keep their menfolk in a fever pitch of rage and discourage cowardice.

A black slave named Wahshi rode with the army. He had a reputation as a marksman with his javelin, and he had come forward primed for battle with the promise of his master, whose uncle had fallen at Badr, that if he slew Muhammad's mighty uncle, Hamza, he should have his freedom. Hind seconded the motion. Whenever she passed Wahshi on the march, she would say, "Come on, father of blackness, satisfy your vengeance and ours!" She said she would give Wahshi all her ornaments—and her legs were shimmering with silver bangles—if he killed Hamza.

In one howdah rode Hubal, on holiday from the Kaaba. Abu Sufyan had well grasped that quite apart from considerations of revenge and caravan routes, he was engaged in a holy war.

It was the spring of 625, one year after Badr, that his army moved northward against Medina. They traveled some distance north of the city and advanced along a wadi, taking up position below the steep hill of Uhud. In the valley where they camped, grain was growing strong, and there they set their animals to feed, and fed themselves.

Muhammad knew of their coming well in advance, for he had a good spy in the Meccan ranks in the person of his Uncle Abbas, and besides he had had a dream in which he saw himself in strong mail. This he interpreted to mean that he should sit tight in the city, using it as a stronghold, and defend it from within. Abdullah ibn Ubayy, the Hypocrite leader, who was fighting with the Muslims in accordance with the terms of the Covenant of Medina that all tribes should join in defense of the city, agreed with him. There were, however, all too many eager people among both Muslims and Hypocrites who preferred to dash out and meet the enemy in the field, and this became a furious demand when their scouts brought word of Meccan camels chewing up their grain. In the end Muhammad yielded to their prodding. He held Friday prayers as usual, and afterward retired to his house to put on his armor. By that time hot heads had cooled, and attempts were made to dissuade him, but he said, "A Prophet who has once taken on his armor must not lay it aside until he has fought." Decisiveness was part of his strength as a leader, and he would not reverse himself again.

The Jews were staying out of these discussions, because although equally obligated under the Covenant to defend the city, they chose to look on the Quraysh squabble as a purely Muslim affair. Besides, they pointed out it was the Sabbath, and they could not be expected to take up arms. However, at the last minute they sent a contingent to join the army, but Muhammad refused their services.

Ibn Ubayy was upset by the decision to move out of the city and also at the rejection of the badly needed Jewish troops. He marched out at night with the Muslims, entreating Muhammad to let him go back for the Jews, but the Prophet said, "We do not need them." He used the word jihad, "holy war," something in which only true believers might share.

Ibn Ubayy said to his Hypocrites: "He won't listen to me. I don't see why we should lose our lives here." He led them back to Medina with Muhammad's parting words ringing in their ears: "God curse you, you enemies of God, for God will make His Prophet independent of you!"

The Muslim force was now badly depleted to about seven hundred men, only two hundred of whom had armor. Two coats of mail were worn by Muhammad himself. He had a sword also, but he gave it to be used by a man who had none. The new owner strutted with it so arrogantly that Muhammad observed, "God hates to see a man walking like that—except on a day like this."

The Muslims had an advantage over the Meccans in knowing the terrain. Approaching Uhud stealthily by a roundabout route, they made their way past the enemy forces, eluding their scouts, and finally gained the steep slope of Mount Uhud rising above the fields. The mountain at their backs lent strength to their tiny numbers. There was one vulnerable point—the gorge whereby they had approached the hillside. Muhammad set aside fifty archers and told them to keep the gorge, not budging an inch from their position no matter what happened. Then he turned to witness in the cracking dawn the enemy's formidable array.

The Battle of Uhud did not begin according to etiquette with single combat between champions. Feelings were too sore and tempers frayed. Abu Sufyan sent to the Helpers saying that he had no quarrel with them and would be glad to see them leave the field. They returned a rude answer to that.

Then battle was joined. Hind and her women moved forward with the troops, scattering about the field as closely as they dared to the fighting men, beating their tambourines with terrible clash and shouting:

"Daughters of the shining Morning Star,
Watching you from silken beds we are,
Thrash them! in our arms we'll fold you;
Run, and nevermore we'll hold you!"

In the very forefront of battle was the Christian monk who had left Medina when the Apostle came. Believing himself to be immune from the blows of his former friends, he had placed himself unarmed at the head of a slave force, but he found to his utter amazement that the Medinans had no objection to attacking him. "Evil has befallen my people since I left them," he said, scrabbling for stones to save himself.

Hamza was fighting with his usual wrath, cutting off the heads and arms of many old friends, among whom was the son of a freedwoman of Mecca who performed the ritual circumcisions for the Quraysh tribe. Wahshi, who was striding about the field with one aim, to find Hamza, found him.

By God, he was killing men, sparing no one like a huge mad camel; then Siba got in my way and I heard Hamza say, "Come here, you son of a female circumciser!" and he struck him a blow so swift and straight that for a bit Siba's head didn't even fall off his shoulders and I thought he had missed.

I poised my javelin until I was sure it would hit the mark and launched it: it got him below the belt and came out between his legs. He came on at me, then folded up and fell. I waited for him to die, then I pulled out my javelin and went back to camp, since I had no business with anyone but him.

Wahshi almost missed his ankle bangles when Hind got in the way of the man carrying Muhammad's sword. He was about to strike her down when she shrieked, and realizing that his quarry was a woman, he turned aside the blade. "I respected the Prophet's sword too much to kill a woman with it," he said. A certain Muslim, noted for his fondness for washing, almost reached Abu Sufyan, but he was killed in the nick of time by a watchful Meccan protecting his commander. "Our friend is being washed by angels now," said Muhammad.

With the mountain and Muhammad behind them and the downslope to give them impetus, the seven hundred Muslims swept the thousands of enemy before them. With a thunderous battle cry of "Allah Akbar—God is Great!" they came down Uhud, raining arrows on men, camels, women, Hubal, and all. The men turned tail, the camels panicked, and Hubal wobbled madly on his screaming mount.

The standard of the Quraysh had been last carried by a Quraysh slave. He fought for it until his hands were cut off, then raised it between his stumps, holding it against his breast and throat until he was killed over it. One of the women ran back to release the banner and get it up again, thus bringing some order to the Meccan retreat, which was now in full swing. "We scattered them like fawns," sang Hassan ben Thabit, Muhammad's poet,

"We attacked them thrusting, slaying, chastising,
Driving them before us with blows on every side,
Had not the Harithite woman seized their standard,
We would have got them all to market and sold them

98

like goats."

The women suddenly gave up, realizing that their songs and their courage were being wasted. They gathered up their skirts and ran from the field with a tremendous show of brown legs and silver ornaments, which the poets duly recorded.

Then suddenly the tide of battle turned. The fifty archers left by the defile, seeing their friends on the plain below falling upon the battle spoils and the women huddled on a hillock, waiting for someone to come and take them prisoner, flung themselves with a whoop of joy downhill—except twenty men who remembered the Prophet's command. A Meccan captain, Khalid ibn al-Walid, having acutely noted how busy the Muslims were at their looting, wheeled around to attack from the rear, and in doing so discovered the gorge. In no time at all he had cut down the twenty staunch defenders. The fleeing Meccans rallied and came storming back with whirling swords, trapping the might of Islam in a vicious sandwich. The women left their hillocks and resumed their persuasive banging on the tambourines. Hind found the corpse of Hamza, slayer of her father, and with a wild yell cut out his entrails to drape and girdle her body. She scoured in his ravaged stomach, wrenched out his liver, and started to eat it. Then, suddenly, she vomited.

A man who resembled Muhammad was killed. The cry went up, "The Prophet is dead!" and shot throughout the Muslim ranks like a deadly arrow. They dropped their weapons and fled before the enemy.

Muhammad was not dead, but he was in dire distress. A group of the enemy had found him and brought a great stone down on his head, so that he fell on his side, one of his teeth smashed, his face ground into the earth. A follower, sobbing, got him on his feet, licking his blood from his face like a desperate mother. The Prophet yelled, "Who will sell his life for us?" Five Helpers rallied to him with a will, making their bodies into a shield against their enemies pressing hard. One by one they were cut down, the last man dying with his face on the Apostle's foot, while Muhammad did as he had done years back in the Wicked Wars—picked up arrows as fast as they fell and handed them to his defenders before God blessed them with martyrdom. Then he seized a fallen bow and shot with it himself. He saw a man with his eye hanging down his cheek and stuffed it back in his head. The man said afterward it was a better eye than the other.

By this time his army was scrambling up the steep hill of Uhud, fleeing before the enemy who were after them, leaping over the bodies of the martyrs. Muhammad turned and fled with his men. But a Muslim warrior caught a glimpse of him, helmeted, flashing-eyed, and this man ran back onto the field, bellowing mightily at his comrades who were sitting inert and shocked among the dead, or else making for the skyline: "Take heart, Muslims—the Prophet is up there shoot-

99

ing with a broken bow!" The closest companions of the Prophet were at that moment hustling him up the mountain with no small difficulty, because in spite of an abstemious life, Muhammad was becoming plump on honey and dates, and moreover he was carrying two coats of mail. They washed him by a spring, and a strong man lifted him on his shoulders to a high rock, where he was able to pause and watch the progress of events—seen by all but in safety. Like a standard over the faithful, he had a magical effect on them. An inflation of strength and savage fury welled up in them. They took up their courage with their curved swords and wielded them both insanely among the enemy, whose women, envying Hind her jewelry, were going mad among the entrails and hacking off men's hands to make garlands of the finger-bones. Hind, her moment of delicacy having evaporated, was enswathed in crimson horror and howling:

"I have slaked my fury and fulfilled my oath,
O Wahshi, you have cooled my burning breast
And I'll thank you while my life lasts,
And until my bones rot!"

For this reason or another, Abu Sufyan had had enough. He climbed a high rock and shouted, "Hubal is victorious! Glory to the great Hubal!"

The Apostle heard him and yelled from his rock, "God is most high and glorious! Our dead are in Paradise, yours are in Hell!"

Abu Sufyan shouted, "Umar! Tell me the truth! Have we killed Muhammad?"

Umar gave reply, "By God, you have not. That was his voice, and he can hear you now!"

"Then let him hear this," cried Abu Sufyan. "There are mutilated bodies among your dead. This gives me neither joy nor anger. I did not order it. I did not forbid it."

He wheeled his horse and scrambled down the slope, turning back to shout once more: "We have a meeting place next year at Badr!" Then he rode off the field, followed by his host.

The Prophet told a Muslim to shout after him, "Yes—it is an appointment!"

The Battle of Uhud ended as ignobly as it had begun, with little heroism and much disorganized slaughter resulting in the death of seventy-four Muslims. Muhammad did not leave the field without being taught a harsh lesson. He walked among the dead until he found the wrecked corpse of his Uncle Hamza, and in a sick rage he swore that if ever God gave him victory over the Quraysh, he would mutilate thirty of them. God sent down a revelation then and there.

If you must punish, punish only in the measure you were punished;

100

But it is better to endure patiently.
Patience rests in God.

And so as well as he could find it in his heart, Muhammad forgave the Meccan women. When later Wahshi became a Muslim, he forgave him too. He forbade the faithful to mutilate corpses slain in battle.

He gave orders for the dead to be buried where they lay. To this day the hel-ter-skelter graves, little heaps covering the men of Uhud, may be seen, with bits of stone marking how they fell.

*Had not God prescribed banishment for them, He would have given them torment
in this world; as it is, they will be tormented in the next with fire. That is because
they opposed God and His Apostle, and verily, God is keen to punish..*

-THE CHAPTER OF EMIGRATION

15

After Uhud:
Farewell to the An-Nadir

U hud was clearly not a victory for the Quraysh. Muhammad was still
alive and master of Medina, while the Meccan caravan trade with the
northern empires was severely crippled. On the other hand, it was far
from a victory for the Muslims. Seventy Helpers were lost and four
Emigrants, and the rest of them knew that the days were numbered before they
could expect another, perhaps better-planned attack.

Public opinion that had been against Muhammad even in the days of his triumph after Badr solidified after Uhud. Within the town of Medina and in the
countryside round about, parties formed, mostly comprising clients and allies of
the Hypocrites and Jews. On every side was heard mockery, muttering, menace,
and grumbling against Muhammad and the umma, and if these died down, there
were secret agents at work to breathe new life into them. Plots were forever thick-
ening and then running into the sand. Now and again in the hinterlands a force
would be mustered, more or less efficiently organized, whose ambition it was to
enter Medina and destroy the Prophet or at least harass the Muslims. They came
to nothing because Muhammad's intelligence system held true to him, and he
would send out armed bands of the faithful to break up trouble at the campfire
stage, before it turned into action.

The two years after Uhud were spent in a wearisome game of spying, counterspying, skirmishing, outwitting, bribing, assassinating. The incessant conspiracies did not really weaken his position. They focused attention on him as a leader whose passage through the life of Arabia would leave things never the same again. He himself was in full control of his powers now. God dealt crushingly with him, knocking him to the ground or forcing him to stand much of the night, listening with all his might for the messages from Heaven to arise in him. Out of this exacerbating period came the dread revelations, bitter vitriol against Jews, Christians, Hypocrites, and all manner of misbelievers. Yet side by side with them are the sober, constructive thoughts on which the umma was being built, a new kind of society which cut across tribal lines, snapped old loyalties, dissolved corrupt habits, and in their place established codes of justice and conduct conforming to the highest ethical principles Muhammad could know or interpret in the centers of his own genius.

He may not have guessed that he was an all conqueror, or that the umma would be a building block of civilization, yet with hindsight we can see that all his actions could have been based on such an opinion.

He trained young men as missionaries to the nomads. They committed the Quran to memory and then went out into the desert wastes and wadis, where the black tents lay, to recite the long, darkly sparkling lines, sounding both menace and comfort to the harsh-living folk. It was a dangerous profession. For a while it was a sport among the nomads to profess deep interest in Islam and request the missionaries to be sent out. Then they were ambushed and their heads—with the whole Quran locked inside—chopped off. Crucifixions took place, too, under the molten sun—and whatever fiendish tortures seemed good at the time. Jewish bribes were behind many of these crimes and behind them the fears rapidly swelling in the Jewish communities, and the ambitions of the Hypocrites and the chagrin of Mecca. It is in the light of this—remembering the young reciters of God's Word barbarously wasted—that Muhammad's own conduct must be understood.

Once Abu Sufyan came riding out of Mecca to witness an execution of a missionary, and as the scimitar was poised aloft, he asked him jeeringly if he did not now wish Muhammad in his place and himself sitting in peace with his family. The young man replied, "By God, I do not wish that even a thorn should trouble Muhammad where he is now, that I might be sitting in peace with my family!"

From the start, tides of men lifted themselves above the ordinary, inspired by Muhammad and his Quran. The missionary groups did not grow less determined for the danger they faced, but larger, and they armed themselves. They were the first Muslims to go out (as they were later accused of doing) with the Quran in one hand and a crescent sword in the other.

One trail of blood in 625 led to disaster for the second Jewish clan of an-

103

Nadir. Muhammad had sent a party of young Muslims, between forty and seventy of them, as missionaries to a nomad tribe with whom he had an alliance, the Beni Amir. They were supposed to be traveling under the protection of the Beni Amir, one of whose tribal chiefs had requested the visit. But a rival leader of the same tribe who wanted nothing to do with Islam persuaded a neighboring clan, the Beni Sulaym—which was not hampered by an alliance—to ambush the band and slay them. This massacre took place by the Well of Maunah.

One man survived to make his way back to Medina. In so doing he crossed the path of two wayfarers of the Beni Amir and in his fury against his erstwhile "protectors" killed them. Thus, when he finally got to Muhammad, he brought him not only the tale of betrayal but a broken alliance, for which blood money would have to be paid if he did not want a war on his hands.

It is quite unclear why Muhammad should have asked the an-Nadir to contribute to the blood money arising from what seems at first sight to be a purely Muslim affair. Perhaps he thought that, since the an-Nadir had an alliance with both the Beni Amir and himself, they should be eager to share the gratification of one and the sorrow of the other. More likely, he thought, or persuaded himself, that the Jews were behind the deed and decided to stage a deadly drama of his own.

With a few companions he called upon the chieftains of the an-Nadir to negotiate the matter. The Jews received him courteously and said they would be glad to come to an arrangement after the Muslims had given them the pleasure of joining them for a meal. They retired to the interior of their house to prepare the food, while the Muslims settled themselves outside the building, their backs against the wall, where they could keep a sharp eye on the surrounding structures and slitted vents, just wide enough for arrows or daggers to be launched. "When an Arab sits with a Jew," Muhammad had counseled his flock, "that Jew is considering the best way to murder him."

Presently Muhammad received a revelation from God: The absent Jews were not preparing a meal at all but his own assassination. Even at that moment they were preparing to take a large stone to the flat roof of the building against which he sat and from there drop it directly on Muhammad's head. He rose suddenly and went home. His companions soon joined him.

This strange tale seems to all but the most devout Muslims to put Muhammad entirely in the wrong, yet he knew that the Jews were waiting for an opportunity to kill him. The idea had been proposed to this same tribe at the beginning of his stay in Medina by the Quraysh, and no doubt there had since been much wishful talk about it. Moreover the Jews had justification—the killing of their poet, Ka'b, a famous and popular man, which could only be expiated by an important death such as Muhammad's. Relations between Jews and Muslims had by this time become such a nervous tangle of animosities that the an-Nadir were probably not

104

at all dumbfounded to receive, soon after Muhammad's visit, an ultimatum. As punishment for having plotted his assassination, they were to leave Medina within ten days, lock, stock, and barrel. Muhammad did not wish to see the face of an an-Nadir in the city streets again.

The an-Nadir were the richest agricultural tribe of the area. To them belonged wide expanses of the splendid date groves that embellished the desert around Medina. They might keep the produce of these groves, Muhammad said, but they must be satisfied to administer them from afar through the stewardship of Muslims.

The Jews would have submitted to this hard demand, for they were well able to assess the situation—that Muhammad was riding a high tide of success that had by no means come to the flood. But at this point their ally, Abdullah ibn Ubayy, injudiciously entered the fray, encouraging the an-Nadir to stand firm against the Prophet and promising them his support. Perhaps he thought, to begin with, that he could do more for them than he could. In the end he could do nothing, and there was no sign of him during the ensuing hostilities when the an-Nadir retreated to their strongholds and there helplessly huddled for fifteen days, besieged by the Muslim force. When, watching through the vents, they saw their groves being vandalized and vindictively destroyed, they could not bear it. They gave up.

The terms were now less favorable. They were to depart from Medina leaving all their arms—of which Muhammad took immediate charge—their dates, palms, stores, produce, and all. These were divided among needy Emigrants.

The an-Nadir departed. It was a grand sight which must have been enjoyed by the Arabs for the sheer spectacle of it—six hundred camels laden with rich stuffs, the tasseled and painted howdahs swaying and bearing great clusters of blazing-eyed wives, daughters, and aunts, who certainly wore all their ornaments on that day, and all around, the well-dressed slaves and pretty dancing girls with orders to beat tambourines and feet for all they were worth until the Arabs blinked their eyes against the noise, the glitter, and the dust.

The an-Nadir departed in defeat, but they knew how to depart in style. They were lucky enough to have large properties in Khaybar where they had yet a while to ply the threads of their lives and dangerous plots.

Did they take with them the wedding apparel, which the citizens used to hire when somebody got married? It was the only wedding wardrobe in Medina and considered very fine.

105

Wives of the Prophet! You are not like other women. If you fear God, be not too familiar in speech lest men of unhealthy mind lust after you: but speak discreetly.

THE CHAPTER OF THE CONFEDERATES

16

Crooked Ribs

A fter Uhud, Muhammad began to expand his household considerably by marriage. Sawda, his senior wife, was but a chatelaine, expending herself in a rather colorless reign over household logistics. Ayesha, brought up by her bridegroom's own hand to fear God, did so in her own way. Being a person of subtle mind, she was one of the few people around Muhammad who could follow his intellect or match his humor. When Hafsa, Umar's spirited daughter, joined the household and became her friend, this pair, allied with Sawda, made up a formidable clique with which subsequent novices in the harem were obliged to pit wits.

Early in 626 Muhammad married Zaynab, a woman of thirty who, like Hafsa, was a widow of one of the Badr heroes, and a woman of Hashim besides, with a special claim on the Prophet's protection. She was a saintly person, devoted to good works and the care of the sick. She may have been an invalid herself. In any case, she died only eight months after her marriage. Still, her existence suggests that Muhammad's many marriages may have another explanation than a compulsion for wife collecting. A fair study of the Prophet's habits shows that he was not as amorous as might be supposed, but an abstemious man who is known to have spent half or more of his nights standing upright on painfully swelling feet, communing with God, and he advised others to do the same.

Up to his marriage with Khadija, he was "like a green virgin." After it, until his fiftieth year, when Khadija died, no blot developed on his moral character, even under the scrutiny of Victorian scholars. As a leader of Muslims, he disapproved of sexual contact outside marriage or the institution of concubinage, and he gently discouraged even flirting among believers.

Still, this part of his complex personality is a puzzle. For all his personal reserve, he had no hesitation in whipping his followers to battle frenzy by painting luscious word pictures of the sensuous delights awaiting them in Paradise, should they have the good fortune to die as martyrs in the way of God. There they would live amid vineyards and gardens, whiling away eternity under the caresses of seventy-two black-eyed beauties "with swelling breasts and the same age as themselves," lovely beyond tiring, since their virginities would be perpetually renewed.

It is odd that he made such a point of virginity in Paradise, since in enlarging his harem he did not insist at all upon this qualification. Out of thirteen wives and concubines, Ayesha was his sole virgin bride.

He learned very much to enjoy the company of his harem. He loved to come home to them and sit among them, or share the household tasks of dusting, milking of animals, and all odd jobs. The tenderness he felt for women would be reflected in the Quran, in laws that put an end to cruel and primitive social conditions in which many women then lived—being lucky to find themselves alive at all and not buried at birth for being female, or respectably married instead of prostituted by their clan heads.

In a harsh "masculine" culture, where a population greater than its food supply survives by physical competition, men take the dominant role. Muhammad's regulations for the umma take male dominance for granted, but he thought women equally loved by God. It is not true that he denied women a place in the Muslim heaven. He told an old lady that she would become young and beautiful the minute she entered Paradise. He was vague, certainly, about the identity of the houris who entertained Muslim heroes on golden couches. They were by no means those gentlemen's dead wives. But once, when his wife Umm Salama remarked that in praising the Emigrants who had shared his exile he mentioned only the men, never the women, down came a Quran from God on the subject: "I waste not the works of a worker among you, be it male or female: one of you is part of the other."

Like every other Arab warrior, Muhammad received after a victorious razzia a choice of women whom he might keep "in his power"—that is, as slaves or concubines. In every recorded case, Muhammad gave such captives the choice of becoming his full-fledged wives should they choose to embrace Islam. Upon his followers he impressed the importance of offering women and children captured

107

in war for ransom by their relatives before consigning them to slavery.

For the first years after the Hijra, Muhammad had been too poor to assume wives and concubines in addition to his three dependents, and to these may be added the support of his related families in the mosque enclosure, such as Ali and Fatima and their children, and Zayd's family. Ali and Zayd, along with Abu Bekr, Umar, Uthman, and others, were his closest collaborators, his cabinet. They and their families had to be considered financially when the household bills came in.

As his circumstances grew easier, the aspect of his household changed, although not extravagantly or luxuriously. He did not disapprove of luxury for others, but he gave all his own surplus to the poor. However, he did assume his normal responsibilities to Muslim widows, and since he was continually foisting widows during his warfaring period on others, he could scarcely avoid similar charges himself. Furthermore, as he grew older and farmed out daughters and granddaughters among his captains, they consequently wished to place their female relatives in his care or in that of his close associates. Eventually Muhammad was bound to the top echelons of his command by a network of harem alliances.

Once someone asked him what he loved most in the world, and he replied, "Of the things in this world that delight me, I love little children and women and sweet scent. Yet none of these can give me the happiness I find in prayer."

If this statement was an honest expression of his taste, and not simply a charming lesson to his questioner, it is surely one of the most revealing statements ever preserved of a historical figure, and yet mysterious because it is so rare. The women in his life, his wives, were equated with children, not sex objects but child objects, or playful joy objects, and both were equated with the delight he took in the pervasive sweetness of a scent.

He liked women the way humorous men often do like women, because they appreciate feminine subtlety. This is expressed in another famous saying of the Prophet: "Be kind to women sprung from your rib. If you try to straighten out a rib, you will break it. Accept women as they are, with all their curvatures."

One suspects that Muhammad had some of this devious femininity in his own nature. He had many "feminine" characteristics, including sensitivity, sympathy, a love of personal cleanliness and order in his surroundings, conviviality and good talk. He liked handicrafts. He patched his own clothes and mended his own shoes.

He restrained vanity in his wives, imposing simplicity in their dress. He once told Ayesha that clothes should never be thrown away as long as they could be patched. The apartments of his wives, even after he had money to spare, continued to be built of mud bricks, and they were furnished with bare essentials: a bed, a mat, a jar of water. Once, exasperated beyond patience by jealous bickering among the wives on the subject of worldly splendor, he threatened to divorce them all. He said he would remove himself from them and their squabbles for one month.

He retired and meditated. They wondered and trembled. He couldn't sit it out, but appeared one day in Ayesha's hut. She had the self-possession to say, "Oh, it's you? I thought you would be gone a month!"

He gave her a hug. "This month is short a few days," he said.

All the same, out of his retirement he brought back to the harem a Quran from God:

O Prophet, say to thy wives: if you desire the life of this world and its vanities, come—I will provide for you generously, and send you out into the world splendidly arrayed. But if you desire God and the Prophet and Paradise, then conduct yourselves as you should. For those who do, God has prepared a mighty reward.

It is believed, though not known, that one or two of Muhammad's wives might have chosen divorce with alimony, after this crisis. If they did, they lost their place in history, and perhaps in Heaven too.

Yet Muhammad was far too humane and observant a man to be unaware of what the vanity of women means to them. One of the most astonishing traditions of the Prophet comes down from a camp follower, a young girl who tagged along adventurously on one of his raids to see the fun. He gave her a ride on the back of his camel, and to her horror she experienced her first menses. Not only did the Prophet—who no less than the ancient Jews had a stern sense of the "uncleanliness" of women in this condition—speak to her tenderly and tell her exactly what to do, but, sensitive to the significance of the event for her, he personally selected from the battle spoils a necklace and gave it to her. She was an old woman when she told the tale, but she said the necklace had never once left her neck.

The first of his "diplomatic marriages" might have been in 626 with Umm Salama, a widow of twenty-nine—not considered young—whose husband had died at Uhud. She was a reserved and lovely woman, and he was very attracted to her, yet her main beauty might well have been that she was born of the Clan Makhzum, his original enemies, and by this marriage he made known his wish to be reunited with the clans of Quraysh.

Ayesha and Hafsa closed ranks against Umm Salama, who nevertheless found a friend in the Prophet's daughter Fatima, a sober young lady who had no use for Ayesha or Hafsa.

In 627 the Prophet married his eighth wife, the only one of his marriages that his contemporaries thought strange. Zaynab bint Jarsh was his maternal cousin. Her father was closely allied with Abd Shams, of which his enemy Abu Sufyan was a chieftain. She had been given in marriage to Muhammad's adopted son Zayd, but apparently against her will from the beginning. It is reported that she

109

had always set her sights on marrying Muhammad. In any case, Zayd was a charmless man, though worthy, and Zaynab could not endure him. One day when the Prophet visited the house of Zayd, who happened to be away at the time, she took the opportunity to display herself to the Prophet in a way that inflamed him—or so the story goes.

Soon after that incident, Zayd came to Muhammad with a proposal. He was willing to divorce Zaynab so that the Prophet could marry her. Muhammad refused the offer at first, but afterward agreed to it, especially when God, who was at that time dictating laws to regulate social conduct among Muslims, including the degrees of kinship in which marriages could be contracted, turned the affair into a handy object lesson. Adopted sons such as Zayd were not in the same category in some respects as natural sons, so that a man might marry the divorced or widowed wife of an adopted son, though not that of a natural one.

"God is surely swift to sanctify your desires," snapped Ayesha when this Quran came down.

Still, the arrangement was unusual. God could not have expected Muhammad to act out all His new laws. It is more plausible to believe that Muhammad wished to relieve Zayd of an impossible wife. If he was infatuated with Zaynab, the traditions show no further evidence of it.

As the household grew, the huts around the courtyard became more numerous, and so did the injunctions (emanating from God and therefore unarguable) that regulated the behavior of and toward women. Such rules became necessary because the courts of the mosque were a place of public thronging, and the privacy of the living quarters, which were separated only by curtains, had to be preserved. No doubt Muhammad was much put upon by people walking in and out, especially as the laws of hospitality demanded that guests be fed and even sent away with gifts. God therefore sent down some rules of etiquette. Believers should not enter the private quarters of the Prophet without an invitation or "observing that he is prepared to receive you, and without announcing your coming—verily that is insulting to the Prophet." God apologized for Muhammad's seeming lack of hospitality: "He is ashamed to say such things to you. But God is not ashamed to tell the Truth!"

When acquaintances had occasion to make a request of the Prophet's wives, they were not to walk freely into their quarters, but should stand outside and speak through the curtain. The women also had to change their free and easy habits:

> Speak to them that they guard their glances and are chaste; and that they display not their ornaments, except those that necessarily appear on the outer garments; that they let their veils fall over their bosoms . . . and let them not strike their feet together, so as to betray their hidden ornaments.

110

Later there came a specific order for the veiling of faces. There is some doubt about the original cause of the command. That it was to guard the ladies against the evil eye seems a strange point of view for God, or even Muhammad, who had little patience with superstition and would have told his wives to guard themselves through pious acts—as in fact the Quran enjoins: "Stay in your houses and do not go in public decked as in the days of your former idolatry, but observe prayer, and pay the poor-rate, and obey God and the Apostle."

Again, the custom is said to have come about to protect the women when in the first hours of dark they emerged from their houses and from the town itself, to find private places among the fields and there relieve themselves. Young Hypocrites took to following them about in the dark with insults, Muhammad's wives being a prime target. God then advised that they should cover their faces to avoid "recognition and insult."

Although only the Prophet's wives were enjoined to hide their faces, other Muslim wives were swift to imitate them. This rule, and others being promulgated by God, were not considered objectionable at the time, since they were the same that prevailed in the most civilized households, for example; those of the Jewish elite whose women veiled their faces in public. It is not likely that either famous lawgiver, God or Muhammad, intended this rule to be stretched into an imprisonment for women, thirteen hundred years long.

"Muhammad was a gentle and noble man who laughed often and smiled much," said Ayesha when he was gone. He enjoyed his wives' company and treated them well, always eating what was put in front of him without argument, waiting on himself on informal occasions and visiting them by night in strict turn. His friends saw with alarm that his mild reign was setting a bad example for Muslim husbands for years to come, and they implored him to beat his wives unmercifully. Once, when Ayesha spoke insolently to the Prophet in the presence of her father, Abu Bekr leaped to his feet, took her by the neck, and began to throttle her, shouting to the Prophet, "Look! This is what you ought to do with her!"

Muhammad made him desist. He said to Ayesha, "You see! I have saved your life."

The Prophet suffered what any man must who tries to handle ten or so wives at a time. God helped occasionally by sending down Qurans, warning the wives on whose side He would be found should they torment His Prophet unreasonably, or reminding them of the fate that befell Lot's wife. When, with God's help, Muhammad framed the laws governing the position of women in the umma, which we may read in the Chapter of Women, a Quran came down directing that a Muslim should confine himself to four wives, and then only if he knew that he could be strictly fair to all of them. If he was not quite sure of himself, he should have one wife only.

Later, another Quran observed, "You will not be able to be fair to several

111

wives, no matter if you wish it."

From this, some learned Muslims have inferred that Muhammad was a monogamist at heart.

Domestic regulations, God-given or man-made, must have been necessary in a household containing Ayesha, who stood not much in awe of the Prophet and sometimes made God Himself look lively in response to her sharp criticism of His Will. In 627 she had good reason to feel annoyed at the influx of entirely too many competitors. Or perhaps it was only a sudden assertion of careless youth—she was fourteen at the time—that made her the heroine of a famous and risky escapade.

In January of 627 Muhammad led an expedition against the Beni al-Mustaliq, a coastal tribe whose friendship or elimination was important to him as they were roaming on ground close to the main caravan route and not far from Mecca, and they were about to conclude an alliance with the Quraysh. On such expeditions women sometimes came along on howdahs as spectators. Muhammad's ladies took turns by casting lots, and in this case the fortune fell to Ayesha.

The Medinans arranged a good ambush and swooped down on their prey by a water hole, settling in short order all ambitions of the Beni al-Mustaliq to form a friendship with the Quraysh. Among the prisoners, Juwayriya, the chieftain's daughter, was assigned as battle spoil to one of the Muslim captains, but she, seizing her destiny by the horns, came running into Muhammad's tent to ask his mercy. She was a captivating woman. Ayesha, who was present at the interview said, "I disliked her the minute I laid eyes on her: I knew he would find her just as beautiful as I did."

Muhammad, indeed, said he would redeem Juwayriya on the spot and marry her. She accepted this proposal, and the marriage was celebrated without delay, all the captured Beni al-Mustaliq being set free as a courtesy, which they returned by confessing Islam. "I don't know any woman who deserves more thanks from her people," admitted Ayesha, but she nevertheless seethed at the marriage taking place just when she had her husband to herself. The events that followed might well have been her recklessly aimed vengeance.

On the homeward journey there was a general halt, during which Ayesha left her howdah and retired behind a suitably distant bush.

I had a string of Zafar beads around my neck. When I had finished, it slipped from my neck without my knowledge, and when I returned to the camel, I felt my neck for it but could not find it. Meanwhile the main body had already moved off. I went back to the place where I had been and looked for the necklace until I found it.

Meanwhile the men in charge of Ayesha's camel arranged the howdah and strapped it down without noticing that Ayesha was not ensconced in it and then prodded up the animal to follow the rest of the army. Ayesha returned to find everyone disappearing into the distance and she alone amid the scrub and sand.

So I wrapped myself in my smock and lay down where I was, knowing that if I was missed, they would come back to look for me where they had left me; and by God, I had just lain down when Safwan came past—he had fallen behind the main body for some reason . . . He saw my form and came and stood over me. He used to see me before the veil was prescribed for us, so when he saw me he exclaimed in astonishment "Why, it's the Apostle's wife!"

Ayesha, the well-mannered child, did not reply. Safwan, with equal decency, then brought up his camel and told her to get on, turning aside while she performed this scramble. Ayesha rode, Safwan walked, and they did not catch up with the army until morning. By that time the Apostle's favorite wife had been missed, and the army was buzzing with the news. Ayesha herself heard nothing of this buzz, especially as upon her return to Medina she took to her bed with an illness.

Yet she knew something was up, because the Prophet, usually so attentive to ailing wives, was extraordinarily distant with her. "How is she?" he asked glumly, addressing her mother who had come to nurse her. Pained at this attitude, Ayesha demanded to be taken to her mother's house and nursed there. "Do as you like," said the Prophet coldly.

In the city every wagging tongue was extending itself over the news that Ayesha had spent the night alone in the desert with Safwan, a personable young man, who had, it was now recollected, previously been seen talking to her in the courts of the mosque. Ayesha was not well liked. She was charming, but too brightly precocious to be popular, and besides everyone knew that Muhammad listened to her more kindly than to anyone else except God and Gabriel. This was resented, especially by Ali and Fatima. Among the wives Zaynab bint Jarsh had her knife into her, and Ibn Ubayy, the Hypocrite leader, was delighted to defame the household of the Prophet. An inkling of Ayesha's position is gained when we learn, surprisingly, that one of her chief enemies in this affair was Hassan ben Thabit, Muhammad's poet and press agent. He was a clever and gifted man, but with political mischief afoot joined in the character assassination of the clever and gifted child.

Ayesha pulled herself quickly enough out of her sickbed when she learned what powerful gossipmongers were against her. "I could not stop crying until I thought that the weeping would burst my liver!" she said. She ran in desperation to her mother and burst out, "God forgive you, Mother, men have spoken evilly of me, and you have not told me anything about it!"

"My little daughter," said the poor lady who along with her husband was drowning in wells of shame over this affair, "when a beautiful woman is married to a loving husband, her rivals gossip about her, and men do the same."

The Prophet was sore with grief, fearing to lose Ayesha, but hating to let criticism fester in his household. He spoke to the faithful in the mosque: "Why do people worry me about my family, telling lies about them?"

He expressed concern about his alleged rival, the young man Safwan, who was ranging about town slashing with his sword at people who looked strangely at him, "By God, I know nothing but good of him, and he never entered my house except in my company."

Some of the congregation, who were of the tribe of Aws, offered to chop off the heads of anyone who had said a word to offend the Prophet. Since everyone knew they had in mind certain heads of the Khazraj, the members of that tribe who were present protested with fury. The conversation became so acrimonious that the wars of the previous decade almost started up again, and the Prophet left the room.

He went to see Ayesha in her apartment. Before entering he called to him Ali and Usama, Zayd's son who was about Ayesha's age. Usama, who liked Ayesha, said outright that the gossip was lies. Ali, furious at the child-woman who was a perennial thorn in his wife's side and now irresponsibly drawing shame on the Prophet, shouted, "Women are plentiful, you can easily change one for another! Get hold of the slave girl, she'll tell the truth!"

Ayesha's slave girl was called, and Ali fell on her, distractedly beating her with his fists and raving, "Tell the truth! Confess the wrong your mistress does!"

The slave, blubbering, said, "When I tell her to watch the dough, she falls asleep and lets the lamb come and eat it!"

The Prophet abruptly left the scene and entered Ayesha's hut. She was out of her wits with weeping. Her parents were there. Abu Bekr bowed low in shame. He wanted to slay this beloved daughter for her foolishness, which might well bring his career to ruin and erase from his life its central meaning. Muhammad sat down and said, "Ayesha, you know what people are saying about you. Now if you have done wrong, repent before God, for he accepts the repentance of His slaves."

Ayesha's tears dried abruptly. She was hoping that her parents might answer for her, but they were silent. "Why don't you speak?" she asked chokingly. They said they did not know what to say. The girl's heart squeezed to watch the misery of her parents that day, and she began to cry again.

At length she collected herself and replied to the Prophet: "Never will I repent before God of this thing you mention. For if I confessed to a sin, God would know that I was confessing what did not happen. But if I denied it, you would not believe me!"

Desperately she racked her brains for some spiritual quotation that would go down well with these assertions. Something floated to her mind concerning

114

Jacob, but his name escaped her. Finally she said, "I'll say what the father of Joseph said, 'My duty is to be patient and ask God's aid.'"

The Prophet, frozen with misery, sat without moving. Then a thing happened that Ayesha never got over for the rest of her life. "By God," she said when she was quite old, "I thought myself too small for God to send down a Quran about me that would be read in mosques and used in prayers. Oh, I had hoped that the Prophet would see something good about me in a dream. But a Quran about me! From God!"

Yet that is exactly what happened. The Apostle fell sideways, pounded down by force and clangor. Someone hastened to put a cushion under his head and cover him with a cloak, for he was shaking heavily and exuding sweat. Presently he sat up, and raising his sleeve wiped his steaming brow.

"Good news, Ayesha," he said. "God has told me that you are innocent."

Ayesha said, "Praise be to God!"

The chief slanderers were flogged, not excepting Hassan ben Thabit, who in addition had to recover from a good cut with Safwan's sword. The Prophet, who was very fond of Hassan, compensated him later with a fine house and concubine. Zaynab had been too astute to let a critical word cross her lips, but her sister who had chattered on her behalf was flogged. Ibn Ubayy, still too influential to be touched, was beyond the reach of Muhammad's justice.

God pronounced further on this matter with a revelation that became part of the Muslim legal code: "Those who cast aspersions on chaste women and do not bring four witnesses, scourge them with eighty stripes, and let them never testify at law again, never, for their words are lies—except such as repent and afterward bear themselves correctly."

115

O ye believers! Remember Gods favor towards you when the great army came to you, and against them was sent a wind and invisible hosts . .
                                    -THE CHAPTER OF THE CONFEDERATES

17

The Battle of the Ditch: Death to the Qurayza

Abu Sufyan and Muhammad had promised each other to meet in the spring of 626 on the field of Badr, but somehow they failed to make contact. Muhammad kept the rendezvous with fifteen hundred Muslims and ten horses, and waited awhile in apparent eagerness to do battle. But a fair was in progress in the town of Badr at the time, so they turned the noses of their steeds in the direction of this event. Abu Sufyan likewise arrived with two thousand fierce men and fifty horses. Then he found something wrong with the pasturage for his animals and insisted upon returning to Mecca. In this way, honor was saved on both sides by a show of beetling brows and glittering scimitars, but nothing at all was lost. Both leaders knew that the clash, when it came, would be decisive, and they wished to save their might.

The year of 626, therefore, while Muhammad was steadying his position by treaty and marriage, was spent by Abu Sufyan and the Quraysh in drawing to themselves all possible strength in men and arms with which to finish the work left undone at Uhud. In this effort they were supported by the Jewish tribes of Khaybar who were sending deputations up and down the region of western Arabia, calling to account old fealties and friendships, and where friendship failed, bribing richly. To the powerful Ghatafan Bedouin they promised one half of the date harvest of Khaybar for mustering to the side of the Quraysh. They poured forth their wealth, generously in the acquisition of black mercenaries from Abyssinia, huge men like Wahshi who would simply stalk about a battlefield throwing spears, never missing a mark.

In the end, by one way or another, the Meccan confederacy comprised about ten thousand men, a fabulous array in a land where hit-and-run was the fundamental tactic of war.

Meanwhile Muhammad's spies had kept him informed of these preparations, and he took counsel what to do. He commanded only three thousand men, and many of these were Hypocrites, an undependable lot in peace, let alone when they stood to get their skins scraped in battle. Besides, even many loyal Medinans did not see the purpose of Muhammad's nonstop quarrel with Mecca. All knew that their paltry force would have no chance against such a foe in open combat. They had no choice but to draw together, dig in, and stand siege in the city itself.

Certain portions of Medina were well fortified by strongholds or even by close-packed houses, which could be defended against bow-and-arrow attack or Abyssinians with javelins. To be sure, those to the south and east were the property of the remaining powerful Jewish clan, the Qurayza. Like the an-Nadir, the Qurayza were master farmers and prosperous. They had every interest in staving off Mecca, and in any case the Covenant of Medina had stipulated that all citizenry, Jews included, should combine to defend Medina under siege. Nevertheless, with the other two Jewish tribes expelled and expressions of the utmost unfriendliness to Jews constantly uttered by God through Muhammad, it is not surprising that the Qurayza did not feel obliged to enter defense plans against the Quraysh, with whom they were on the best of terms as business associates and clients.

Muhammad knew all this. Besides, he had made up his mind that he was waging jihad, and he did not want Jewish help. He therefore negotiated with them, asking only for a promise of neutrality, and it appears that this arrangement was agreed between them—the Muslims and Medinans to defend, the Qurayza to sit tight.

The most vulnerable part of the city was in the north, where the streets opened onto gardens and date groves, and thence to the extremities of the irrigation channels that stretched green tendrils across the desert's hard face. The wide expanse was impossible to cover with a small force. Now in the full beauty of their growth, the fields looked to the Muslim commanders surveying them like the highroad for death to enter the city.

There was, however, among the faithful, a Persian convert named Salman who had fought with the imperial armies, and he advanced an altogether foreign and sophisticated idea. They should build a Persian trench, khandaq, he called it, all along the northern front, blocking access to the city. This suggestion was adopt-

117

ed with electric speed, because word was received that Abu Sufyan and his mighty host had already started northward from Mecca.

It was March, 627, or A.H. 5. Every able-bodied male in Medina pitched into the task of digging the khandaq, except the Qurayza, and even they lent their digging tools. The Prophet was down in the mud with the rest, and in later years many a tale was told to their grandchildren by men who were boys then of how the Prophet worked harder than anyone and how God helped by causing the dates at lunchtime to multiply miraculously so that all the workmen could eat, and how poor workers were invited by rich workers to dine. And they told how many a secret Hypocrite revealed himself by tiring too easily of hard work and sneaking off on some false excuse, while second by second Abu Sufyan bore destruction closer to Medina. God saw these malingerers clearly enough, as one may hear in the Holy Quran: "Do not treat the Prophet's call as if it were only one of you calling to another. God knows those who steal away and hide themselves. Let those who conspire to disobey watch out for trouble and painful punishment!"

The young ones privileged to learn of these heroic days first hand from their forefathers would say in awed tones: "But if we had been there, we would not have let the Prophet work. No, we would have borne him on our backs before we would let his feet touch that mud." But they did not know Muhammad. He would not tolerate anyone to spare him, it was not his way. He may have been a little plumper with the years, but he was energetic as a young man, and when there was a stone so hard that everyone gave up the hope of breaking it, he leaped into the mud and banged away, singing out, "That for Yemen! That for Syria! That for the east! That for the west!" Those who saw him never forgot the vibrant man laboring amid a fireworks of sparks, and when years later these places fell before the Muslim armies, they reminded their generals: "Conquer where you like, conquer until Resurrection Day, and you'll not conquer a place whose keys God did not give to Muhammad at the ditch!"

It took them six days to dig the ditch, and none too soon. They packed the women and children away in the fortresses, sharpened their stocks of arrows, and sat down to wait. The enemy came, and as they had done before took a winding path around the city to the plain of Uhud. Then they came on their camels and horses, surging across the grains and gardens to have a look at the first wonder of Arabia, khandaq, the ditch.

They sat down. There was nothing else to do.

Abu Sufyan made contact with the Jews. He sent to the Qurayza their associate of days gone by, Huyayy ben Akhtab, a chieftain of the exiled an-Nadir, to persuade them to sedition. At first the Qurayza slammed their doors in his face. He stood outside and taunted them, saying that they were too stingy to invite him to eat a dish of grain, so in fury they let him in. "Great Heavens!" cried

Huyayy, "What's wrong with you? Here I am, come with revenge, bringing you eternal fame and a great army!"

The Qurayza chieftain replied rudely, "By God, you have brought us eternal shame in an empty cloud which goes on thundering and lightning after the rain is squeezed out of it!"

This chieftain was to prove himself in the next days to be one of the most indecisive persons ever to show up in history. At first he seemed to wish to hold fast to his given word to Muhammad, but as Huyayy talked, describing the immense force surrounding the town, naming the great tribes of the confederation which would surely prevail and restore the Jews to their former status, his determination faltered. The Qurayza indeed stood to gain too little from a Muslim victory and too much from their defeat. The chieftain was persuaded to promise that at the proper moment his tribe would attack the Muslims from the rear.

Muhammad got wind of these dealings, and he sent to the Jews two emissaries. Both were called Sa'd, and one of them was of Aws, the other of Khazraj. The Qurayza, traditionally, were confederated with Aws, therefore it was Sa'd ben Muadh, a sheikh of that tribe, who hoped that his words would weigh with them. But he found the situation graver than he had supposed. The Qurayza chieftain said to him, "Who is this Apostle of God you are talking about? Muhammad? We have no agreement with Muhammad!"

Hot words broke out, but the other Sa'd said abruptly, "This matter is too serious for insults," and pulled his companion away. Both Sa'ds returned to the Apostle and let him know that he could not rely upon Qurayza.

The vast numbers of the besieging tribes made them seem like a heaving sea of men stretching across the orchards and fields, obliterating all signs of the richly sprouting crops, which in any case the animals were devouring. As day followed day and supplies ran low, the hearts of the faithful shivered. The Hypocrites did more than shiver. They wailed and lamented, asking everyone why they were sitting there waiting to starve to death or be overwhelmed the moment they moved from behind the ditch. The Quraysh, the Ghatafan tribesmen—these were not enemies, but friends of Medina, customers in fact.

Hardly any fighting was taking place. It was as if, in stumping the confederates' cavalry, all initiative had been stumped by the ditch. Some arrows were exchanged, but the besiegers could not find a way to hurl themselves across and make their huge numbers felt in an unusual celebration of steel and blood. A few forays were made at night, and at one point some enemy horsemen made a dash, but they were repulsed. The brave Ali was the hero of this skirmish, cutting off the leg of one of the Meccan warriors. The man leaped about on one leg until he retrieved the other, which he then used as a club to batter Ali—or so the apocryphal story goes.

It was not fighting but waiting that exhausted the Medinans, the long-drawn-out contemplation of their fearfully obvious future when the Qurayza should leave their strongholds and press them from the rear. Then nothing would prevent the screaming tide of men from scrambling across the ditch to murder them, half starving as they were.

Even Muhammad felt forced by inaction to think up an alternative to sitting and waiting. He tried subversion. He had a note drafted to send to leaders of the Ghatafan, pointing out that he had no quarrel with them and offering them one third of the Medina date harvest if they would leave the field. He called the two Sa'ds, showed them the note, and commissioned them to take it secretly across the ditch. The two Sa'ds said to him carefully, "Is this God's idea or yours?" Muhammad admitted that it was his own.

"It is for your own sakes," he said.

Then Sa'd ben Muadh said, "When we were idolators, we made the Ghatafan pay for our dates. Now that God has honored us by guiding us to Islam, are we to give them free? By God, we'll not! We'll give them the edges of our swords!" Muhammad said, "Then let it be so." Sa'd thriftily erased the words from the paper.

The Muslims were badly armed. Sa'd ben Muadh's armor did not even cover his forearm, and all were suffering the weakness of hunger. The women and children, who had retreated into the tribal fortresses which were near those of the Qurayza, were famished and frightened to death of what the Jews would do next. One of Muhammad's aunts did not help matters by leaping out on a passing Jew and clubbing him to death.

The far-flung army of the confederation were in equally desperate case because their animals, having eaten the land clean, were now dying.

As for the Qurayza, under their vacillating leadership, they were having second and third thoughts, torn between the force of their word to Muhammad, their fear and mistrust of him, and ordinary self-interest. They were sending messages back and forth to the Meccans and were up to their ears in plots without arriving at any effective course of action, for they were also fearful that Ghatafan and Quraysh might suddenly melt away in the night and leave them to face the dawn alone with Muhammad.

Muhammad was keeping track of all conspiracies by means of his spies and handling them cleverly by sending out secret agents to create rumors and sow distrust on every side.

Thus, matters stood in a miserable paralysis. Everyone concerned might well have suffered a nervous breakdown if God had not intervened in His simple decisive way. He caused to move down on them all a great cold—straight from the steppes of Asia, from Siberia even, an unheard-of cold, bitter weather such as no Arab alive had known or imagined or any poet ever dramatically described—and it was borne on a wind sharp as a blade and wild, swinging madly at tents and toppling them, smashing the cooking pots and scattering the fires. The Medinans huddled in the ditch. The Meccans, shuddering in the open, would have joined them gladly.

Abu Sufyan glumly said, "O Quraysh, we have no permanent camp here. The animals are dying, the Qurayza have broken their word, and I am going home." This he did, and so did Ghatafan, and all the confederated tribes and the giant men from Abyssinia.

A young scout of Muhammad's saw them go like a plague of locusts lifting from the fields, and he came with the news. He found the Prophet in prayer, wrapped in a mantle belonging to one of his wives. Muhammad did not let the boy speak, but he signaled him to sit at his feet where he flung part of the cloak over the lad's head. He bent and knelt and prostrated himself on the ground, yet doing all as carefully as he could without removing the warmth from the shivering boy.

Only when he had finished his exaltation of God, did he learn that the siege was lifted.

The revenge on Qurayza was terrible. The Jews were besieged in their stronghold for twenty-five nights. Even in this extremity their leader could think of nothing but alternatives. He said to them, "O Jews, I offer you choices, do as you please. The first is: We will follow this man and accept him as a true Prophet— for by God, we have seen with our own eyes that God is standing by him. In that way our lives and our property, our wives and children will be safe."

The Jews were horrified. They said they would never abandon the Torah or exchange it for another Book.

The chieftain said, "Then let us kill our wives and children and go out with swords drawn and fight the Muslims to the last man."

They said, "How can we kill them—and suppose we did, what heart would be left in us to fight?"

"All right," said the chieftain, "then I suggest this. Tonight is the Sabbath and Muhammad will not expect any movement from us. Let us steal down in the dark and take them by surprise."

The Jews were stunned. "What! Profane the Sabbath? And have you forgotten what happens to people who profane the Sabbath? They are turned into apes! No! Never!"

So the Jews sent to Muhammad for an ambassador. One came, an old friend whom they trusted. He entered the Jewish stronghold, and the women and children came to him weeping so that his heart squeezed. The Jewish chieftain said, "What do you think? Shall we come out and surrender to Muhammad?"

Aloud the ambassador said, "Yes!" But silently, perhaps out of sight of the women, he drew his finger across his throat. His meaning is not explained in the traditions, and Muslim historians are hard put to deny that a decision had already been taken for massacre of the Qurayza, but that conclusion is hard to avoid.

"My feet had not moved from that spot," said the ambassador afterward, "before I realized I had betrayed God and His Apostle." He went straight from the Jewish fortress to the mosque where he bound himself to a pillar, vowing that he would not leave it until he knew that God had forgiven him.

The Qurayza came from their fort and gave themselves up. They asked for the same terms as had been given to the Qaynuqa after Badr when Ibn Ubayy had intervened on their behalf. The chieftains of Aws, bound to the Qurayza by treaties of long standing, came forward to support them. "O Apostle, they were our allies. Treat them as you treated the allies of our brethren, the Khazraj."

Muhammad said, "Will you be satisfied, O Aws, if one of your own number pronounces judgment on them?" Joyfully they agreed, and the Qurayza breathed huge sighs of relief.

Muhammad then sent for Sa'd ben Muadh. He was lying in a tent inside the enclosure of the mosque, carefully tended by a skillful nurse. For his forearm, where the armor had not reached, had suffered a bad arrow wound, and it was festering. He had not many more days to live and knew it, and so did everyone.

He got up from his bed to pronounce judgment on the Qurayza. His fellow tribesmen of Aws surged around him, "Deal kindly with our friends. Remember our alliance. The Prophet has named you, knowing your mercy."

Sa'd faced the Qurayza and said, "The time has come for me to think of God's cause and care not for any man's blame." He then condemned every man of them to death. Their property was to be divided and their women and children sold into slavery.

Trenches were dug in the marketplace and the Jews made to sit on the edge, so that they would topple when their heads were lopped off. Six hundred men, at least, died in this way, every one of the Arab tribes and clans participating in the executions so that no one of them would bear blood guilt. Huyayy, the an-Nadir chief, had been captured, and he met the same fate. He came in grand an-Nadir style for his killing, wearing a glorious flowered robe, but he had made little holes all over it, so that nobody would feel tempted to despoil him of it.

The women and children were allotted as slaves. A rich Jew of a weaker tribe—for there were still Jewish tribes in Medina—came forward and spent a fortune buying women and children.

A woman called Rayhana was chosen by the Prophet. He cared for her and would have married her if she had agreed to become a Muslim. But she felt a repugnance for Islam and said to him, "Nay, let me live in your power—that will be easier for me and for you."

One day, walking in the street, Muhammad heard the sound of sandals behind him. His face lighted up with joy, and he said to his companions: "Listen! That is someone coming to tell me that Rayhana has confessed the faith." But for once his clairvoyance was false to him. Rayhana died as Muhammad's Jewish concubine.

Sa'd lived only a few days after the massacre. Muslim historians in relating this terrible event blame it on the painful wound which they say had impassioned the mind of Sa'd and made him vengeful, so that he betrayed the Prophet's kindly intentions. But the man who really betrayed the Prophet—or thought he had—was even then oiling his arms where the ropes that bound him to a pillar in the mosque had chafed them. Muhammad himself had untied the erstwhile ambassador as he passed to morning prayer.

Western historians condemn this whole episode, blaming the Prophet. What might be said in his defense is that the Qurayza, by breaking their word, had become outlaw, and by doing it in war, they were punished in the extreme way we still punish traitors.

It is really quite fruitless to fix blame on a desert chieftain for behaving according to the customs of his kind or to wonder why God should choose to speak to us through such a man. It is better to look at the deeds of man at large and wonder that God should choose to speak to us at all.

123

Verily, those who swear allegiance to thee, do but swear allegiance to God; God's hand is above their hands . . .

-THE CHAPTER OF VICTORY

18

The Pledge Under the Tree

The year 628 was spent by Muhammad in launching raids against or being raided by Bedouin tribes allied with Mecca. He would have preferred to send to them missionaries instead of pirates, but their treaties with the Quraysh now carried a brand-new clause: They were not supposed to listen to recitations of the Holy Quran.

Nevertheless there was a breathing spell in the quarrel with Mecca, and Muhammad is believed to have turned his attention for the first time northward in this year, sending an envoy to the governor of one of the Byzantine outposts in Syria. Possibly he wanted to explain his political position as a first step to sending his caravans into that country. In fact, he did this at the end of A.D. 628, A.H. 6. It was the first trading journey entirely Muslim-owned and led. Another set out a month later. We do not know how far Muhammad could foresee a time when his Quran would travel northward along with his skins and dates, but he was not a man of timid vision, and perhaps it was even then expanding. These caravans, passing within a few miles of Khaybar, were probably regarded with more fear than greed by the Khaybar Jews and the Jewish cultivators of other oases of the area. So far they had felt safe on their flourishing estates, and would certainly have preferred to see Muhammad contain himself in the peninsula. Now they felt obliged to continue their dangerous friendship with Mecca and expend huge quantities of dates on Bedouin tribes who remained enemies of Islam. They were the more successful because it was a year of famine in Arabia, and they opened their great stores, hoarded as their Scriptures had taught them, during fat years against lean years.

Throughout this decade of contention, Muhammad had kept paramount in his heart and mind a determination to persuade his relatives of the Quraysh to give up idolatry. Every Emigrant follower of his felt the same longing to be reunited spiritually with home, and they yearned also to follow once again the footsteps of their ancestors in the strange rite of walking around the Kaaba and touching the Black Stone. For the Beit Allah, stuffed as it was with blasphemous idols, was still a blessed structure to them, imbued with ancestral magic by the very hand of Abraham, and oddly enough it was becoming even more sacred to Muslims than to other Arabs, since several times a day they turned to it in prayer. It was quibla, the niche, the navel of all creation.

Muhammad's own feelings for the Quraysh are easy to understand, for they are built into every human nature. Quraysh bitterness against him is more complicated. Certainly some tribesmen prized ancient gods and old customs, but these loyalties were weakening before Muhammad came on the scene. The commercial value of the Kaaba, the excellent pickings from the pilgrimage trade, control of Beit Allah, Well Zem-Zem, and all the paraphernalia of idol worship—in short, the economic considerations—were an element in Quraysh hostility, as was the usual mob hatred visited upon a maverick in the group.

The "generation gap," also, emerges from the traditions surrounding the pledge that Muhammad took in 628 from his men under a tree near Mecca.

At the beginning of 628, the Prophet had a dream in which he saw himself making the lesser pilgrimage to the Kaaba, unopposed by any enemy. Because he trusted his dreams, he could hardly wait to get an expedition together, and he called the faithful to join him along with animals for sacrifice. His appeal was not well received. About fifteen hundred men answered him, apart from his faithful Emigrants and Helpers. Mostly, they were Bedouin, eager for loot. Not many people believed that Mecca would not offer opposition, even though, on the face of it, there was no reason why Muslims should not be admitted to the Kaaba under a truce, as other foes of the Quraysh were privileged to do in time of pilgrimage. To establish this thought, Muhammad proclaimed loudly in the presence of all possible spies that no one would bear arms, excepting their swords as a necessary implement of everyday use, and he himself donned a pilgrim's garb.

The doubters were quite right. The Meccans did not believe Muhammad was a pilgrim, even though he dressed like one and traveled in a holy month when killing even one's worst enemies was a crime. He was not famous for observing holy months. They therefore sent out two hundred horsemen to bar his way, announcing that they would never let him into Mecca, and they wore their leopard skins as a sure sign they meant to fight it out. The Apostle, when he heard of this, said, "Alas, the poor Quraysh, war has devoured their minds. What harm would it do if we peacefully did what we came to do? As for me, by God, I'll fight for the mission God has given me until He makes it victorious or I perish."

Then, being a clever leader, he added, "Now who knows how we can get around these horsemen?"

Somebody knew a way over the mountains, so they eluded the enemy cavalry and arrived at a place close to the outskirts of Mecca, the vale of al-Hudaybiya. Muhammad's camel selected it, refusing to budge farther, and since the Prophet always did as al-Kaswa directed, they made camp, though there was no water hole to be seen. After some poking around in the ground, though, a good spring bubbled up, which goes to show how right Muhammad was to trust his camel.

In the meantime the Quraysh in their leopard skins had returned to Mecca and were collecting intelligence data about Muhammad's movements from the local Bedouin. "Maybe he doesn't want war," they said, "but, by God, if he comes here, he'll get it!"

They sent one of the Bedouin as an emissary to talk to the Prophet. Muhammad didn't like the looks of him and said, "This is a treacherous fellow." All the same, he received the man, saying coldly that he had come to make pilgrimage and nothing more.

Not satisfied with this, the Quraysh sent another of their untamed allies, a black sheikh named Hulays. Muhammad, seeing him in the distance, said, "Now here is a good man, so let him see the camels." They drove out across the sheikh's path the sacrificial animals all garlanded and braided as befits camels about to meet their Maker. Without bothering to ask questions of Muhammad, Hulays rode back to Mecca and reported what he had seen. The Quraysh thought his assessment far from thorough. "Oh, sit down and be still, Hulays—you are nothing but a stupid bedou, after all."

"What's the matter with you, you Quraysh?" shouted Hulays in wrath. "Is this the way you talk to an ally? What harm is there if this man comes to do honor to God's house? Is he to be shut out? By God, let him enter here, or I'll take away my black troops to the last man!"

They said, "Shut up, Hulays. We've got to think."

They thought and then sent another envoy, Urwa, and this man faced the Prophet. "O Muhammad," he said, "what are you doing here, followed by this raggle-taggle crew? Have you come to make trouble for your own kind? If so, know that the Quraysh have put on their leopard skins and have sworn to fight you, and, by God, when they do, this gang of yours will turn tail and leave you flat!"

126

"You can go and suck the breasts of al-Lat!" cried Abu Bekr. Urwa was so angry at this vulgar retort that he leaned forward and seized the Apostle's beard, shaking it to and fro to lend force to his arguments. A companion of Muhammad began to hit sharply at the man's hand, bellowing that he should let go before he cut it off. "You're a rough and rude one!" exclaimed Urwa, snatching his hand back. "Who is the fellow, anyway?" he asked the Prophet.

"It is your brother's son," said Muhammad, very amused.

"Confound you," cried Urwa to his nephew, "it was only yesterday that I was wiping your bottom!"

Al-Hudaybiya is famous in the history of Islamic diplomacy, but not for the diplomatic language used there.

Urwa remained awhile in the Muslim camp. He returned to the Quraysh and reported, "I have seen the king of Persia in his kingdom, and Caesar in his kingdom, and the Negus in his kingdom, but never have I seen a king among his people as Muhammad is among his companions. They will never desert him, that is certain."

The Quraysh sent a party to raid Muhammad's camp. The raiders were captured and brought before Muhammad. He let them go back to Mecca, telling them mildly that he had only come to perform the circumambulation, not to fight. He then sent Uthman, his son-in-law, to Mecca to reiterate this statement. It was a mission of grave danger, for the Quraysh might well have decided to revive the ancient custom of human sacrifice in the case of Uthman, but instead they told him he might perform the circumambulation if he wished. He said he did not feel free to perform the rite before Muhammad had done so, so they held him prisoner. But they gave it out that he had been killed, probably to provoke Muhammad into unmasking himself as an armed enemy.

But Muhammad was playing a subtler game than they guessed. For the time being he was in dire peril of his life, and he knew it. It is hard to understand the hesitation of the Quraysh in not emerging and dealing with the Muslims as they lay defenseless in their flimsy tents at Hudaybiya. It was a sacred month, of course, but they could have argued that Muhammad's blasphemy had forfeited all consideration. As a matter of fact, no argument would have been necessary, since affairs involving sacrilege were in the hands of Hubal, and Hubal would have rejoiced at the deed.

There is only one explanation—the knowledge that those flimsy tents contained a good number of their brother's sons, not to mention their own.

Muhammad could not count on their forbearance. As soon as he was told Uthman had been killed, he realized that he might not leave that place without a battle and it might mark the end of Islam. Many of his men were truly raggle-taggle Bedouin of the Khuza'a tribe, and he could not be sure that they would not evaporate when trouble brewed like a mirage at sundown, or that they might not

127

start trouble where it was not wanted.

On the following day he selected a good acacia tree and stood with his back to the trunk. He called his people around him and demanded of them a renewed oath of loyalty. One by one, fifteen hundred men filed past and swore. The precise terms of the oath are not known. Logically, we suppose they would vow not to desert him if battle ensued, but it is possible that he also exacted quite an opposite promise—that is, if battle did not ensue, they would cause no difficulties. The Khuza'a might think Muhammad was a magical sort of sheikh, but they had joined this expedition in the hope of sacking Mecca, and they had taken the trouble to secrete a quantity of weapons with which to do so. They would be annoyed to find they had really come on a holy pilgrimage.

The Pledge Under the Tree is also known in Muslim history as the Pledge of Good Pleasure—that meant Muhammad's good pleasure, whatever it was, for peace or war. One man positively refused to swear his freedom-loving soul away. While the others filed under the tree, this enemy of God hid behind his camel.

Enormous relief was felt when the next emissary from Mecca turned out to be one Suhayl, a man known to all for his persuasive and diplomatic gifts. By this time Muhammad had learned that Uthman was safe, and he realized that the Quraysh were going to be sensible. He greeted the envoy. There followed a long argument in which terms were reached that would avoid bloodshed for the present. Ali, who acted sometimes as Muhammad's secretary, was sent for to set the matter forth on paper.

"Write!" said Muhammad to Ali. "Write—'In the name of God, the compassionate and merciful!'"

Suhayl considered this. The phrase had an unpleasantly Muslim ring in his ears. He said, "No, let's just begin, 'In Thy name, O God!'"

Muhammad told Ali to write as Suhayl wished. Then he said, "Write, 'This is what Muhammad the Apostle of God has agreed with Suhayl ben Amr.'"

"Oh, no," interposed that gentleman. "I do not recognize you as God's Apostle at all. If I did, I should never have fought you. Cross that out."

"Never," cried Ali, working up to a rage.

Muhammad leaned toward Ali and looked over his shoulder. He asked him to point out the objectionable passage. Then he took the pen from Ali's hand and struck it out. He said, "Now write: 'Muhammad ben Abdullah has agreed this with Suhayl ben Amr . . .'"

The diplomatic atmosphere was not only drawing scowls from the Khuza'a, but it was getting on the nerves of Muhammad's fiery companion Umar, who finally burst out to Abu Bekr: "What is all this? Is he God's Apostle or isn't he? Are we Muslims or aren't we? Are they idolators or aren't they? Why should we agree to what demeans our religion?"

Getting no satisfactory answer to this, Umar in his anger interrupted the deliberations and put his questions to Muhammad. The Prophet fixed him with a calm gaze and said, "I am God's slave and His Messenger. I will not go against His commands, and He will not let me down."

So Umar fell silent, and the writing of the armistice continued. The terms were these:

Peace was to be established for ten years, during which time there would be an absolute taboo on hostilities between Mecca and Medina.

Muhammad was to lead his force of so-called pilgrims away from Mecca that year, but the following year he would be allowed to return and circumambulate the Kaaba, remaining for three days in Mecca, armed only with swords. During the time the Muslims would be in Mecca, the Quarysh undertook to vacate the town—they would all go and camp out in the mountains.

During the period of truce, Muhammad was to have a free hand among the Bedouin. He might make bonds, agreements, and alliances with them without interference from Mecca. The Khuza'a took this opportunity to jump enthusiastically to their feet. "We are in bond and alliance with Muhammad!" they yelled.

"Yes, I know," said Suhayl in dulcet tones, "and now he has just promised to lead you away from Mecca this year and bring you back next year."

It was in this way that the Khuza'a learned the meaning of the mysterious expression "Pledge of Good Pleasure."

One more interesting condition was agreed upon, and the entire armistice hinged on it. It was this: If any young man from Mecca should try to join Muhammad's Muslims in Medina without the permission of parents or guardians, the Prophet was to return him to the bosom of his family. Of course, the agreement worked both ways. Apostate Muslims taking refuge in Mecca would be returned to Medina. This promise was fairly empty, for the situation rarely arose.

As if to give point to the problem, while this very document was being dictated, there arrived in the camp an exhausted and wretched refugee, a very young man hardly out of his teens, hobbling and stumbling, his legs bound in fetters. His name was Abu Jandal, and he was the son of none other than Suhayl, who, upon learning that Muhammad was encamped in the vicinity, had like other prudent fathers promptly put fetters on his son and locked him up. Abu Jandal had contrived his escape and made his horribly painful way to al-Hudaybiya.

The moment his father set eyes on him, he turned the color of sunset, rose from his labors over the document, and slapped the boy in the face. He seized his son by the collar and turning to the Apostle said, "Muhammad, the agreement was reached before this youth came here!"

Sadly Muhammad agreed. The father tugged at his son's collar and, throwing his reputation as a diplomat to the four winds, began to shake him to and fro, dragging him vaguely in the direction of Mecca, while Abu Jandal shrieked, "O Muslims, save me! He is taking me back to worship those old gods!"

129

The Prophet ran after him saying, "Abu Jandal, control yourself! God will provide the way for you and other helpless ones. We have made a peace with Mecca—we have invoked God! We can't go back on our word now for your sake!"

Umar took up where he left off, getting next to the youth and saying, "Be patient, what are they but idolators? Their blood is the blood of dogs!" He drew out his sword and offered it to the young man. He said afterward, "I hoped he would take it and kill his father."

But Abu Jandal decided to leave his case in God's hands. He could not have left it in better. After this armistice was signed and sealed, there were many like Abu Jandal wanting to join the Apostle but prevented from doing so by the terms of the peace. One day a refugee showed up in Medina after a dramatic escape from his family and a solo journey through the desert. He had to be put under guard and sent back to Mecca. But on taking leave of him, Muhammad said, "Oh, what a man! If only he had a few people with him like himself, he might have started a war!"

It was a very roundabout remark, but it sped like an arrow to the brain of the fugitive. He escaped from Muhammad's guards without too much difficulty and set up camp in the coastal area near the caravan route. This settlement acted like a magnet and a refuge for other malcontents from Mecca—slaves on the run and mistreated youths who arrived with fetters dangling around their mangled legs. They formed a sort of bandits' lair on the caravan route, preying on the caravans going past. Since these were mostly the property of their own clans, they could not even be considered outright thieves.

By and by the Quraysh approached Muhammad and offered to eliminate the sensitive clause. Meccan youths might now join the Prophet in Medina and he could keep them—with pleasure, more or less.

Muhammad on his side had now a free hand with the Bedouin. Friend or foe, no matter whose allies they were, he could conclude treaties, truces, pacts, and so on without hindrance from Mecca. He had not emphasized this in his conversations with Suhayl, but it now became evident that he felt free to preach up and down the Hejaz, sending missionaries out with the Quran to bring whole Bedouin tribes under the influence of that mesmeric Book.

130

God was pleased with the believers when they swore allegiance to you beneath the tree . . . and He rewarded them.

-THE CHAPTER OF VICTORY

19

Khaybar and the Road North

With menace removed from his southern interests, the Prophet could now turn his full attention northward in the direction that his acute instincts told him the impulse of events was taking him. The first main obstacle on the road to Syria was Khaybar, whose Jewish inhabitants had watched developments to the south with the utmost dismay, knowing full well that he had unfinished business with them for their role in uniting the confederation against him. The man chiefly responsible for this diplomatic feat had been an an-Nadir leader, Sallam ibn Abu'l-Huqayq, and shortly after the siege, Muhammad had sent five men to assassinate him. Muslim historians regard this not as murder but as an execution.

Since the Aws had had the honor of executing the dangerous satirical poet Ka'b, the Khazraj were entrusted with that of Sallam. Muhammad saw them on their way to wish them luck and bless them. They planned to enter Sallam's house and kill him in his bed—a somewhat unusual plan, for it was thought more honest to kill people in the open. At the last minute Muhammad had a qualm about it, and he said to his men, "Be careful you do not harm any women or children."

The five men journeyed northward and entered Khaybar by night. Sallam, they knew, would be sleeping in an upper chamber of his house, which was reached by a ladder from outside. They climbed the ladder and made a noise at the window, bringing Sallam's wife there. They were wayfarers, they told her, and needed food. Rigid laws of the desert gave privileges to wayfarers, and she let them in. In the dark they perceived a lumpy mass—Sallam lying on a mat on the floor. With drawn swords they leaped upon the Jewish sheikh, but his wife was too quick for them and interposed her body between the assassins and their victim. There ensued a strange interlude, a grim ballet in the dark, the five men intent upon a murderous deed but fearing to graze the body of one woman because of the Prophet's last injunction. Warily and clumsily they lunged back and forth. They finally found their way around Sallam's wife and killed him.

Sallam's grandson, Kinana ben al-Rabi, succeeded him as sheikh of Khaybar, and he carried on with renewed vigor his grandfather's policy of subverting the minds of Bedouin with dates. These Bedouin controlled the northern regions stretching into Syria.

Urwa had rightly called Muhammad's men at Hudaybiya a "raggle-taggle crew." Cheated of their pious hope of launching a razzia against Mecca, the Bedouin faithful, mostly Khuza'a, had felt disgruntled by the armistice and suspected that they had been hoodwinked by the Pledge Under the Tree.

Muhammad knew he had nebulous disaffection in the Bedouin ranks and that, unless he wanted them to slip through his net, he must give them a razzia they could write poetry about. An obvious target was Khaybar, the richest oasis in the whole of the Hejaz, a paradise of date gardens, almost wholly worked and operated—indeed, established and settled—by his dangerous enemies the Jews. Even had they not been his enemies Muhammad would have had to bring this settlement under control if he wished to run his caravans under their noses.

About six months after Hudaybiya, he struck. Only the men who had taken the Pledge Under the Tree were privileged to participate in this first-class razzia. The force was mustered in admirable secrecy, and swiftly it marched northward without the Jews having an inkling of the dark menace coming their way. Muhammad brought his men over a well-spied mountain route so stealthily that on a September dawn they could stand above the city with their prize tranquil below—all inhabitants sleeping soundly amid their treasure of gardens, a great scattering of magnificent emerald groves well set in golden coils of sand. It was the Prophet's habit always to pause thus at dawn over a settlement or camp he proposed to raid. If he heard the call to prayer, he did not attack.

The sun went up and no muezzin called. The Prophet prayed as he always did before a raid, for these were holy raids:

O God,
Lord of the skies and what they know,

And Lord of the lands and what they grow,
And Lord of the jinn and the sins they sow,
And Lord of the winds and what they blow—
We beseech Thee for the good of this town
For the good of this people
For the good that is in it;
We take refuge in Thee from the evil in this town,
And the evil of this people,
And the evil that is in it.

Then he uttered, "Forward, in the name of God!"

The farmers coming into the field at daybreak saw them first as they swooped grandly down the slopes with the rising sun striking their swords like red lightning. Not much came of this splendid entry. Khaybar was a spotty oasis, every separate settlement possessing a stronghold that very quickly filled in response to the farmers' screams, while Muhammad's men pitched camp in the groves. The Jews were confident at first, because they had managed to send out an early appeal for help to their confederates, the Ghatafan, who lost no time in sending a strong force to help them. Muhammad, however, was not on his way to becoming a world conqueror for being slow-witted. He had left rumors all along his route that a strong force of Muslims was making for certain unprotected Ghatafan oases to destroy them, and when they heard this, the tribesmen turned back in their tracks.

It shows what a vogue Muhammad had started in Arabia that afterwards the Ghatafan leader excused himself by swearing that he had heard this rumor, false though it was, in a Voice from Heaven.

The weaker strongholds of Khaybar fell easily to the Muslims. Few champions emerged from these forts to withstand the young lion, Ali. The Jews, being farmers and settled people, were rusty in the warlike arts so dear to desert Arabs. One fort produced a famous hero, Marhab, who came out bristling with weaponry and spouting poetry like a Homeric warrior:

Everyone knows who I am: Marhab,
Armed to the teeth, artful in war,
Piercing and slashing
Like the charge of a lion in anger . . .

Prancing out against him, the Muslim champion, Ka'b ben Malik, had equal claims:

Everybody knows that I am Ka'b
Bold as can be and grim,

Difficulties simply become smooth in my
path . . .

When voices wore out, there was a memorable combat around a fallen and decaying tree, whose branches were lopped off one by one until the two confronted one another. And then Ka'b killed Marhab.

The invaders progressed toward the heart of the oasis, fort by fort, some of them holding out for only a few days, others for ten. Stronger resistance was not possible, because the Jews had been taken by surprise and were not able to get fresh water to their strongholds. The Muslims were feeling a pinch, because not much in the way of stores was coming out of the outlying forts, and they were hungry. It was a welcome day in the tents of the Muslim high command when a companion of the Prophet raided an enemy sheepfold: "I went out running like an ostrich, and when the Prophet saw me running back, he said, 'O God, long may we have the pleasure of this man's company!'" By this, he meant that he wished the man long life, and no wonder, because he was carrying a sheep under either arm, carrying them as if they were but feather pillows, and he dropped them at the feet of Muhammad. The man had occasion to remember the episode with tears his whole life long, for he was the last of the Prophet's companions to die. "They did have the pleasure of my company for a long time," he used to say.

The Bedouin were elated one day to capture a flock of twenty donkeys, which they slaughtered at once and put to a merry boil in their pots. The Prophet, attracted by the savory odor, came to see what they were doing. A fastidious man about food, he was appalled at the thought of eating donkey meat, and he pronounced on the spot a prohibition against it. The starving Bedouin had to watch their cooking pots being overturned before their eyes.

Eventually, after stout battle had been fought with the defenders around the food stores, they fell to the Muslims, and so at last did the fort of al-Qamus, commanded by the Jewish leader, Kinana ben al-Rabi, grandson of the assassinated Sallam. In his custody was the main wealth of the Beni an-Nadir, the exiles from Medina. When he was dragged before the Prophet, Muhammad asked him where the treasure was, and Kinana said that he did not know. A traitor came forward to tell Muhammad that he had seen Kinana frequenting a certain ruin. "You know," said Muhammad to the sheikh, "that if I find it there, I shall have to kill you."

Kinana agreed. The ruins were searched and part of the treasure was found, though not all of it. Muhammad gave orders that Kinana was to be tortured until he divulged the true hiding place, and so a fire was built on his chest. But he did not reveal it. At last the Prophet allowed him to be killed, granting the privilege of execution to a man whose brother had been killed by the Jews.

In the end all forts fell, and the people emerged, asking for their lives. Beyond Khaybar, God struck terror into the hearts of other Jewish oases, and their deputations began to arrive, surrendering and suing for peace. The inhabitants of Fadak had the sensible suggestion that they be allowed to continue working their lands, owing him one half the produce. "We know more about date farming than you do, and we are better farmers," they said temptingly.

Muhammad agreed, and these peace terms were made with all Khaybar and Fadak, depending on one prime condition—that "if we wish to expel you, we will expel you." From this, some historians have inferred that at this time Muhammad had already formulated his principle that "two religions should not be permitted to live side by side on the peninsula of Arabia."

The next days were spent in the enjoyable business of dividing up spoil. Muhammad had his fifth, but he was by custom not entitled to all the spoil of Fadak and other oases that had surrendered without being "attacked by horse or camel"—that is, without a battle. He had some difficulty with his Bedouin, who were Muslims but had not been greatly gentled by a religious education. Revelations were pouring on the Prophet plentifully, correcting their misdeeds. The Bedouin were not to rape pregnant women. They were to bring all spoils to the common pool. They were not to ride captured horses until they dropped dead before turning them into the pool. They were not to wear fine garments to rags before turning them in. And so on. All the same, the Prophet's sense of humor did not desert him. When a lad was discovered stealing a bag of lard to share with his half-starved comrades, he said to the overseer who was beating him, "Let him have it, confound you!"

A Jewish woman, Zaynab, filled with the spirit of the heroines of the Old Testament, attempted a very risky deed. She invited the Prophet to dine at her table along with some of his companions, and for this purpose she roasted a whole lamb. Having inquired what portion of the lamb the Prophet preferred and finding that he liked the shoulder, she injected into the shoulder a large dose of poison. Then she poisoned the rest of the lamb.

The meal was served. Muhammad seized the shoulder and took a bite. As we know, he was a sensitive man about food, and noticing a peculiar taste, he spit it out. A companion swallowed his piece, and the pains soon overwhelmed him. The hostess was called for, and she confessed.

The Prophet asked her what had induced her to do such a thing, and she replied honestly but with cunning, "Because of what you have done to my people. Yet I said to myself, 'If he is only a chieftain, we'll be rid of him. But if he is a prophet, he'll know the meat is poisoned.'"

Muhammad did not punish her, even when his companion died. He always forgave people who wanted to kill him. It was only those who interfered with the faith and the Holy Quran to whom he was merciless.

Of the Khaybar spoils there was a most beautiful woman, Safiyya, the wife of the Jewish sheikh Kinana. One of his captains had asked for her, but Muhammad preempted her for himself even before he saw her. She was led up to him with another woman past a field of slain Jews. The other woman shrieked at the sight and began to pour dust on her hair. "Take this she-devil away from me," said Muhammad irritably. But he threw his cloak over the silent girl Safiyya as a sign that he placed her under his protection, and he reproved Bilal, who had charge of the prisoners: "Have you no compassion, bringing these women past the sight of their dead husbands?"

He noted that Safiyya's looks were somewhat marred by a black eye, and when he inquired the reason, he received a most pleasing response. It seems that some nights before she had dreamed that a moon fell into her lap. When she told her husband of it, he gave her a great blow in the face, saying, "That must mean you have a crush on that king of the Hejaz, Muhammad!"

Perhaps she did have a crush. She embraced Islam and became a contented member of the harem. She happened to be the daughter of that an-Nadir chieftain who had gone to his execution so gaily bedecked in a flowered robe, and Muhammad meant to announce by this union that he was ready to bring to an end his hostility to the Jews.

Muhammad apportioned some of his new riches to the household needs of his wives and for himself claimed a longed-for luxury—a pulpit for the mosque. Never again would he preach to his congregation while leaning up against a palm-trunk pillar. It was axed down to make way for the pulpit, and the story goes that it gave out a groan like a human thing, so that the builders gave it a decent burial underneath the pulpit.

The summer of 629 brought some notable converts from Mecca. One of them, Amr ibn al-As, had been among Abu Sufyan's chief captains at the Battle of Uhud, and in times yet to come he would carry Islam to Egypt. Another important addition to the flock was Khalid ibn al-Walid. We know the stuffing that was in this young man. He was the son of that very tribesman who long ago had been the first to walk up to Beit Allah and inform the gods that the old walls were going to be pulled down. Later, at the Battle of Uhud, it was Khalid who had turned the retreat of the Meccans by leading a splinter group through the gorge to the Muslim rear.

Neither of these men were uncertain youths groping their way with crude violence through changing times. They were solid, successful citizens, but they saw the direction in which history was moving, and they were not the men to be left behind. Both became Muslim generals of historic accomplishment.

It was about the time of Hudaybiya and Khaybar that Muhammad began to establish communication with the princes and governors of the surrounding kingdoms, empires, and provinces by sending out emissaries to call these various rulers to Islam in rousing terms. There are popular stories about these diplomatic forays, very heart lifting in the picture they present to the mind's eye of the Prophet's messengers riding forth in all directions, amid a fine glitter and thump of sand and hoof.

The facts were probably more prosaic. Muhammad, as a statesman, was not romantic but always behaved realistically and with self-interest. He certainly owed his neighboring rulers an explanation of the Arabian squabbles, and he attempted to allay any anxiety they might have nursed about their caravan routes as much as to provoke their curiosity about God. Moreover, all these rulers were People of the Book, Christians and Zoroastrians, and Muhammad so addressed them: "O People of the Book! Let us agree! We shall serve no other god but God, nor set up any god beside Him, or take each other for gods instead of God!" This is not a call, specifically, to Islam, only to peaceful relations with Islam, but it is a bold attitude for a Quraysh tribesman to adopt in addressing the mighty emperors of Byzantium and Persia.

Besides these monarchs, the messengers are said to have gone to the rulers of Syria, Egypt, Yemen, and Abyssinia. The Negus of Abyssinia, who had previous experience with Muslims, received the communication in a friendly spirit. It is thought likely that Muhammad arranged with him at that time for the return of the original emigrants to Abyssinia, who were now, after fifteen years, to rejoin the main body in Medina. One of their leaders had died, leaving a widow, Umm Habiba, whom Muhammad claimed in marriage. This was indeed a marriage of diplomacy, for Umm Habiba was the daughter of his chief enemy, Abu Sufyan. The Negus provided sound boats and safe passage across the Red Sea to all Muslims, and he decked and trousseaued Umm Habiba splendidly as a compliment to Muhammad. She was waiting for her wedding day when he returned from Khaybar.

The ruler of Alexandria also replied courteously, sending great gifts, which included a beautiful white mule and two Christian slave girls who were sisters. One sister was presented by Muhammad to the poet Hassan, the other he took to himself. She was Maryam the Copt, the only member of his harem to give him a child, his son Ibrahim. He would gladly have married Maryam, of whom he was very fond, but like Rayhana she refused to give up her religion.

If such high dignitaries as the emperors of Byzantium and Persia ever received letters from a desert chieftain, they paid no attention. In any case, they were at that time occupied in rending one another to pieces. Various legends adhere to their reception of Muhammad's communications, among them that the Persian emperor contemptuously tore his letter up and sent to his vassal, the governor of Yemen, to arrest Muhammad at once. When the governor's soldiers arrived in Medina, Muhammad was able to tell them, clairvoyantly, that the Persian emperor was dead, and that they should go home.

The governor of Basra, in Syria, whose territory lay across the trade route from Arabia, decided upon a spectacular show of his contempt for the upstart Muhammad and his insolent letters. He killed the ambassador. There was only one possible response. Muhammad, with only the grudging peace at Hudaybiya to hold Mecca at bay, had to send out an avenging army. Three thousand men were marshaled, and they marched northward under the command of Zayd, seconded by Ali's brother Jafar, recently arrived with the Abyssinian group, and a third commander, Abdullah, who had a fateful presentiment which kept him reciting poetry through tears as he said good-bye to his friends. He was a man of unusual sensitivities. On taking his leave of Muhammad he remarked, "I perceive in you a natural gift of goodness—and I am a man who sees deeply. You are indeed God's messenger."

The avenging army rode off bravely into Syria, six hundred miles from home, a glorified band of desert raiders. Muslim historians still tend to call the Battle of Muta a "raid," as if there was anything that these "raiders" could do except let themselves be slaughtered by the hundred thousand men the Syrian ruler had lying in wait for them. Even allowing for gross exaggeration of these numbers, the Muslims faced a force of the best kind of fighting men, drilled in the Roman style, who moreover commanded the surrounding countryside and were on home ground.

As the Muslims approached their deadly peril, they wondered desperately if they should write back to Muhammad, seeking to be released from their fate, but it was too late to retreat with honor. Fortunately Abdullah, the golden-tongued poet, was there to put heart into them, reminding them of the pleasures awaiting martyrs in Paradise, and as they approached the enemy in the night, he continued to entertain his camel, painting this stirring preview of the situation:

> "Forward they bear us, the free-reined steeds,
> The hot wind burning their nostrils.
> If God wills, we'll come to Moab,
> Stand up to those Greeks, the Arabs too!
> Now! We catch the reins, they are furious at us,
> Stamping the dust up!
> And their helmets, point after point of light
> Burst out like stars in the distant sky!
> Ah, women we have loved, our spears now divorce you . . ."

A young orphan Abdullah had adopted, who was riding on the back saddle, began to cry. Abdullah flicked him with his whip: "Why worry, you young wretch? I am for martyrdom, you for a safe homecoming in the saddle."

The stand came at Muta, and it was very much as Abdullah had told his camel. Zayd took the Apostle's standard and was killed almost at once, the first Muslim to die for the faith on foreign soil. Jafar, the second in command, caught the standard as it fell. He hamstrung his horse so that it could not run away and fought there, upholding the standard until he died. Abdullah, next in command, having spent his slender battle lust in versifying, was horrified to find himself with no heart left in him. He said to his cowardly soul:

> "By God, you'll fight,
> Or I'll make you fight!
> Men are screaming around you,
> And you dodge Paradise!
> Pah! You are an easy, sleazy
> Blob in a worn-out skin!"

A relative of his, seeing him dismount, perhaps the better to solve a point of rhythm, brought him a bone to gnaw. "Strengthen yourself with this," he said.

Abdullah gnawed for a bit and then exclaimed in self-disgust: "Are you still alive?" He seized his sword, jumped into the fray, and within minutes was being carried up to Paradise in a bed of gold. Muhammad, in Medina, was seeing all this on the screen of his inner eye.

Another warrior caught the standard and called the Muslims to rally, not to himself, but to another whom most of them had barely heard of, the new Muslim, Khalid ibn al-Walid. Khalid seized it and did a strange thing. He fought only to keep the enemy off, and when he saw his chance, he withdrew from engagement, leading the Muslims into retreat.

Muhammad had news of the deaths of his two close companions, Zayd and Jafar, before the army's return. The wife of Jafar describes how he broke the news.

The Apostle came into my house when I had just tanned forty skins and kneaded my dough. Then I had washed, oiled, and cleaned my children. He asked me to bring him Jafar's sons, and I did. He held them close as if sniffing at them, but his eyes filled up with tears.

I asked him whether he had bad news about Jafar and the others. He said that they had been killed that day.

Jafar's wife cried aloud at that and other women in the household came running to her. The Apostle rose to leave, but he admonished them, "Take care of Jafar's family. See that they have food. Prepare their food for them today, for they are filled with tragedy."

He then left to break the news to Zayd's children.

When the army came riding home, he went out to meet them, Jafar's son on the saddle before him. It was a terrible homecoming for these men who had returned from battle alive, following Khalid, while the Prophet's own relatives and beloved companions had fallen. The people of Medina picked up sand and dirt along the way to throw at the returning force, shouting, "Cowards! Runaways! You fled from God!"

Muhammad put a stop to it. He said, "They are not runaways. They are come-agains, if God wills."

However, the incident cured Khalid ibn al-Walid forever of taking cool wits to battle with him. From this time on in his career there was no enterprise too irrational or dangerous for him, and he acquired the title "the Sword of Islam."

God truly granted His Apostle's dream: that you should enter the sacred mosque,
if God please, in safety, with shaven heads or cut hair, and without fear.

-THE CHAPTER OF VICTORY

20

Home to Mecca

For the present the Prophet's hand was restrained from Mecca by the Peace of Hudaybiya. He bided his time. Meanwhile, with enormously increased prestige, he had no difficulty in bringing many Bedouin tribes into the faith, even Ghatafan.

In 629, the seventh year after the Hijra, the Prophet made his pilgrimage to Mecca followed by the men of Hudaybiya, who, by this time fat with the loot of Khaybar, considered themselves something of an elite guard. As they approached, the inhabitants of Mecca, honoring the terms of the treaty, moved out of their city, leaving it empty. They camped in the hills round about, but without doubt peered through the shimmering air to catch glimpses of long-lost clansmen and perhaps beloved runaways following the Prophet. The Emigrants in their turn would have raced up and down the streets, remembering the places where they had lived and played as youngsters before they ever heard the will of God or saw death on the ground.

Uncle Abbas alone, as head of the Hashim family, was delegated to remain in town and receive the homecomers. It was he who described the never-to-be-forgotten scene at the Kaaba, when the Prophet led them, perched on the high hump of his inspired camel al-Kaswa, to the holy place of Beit Allah. He threw his cloak over his left shoulder like a toga, leaving his right arm free. He raised it and said, "God have mercy on this man and show them that he is strong this day." He dismounted and walked up to Beit Allah. He embraced its walls with both arms and kissed it. Next he performed the circumambulation, using for three circuits a special sacred walk, moving his shoulders up and down as if walking on sand, though lightly, like a dancer. When he came to the southern wall, he kissed it again. Then he kissed the Black Stone.

He lodged with Uncle Abbas. Abbas is said to have embraced the faith then and there, although he assured Muhammad that he had been a secret Muslim all along. Certainly he had been a secret Muslim spy all along. He was a man who did not feel easy without holes in his fences. To cement their ties, Abbas now proposed marriage to Muhammad on behalf of his wife's sister Maymuna, to which Muhammad happily agreed, first because he liked marrying people, and second because he loved Abbas, loved the Hashim, and loved being home again.

On the third day, some Meccans came down from the mountains and told Muhammad firmly that his time was up. "What harm would it do," asked the Prophet wistfully, "if I celebrated my marriage here in Mecca with a feast, and invited all of you?"

They replied with the utmost ill humor, "We don't need your food, so get out!"

The Apostle got out and was married on the road in a valley now called Wadi Fatima. It was not much of a wedding in any case for Maymuna. There was a shortage of camels that year, so they had to kill an ox instead. She was Muhammad's eleventh and last wife—the two concubines Rayhana and Maryam make up the full roster of his thirteen crooked ribs. She was to outlive all of them, and when she died, she asked to be buried in Wadi Fatima.

This pilgrimage to Mecca had been a marvelous stroke of press-agentry, for news of it went far and wide, making a deep impression on every thoroughgoing Arab. For now it was clear to everyone that Muhammad's new religion was Arabian to the core, a homespun product, attached by strong threads to the venerated shrine. Never again would an Arab need to comfort his soul with harebrained superstitions, still less with the foreign ways of worship, Christian or Jewish, nor the even stranger teachings of the Persian Magi. What was more, a fantastic change had come about. Arabs could now call themselves "People of the Book."

Before the end of the year 629, certain events came to a satisfactory boil, making it possible for Muhammad to break the Treaty of Hudaybiya. No doubt he had been waiting for the opportunity with catlike patience. An argument arose between two Bedouin tribes, the one loyal to Muhammad—it was in fact the "rabble" of Hudaybiya, the Khuza'a—and another tribe loyal to the Quraysh. With incredible recklessness, the Quraysh saw fit to supply their excitable allies with weapons. It was not until the fighting was transferred from the desert to the city of Mecca itself, where some riots broke out in the streets, that they came to their senses and banished both warring groups from the city limits.

They then held agitated discussion, wondering how they had best explain the matter to Muhammad. Since some of the Khuza'a had been killed, he might demand blood price, but to pay it would be as good as admitting that they had supplied the weapons. They could disown their allies, but that would not be honorable. They might declare war on Muhammad—but they had tried that before.

They sent an envoy to persuade Muhammad that the unfortunate affair had been totally beyond their power to control. It might seem strange that they chose for the task that sworn enemy of God, Abu Sufyan, commander of the late-lamented confederation, until one reflects that he was now a father-in-law of the Prophet. Muhammad himself chose not to recollect this fact. When Abu Sufyan arrived in Medina, he ignored him and did not invite him to visit.

The Muslim traditions cherish a satisfying legend about the Meccan commander's reception by his daughter, Umm Habiba—how he went straight to her apartment to gain her support for his intended diplomatic negotiations and was just about to sink down in the place of honor on the mat when Umm Habiba made a swift dive for it and pulled it out from under. "My dear," said her surprised father, "I am wondering whether you think the carpet is too good for me, or that I am too good for the carpet?"

She answered him straight: "This is the Apostle's mat, and you are an unclean idolator."

The father stared in humiliation and despair. "By God," he said, "since you left my house, you have gone to the bad!"

He approached Abu Bekr, asking his aid in gaining access to the Apostle, but Abu Bekr refused. Abu Sufyan then went to Umar, who said, "What, I be your go-between? If I owned only an ant, I'd fight you with it!"

His next stop was at the house of Ali, whom he found playing with his small son Hassan. Ali was not encouraging. He said that Muhammad had made up his mind not to receive Abu Sufyan or listen to Meccan excuses. Still, he offered good advice. Abu Sufyan should go to the mosque and pronounce a certain traditional formula granting "protection between men." Abu Sufyan did so. He entered the mosque, arose before the worshipers, and said, "O men, I grant protection between men." By this he announced that in the event of forthcoming hostilities, he held himself responsible for the safety of all Muslims who might seek his protection. It was a friendly thing to say, and having said it he rode back to Mecca.

Modern scholars look with a cynical eye on this story, which they call too pat. They say it is obvious from the ensuing events that not only was there a meeting in Medina between Muhammad and Abu Sufyan but that a specific procedure was

143

planned whereby the old differences might be dissolved with the minimum loss of face on either side.

Whatever was the case, the next magic-lantern slide displayed to us by the Arab traditionists shows Ayesha, now sixteen, skipping about as she collected the Prophet's things together for a razzia. But when her father, visiting, asked her where Muhammad intended to raid next, she said she did not know, nor did any-one else—it was a huge secret. The announcement was made to a trusted few that night. They were going home to Mecca. "O God, take away the eyes and ears of the Quraysh," prayed Muhammad, "so that we may take them by surprise!"

There must have been a swift and stealthy ride-out of messengers, a speedy mustering of forces. It was January of 630 and the month of Ramadan, and all the way southward one may imagine the faithful came swarming in from the desert, silent as shadows and dodging all who might give them away. Such was Muhammad's prestige now that even tribes that had been previously hostile joined the great march toward the center of the world. By the time they arrived two stages out of Mecca, ten thousand warriors followed the Prophet, and still the Quraysh did not know they were on the march. However, Uncle Abbas must have had an inkling, because very soon a column of dust appeared to the south, moving smartly toward the camp. It was Abbas, getting on the right side as usual, and the following day he moved southward with the army, moving out ahead of it on Muhammad's white mule.

That night he took it into his head to go stumbling about in the dark, and who should he stumble on but Abu Sufyan? A suspicion can be entertained that this meeting was arranged. Certainly, the presence of the white mule, shining under the moon, would have facilitated a prearranged meeting. In any case, it was now time to stage a little drama that would force Abu Sufyan to decide whether he was a sheep or a goat. Abbas told him to get up behind him on the mule, and he would take him to the Prophet, on whose mercy he would do well to throw himself. Otherwise, he said bloodthirstily, "Muhammad will have your head chopped off."

Abu Sufyan climbed on the mule. The animal did not know it, but it now had on its back the ancestors of two splendid dynasties of Islam, the Umayyad caliphs descended from Abu Sufyan, and the Abbasids founded by Muhammad's clever uncle. After a little they entered the Muslim camp, unchallenged because of the familiar mule. Muhammad allowed the Meccan general to be brought before him, but he stared coldly and did not speak to him. "Take him away for now," he told Abbas grandly. "I'll see him in the morning."

The next morning Abu Sufyan came again before the Prophet, who said to him, "And now! Isn't it high time for you to admit that there is no God but God?"

"If there were," replied Abu Sufyan, "I should not be here."

"And shouldn't you also admit that I am the Messenger of God?" asked Muhammad.

"As to that," replied Abu Sufyan, "I still have my doubts."

"For goodness' sake," interposed Abbas, "say there is no God but God and Muhammad is the Messenger of God, otherwise you will get your head chopped off."

That, therefore, is what Abu Sufyan said next, and when he had said these words, it seemed that a load of hatred was lifted from his heart, and he was again a man with a direction to his life. "It is strange," he said to the Apostle, "that He who overcame me was the One I had been fleeing from all my life."

Muhammad gave him a great punch on the chest. "Indeed you did!" he said, laughing. There was no joy for him like the netting of a new Muslim, and this was a rare catch.

They agreed on peace terms, and Abu Sufyan and Abbas left the camp carrying them to the Meccans. They were simple. All who locked themselves in their houses or went to the enclosure of the Kaaba were to be spared, and so were all who claimed Abu Sufyan's protection.

Fast on their heels the army struck camp. On the Prophet's orders, Abbas detained Abu Sufyan at a spot where he could see the army pass by—all the squadrons with their standards, and finally Muhammad's squadron, clothed in green and black, and around the Prophet helmeted, armed warriors under the flying banner. "By God," exclaimed Abu Sufyan to Abbas, "but your little nephew has jumped up!"

He hastened then to Mecca and bellowed to the citizens: "O Quraysh, I come from Muhammad who is on his way here with a force you cannot resist. And these are his terms: All who enter my house and claim my protection will be safe!"

His wife Hind, who very often disagreed with him, was opposed to this invasion. She went up to him and seized his beard and moustaches, shaking his head about. "Slay this fat, greasy bladder of lard," she screamed. "What sort of a public protector does he think he is?"

Abu Sufyan extricated himself and said, "Hear me further! Whoever shuts himself in his own house will be safe!"

"God slay you," yelled someone in the crowd. "What good will houses be when that lot enters the town?"

"And further," pursued Abu Sufyan, "he who shelters in the holy enclosure will be safe."

Perhaps it was the very gentleness of these terms that stilled the violence of the crowd. Tempers fell, and the Meccans dispersed to their houses and the grounds around the mosque to await what should befall.

Meanwhile the Prophet was riding toward his home as if it were already a victory progress, slowly, enjoying every stone of the countryside becoming more familiar by the hour, stopping to receive the homage of people dear to him. As they passed through one village, Abu Bekr's father came out to see him, or rather to touch him, for he was old and blind, his hair white as a cloud, and he was gravely reverent toward the man who filled his son's life. "Why didn't you leave him in his house so that I could come to see him there?" the Prophet reproved his attendant. He made the old man sit before him, and he gently stroked his chest as he spoke to him and asked him to accept Islam. After this ceremony was over, he looked at the old man's hair and said, "You ought to have it dyed."

That night he camped his army in the hills surrounding Mecca. He commanded every single man to build himself an individual campfire, so that the Meccans, looking fearfully toward the horizon saw a host of ten thousand fires poised above them like doom.

In the morning the Prophet rose, and we imagine him as the call to prayer went forth gazing down at his city emerging from the long shadows. He had already divided his army into four columns, each of which knew what portion of the city they were to take. He now repeated his orders. They were to offer violence only to those who resisted. There was to be as little bloodshed as possible.

There were a certain number of people whom the Prophet told his columns to kill on sight. The reasons for his severity are revealing. First, there was a certain young man who had been a Muslim, Muhammad's own secretary in fact, with the privileged task of writing down revelations. Yet homesickness had proved too much for him. He had finally given up the faith and returned to his family in Mecca. Him the Prophet wanted dead.

Another was also an apostate. He had killed his freed slave, who happened to be a Muslim, thus becoming guilty of murder. Fearing to stay in Medina, he had fled the faith. He owned two clever dancing girls who used to comfort him by singing funny songs about the Prophet, which had become quite popular in Mecca. These girls, along with their master, Muhammad said, must be killed.

There was another who had insulted him long ago in Mecca, and another who had murdered a Muslim. There was Ikrima, the son of his old enemy Abu Jahl, who had fought hard at all the battles after Badr and had inherited his father's hatred of Muhammad. Now that the Prophet was at the city gates, he fled to Yemen.

There were others of the Clan Makhzum whom he ordered to be executed.

These commands given, the Prophet walked down on Mecca followed by ten thousand men, most of whom, having come in the hope of gaining the richest spoils in the Hejaz, were wondering why they were there. They entered the silent city causing hardly a flutter from the populace which, taking the Prophet at his word, had locked themselves snugly indoors. Only one column under Khalid ibn al-Walid met with opposition. That young man could always stir up a battle and win it as well.

Muhammad went straight to the Kaaba. He encompassed it seven times on his camel, each time touching the Black Stone with a staff which he held in his hand.

146

Then he summoned the keeper of the keys of the Kaaba and told him to open the door. He entered. The first thing he laid hands on was a dove carved of wood, rotten and decayed. He carried it outside and let all behold how it crumbled in his hands. He scattered the remains on the ground.

Three hundred and sixty idols inhabited the House built by Abraham. "The truth has come," Muhammad told the crowd, "and falsehood has passed away." He got the images out of the holy place and threw them on the ground. He erased the pictures from the walls—some are said to have represented Christ and the Virgin Mary. He did not stop until the house was empty as the day it was first built, while outside the people blinked and trembled in their smallest ancestral bones.

He stood at the door of the Kaaba and spoke to his tribe:

"There is no God but God
Nothing exists beside him;
He has made good His promise to His servant;
He has put to flight His enemies.
Quraysh! God now takes from you your idols
And your ancestral haughtiness is no more,
For man springs from Adam,
And Adam sprang from dust."

He pointed to the idols on the ground and told them to build a fire and burn them. When noon came, he turned away and prayed the noon prayer.

Afterward he called the people together and said, "O Quraysh, what do you think I am about to do with you?"

"You are a noble brother, and the son of a noble brother," said a leader with extreme caution.

Muhammad then abolished all blood claims or property claims the Quraysh might have for losses sustained in battling the Muslims. He abolished some of their shady profiteering practices. He kept in his gift the custody of the temple but confirmed the present keeper of the keys in his office, even though Ali had craved the privilege for his own family. He permitted Uncle Abbas to go on selling the waters of Zem-Zem to pilgrims.

Then he said to the Quraysh: "Go your way. I set you free."

The Quraysh were dumbfounded by this generous action and a mood of rejoicing struck up as families sundered by the breach were reconciled. The following day, and for many days after, the Apostle received the people of Mecca on the hill of Safa as they came to do homage and be received into Islam. When he had finished with the men, he started on the women.

In Medina, a number of pious ladies had begun to imitate the Prophet's wives

147

by veiling their faces in public, and in Mecca he might have been pleased to see one woman, at least, in the listening crowd thus religiously attired. It was that vixen Hind who, having eaten his Uncle Hamza's liver, was not eager to be recognized. However, she was a free spirit who was incapable of holding her tongue, and when the Prophet, instructing the women, forbade them to carry talismans or charms about with them, or set up little shrines in the corner of their houses, as housewives like to do, she brayed, "Aha! So you are forbidding us to do something that you didn't forbid the men!"

The Prophet overlooked the remark and continued. He said that it was not lawful for wives to act as plunderers in the family cashbox.

"By God," cried Hind before she could catch her tongue, "I have always taken Abu Sufyan's money, lawfully or not!"

Abu Sufyan, who was present, took this opportunity to inform his wife that while her riflings of the cashbox had been lawful in the ignorant past, they were no longer so when she was going to be a Muslim.

Muhammad looked narrowly at the mysterious veiled lady and said, "You are Hind? Utba's daughter?"

"I am," said Hind suddenly queasy. She added, "Forgive me what is past."

The Prophet ignored her, but his further educational efforts seem pointed. "Do not commit adultery," he said.

"How can a free woman commit adultery?" asked Hind proudly.

"And do not kill your babies," said Muhammad.

"I? Kill my babies?" exploded Hind. "When my children were babies, I cared for them. And when they were grown, you killed them on the field of Badr!"

Umar, who was present, began to heave with laughter at this reply. Patiently the Prophet proceeded. "You are not to tell lies and slander people," he said.

"By God, slander is vile," agreed Hind. "Everybody should ignore slander."

"Do not disobey when I order you to do good."

"Should we have sat and listened all this time if we wanted to disobey you?"

Muhammad said to Umar, "Accept their oath." Umar did this by touching the hands of the women of Mecca. The Prophet would not do this himself, since he never touched the hand of any woman not his wife. However, he caused a bowl of water to be placed in which he plunged his hand, and every woman coming by, as she accepted Islam plunged her hand in the same water.

As it happened, few of the executions he had ordered were actually carried out on the minor Judgment Day when Muhammad took Mecca. His former secretary's foster brother asked for the young man's life, and it was granted. Ikrima's wife asked mercy for Ikrima and received it. He returned from exile in Yemen and became a historic Muslim leader. One of the witty dancing girls was killed, the other was forgiven. Some murderers had to die the death. The condemned men of Makhzum fled through the streets of Mecca with Ali fast on their heels wav-

148

ing his moon-bright sword, but they took refuge in the house of a quick-minded lady who locked them in, got Ali off in a wrong direction, and ran to the house where Muhammad was lodging. She found the Prophet bathing rather thoroughly, his form shielded from public scrutiny by his daughter Fatima holding up a garment. He made the woman wait while he prayed the morning prayer with eight prostrations. Then he told her to tell Ali not to kill the men of Makhzum.

So it was that, almost bloodlessly, Muhammad's long-sought battle with his tribe was over, and God allowed him to bring to his people a magnificent blood price for the loss and pain of Badr, Uhud, and the rest. It was the gift of thought, which would grow in them and in their remote children, inspire them to greatness, endow their works with grandeur, bless every mind it touched, and raise their consciousness toward God. A poet was there to tell us how it all started:

> You should have seen Muhammad when he came,
> You should have seen those idols how they burst,
> You should have seen God's light fill the scene,
> And darkness smother ignorance.

149

Islam

O thou Prophet! Urge on the believers to fight! If there be of you twenty patient men, they shall conquer two hundred; if there be of you a hundred, they shall conquer a thousand of those who misbelieve . . .

—THE CHAPTER OF THE SPOILS

21

The Battle of Hunayn

Muhammad might have hoped that in accomplishing his dear dream of winning Mecca and overcoming the stubborn polytheism of his near relatives, he might rest and consider his mission accomplished. God did not, however, as long as Muhammad lived, lift the scourge of action from His messenger. No sooner had Mecca submitted than to the east the Bedouin rose in outrage, not only at the fate of the unfortunate Hubal, but in dread of what would surely happen next to his wives and daughters, al-Lat, al-Uzza, and Manat, if Muhammad was not quickly stopped.

Muhammad sent his bright young general Khalid ibn al-Walid out to do some missionary work. He was to take no lives, the Prophet said, only to explain to people at first hand the events in Mecca. Khalid, however, was not good at explaining. He had a trick of asking people to lay down their arms in order that he might hear their confession of faith. Then, when they had laid them down and prostrated themselves on the ground after the manner of the faithful, he had their hands seized and tied and their heads lopped off. In that way he rid Muhammad of a number of God's enemies, but the Prophet had a difficult time explaining to God what had become of them. Moreover, he had to pour out his own money in blood price. Honest Ali had to go out in Khalid's tracks and pacify the tribes.

Khalid made amends for his mistake by disposing of the shrine of al-Uzza, which occupied a hilltop at Nakhla. The guardian of the shrine saw him coming, climbed the hill, and exhorted his great mistress:

"O Uzza, now's the time!
Throw off your veil, bind up your skirts,
And slay this man Khalid!
And if you don't,
You had better become a Christian!"

Al-Uzza did neither. After a brief encounter with Khalid's forces, she joined her father Hubal in limbo.

Even within the fifteen days that Muhammad remained in Mecca after the conquest, the vast tribe of Hawazin were thronging to the east, having mustered, after fast riding and mighty persuasion, confederates to the tune of twenty thousand men. As a deterrent to cowards who might not want to make a stand in battle, they obliged everyone to bring along his women, children, camels, horses, goats, skins, grains, dates, and household goods—in other words the sum total of his earthly goods—and these were arranged on the slopes of a wadi, so that whoever ran away would have to run right past them. They also brought along an old sheikh named Durayd, who in his day had been one of the best heroes and noblest men in all Arabia and an expert in razzia. Now he was old and had to be carried in a howdah like somebody's concubine. He looked with disdain at the horde of women and children in whose persuasive value he did not put much faith. "You sheep-tender," he said to the Hawazin general, Malik, "do you think anything is going to stop a man who has made up his mind to run?"

He had the time of his life picking fault with everything the younger man had done, until finally General Malik called him an old dotard and had him carried out of earshot. He then told his twenty thousand men that the minute the Muslims showed their faces in the wadi, they were to fall upon them as one man.

Muhammad received notice of these dispositions from one of his spies. Umar simply refused to believe there was such a thing as twenty thousand Bedouin with wives, children, goats, and the rest all in one spot. Against this host they could bring the ten thousand men who had marched with Muhammad from Medina together with about two thousand new converts from Mecca. Not all the Meccans had embraced Islam, nor had Muhammad insisted that they should, being willing to bide his time patiently. Even the Mecca chieftain Safwan, the chief rival of Abu Sufyan, remained an idolator, although he rented to Muhammad armor, weapons, and transport for this battle.

They marched out from Mecca toward the Hunayn Valley, close to the city of at-Taif, where many years ago Muhammad had gone in peril of his life as a refugee. They passed a certain green tree, sacred to the Meccans, on which when they went to battle they used to hang their arms for blessing, while sacrificing to the tree. Muhammad's new converts shouted to him, "Hi, Apostle, can't we have our own tree now?"

"Great God Almighty!" Muhammad blazed at them. "You are as bad as the Jews when they said to Aaron, 'Make us a god!'" He added, "What an ignorant lot you are!"

Thus they advanced toward the battleground, the Prophet contentedly badgering his new converts, hammering home Islam when he should have been listening to his spies with all his six senses alert. They camped short of Hunayn Valley and at dawn advanced on the enemy through a defile. Umar's son described what happened then:

We came down through a wadi, wide and sloping. . . descending gradually in the morning twilight; but the enemy was there before us and had hidden in the bypaths, side-tracks, and narrow places. They were there in force, fully armed and knowing exactly what to do, and by God, we were terrified when we descended and suddenly the Hawazin came down on us as one man!

The Bedouin attacked with stones, boulders, arrows, lance, and sword. Muhammad's van, under General Khalid, broke, the camels jostling and crashing, screeching and tangling up their long legs. The Prophet might well have been trampled to death in that mad rush to backtrack from the defile, but he was fortunate enough to find a foothold at the side from which he could climb to rising ground. There he could be seen by the panicking host, his red cloak flapping under his white standard, and his voice borrowing volume from the superhuman passions that guided him: "Where are you going men? Come back! Come to me! I am God's Apostle . . ."

He saw among the fleeing men his new converts from Mecca, and he called to them as one of their own: "I am Muhammad, son of Abdullah!"

Not one of them heeded, and why should they? There was a Hawazin warrior after them on a russet camel, his standard flying from a long lance, and every time he dipped the blade of that lance it showed up on the other side of someone's chest. The Prophet's voice was drowned in the uproar of men, the clamor of camels. He asked his Uncle Abbas, a man with a mighty lung, to take up the cry, "O comrades, remember the acacia tree . . ."

This reminder of the Pledge of Good Pleasure had the effect of staying some of the stampeding men, but even those who strained to bring their beasts up short could not control them in such a swirl of motion. Nevertheless the veterans of Hudaybiya, mastering their panic, left their steeds, shed their heavy armor, and seizing sword and shield gradually made their way to their Prophet upon his little hill.

The Emigrants, those old and tried companions of a decade of trouble, and the Helpers too who had made his determinations their own, stood by the Prophet on that day, and even some old enemies stood fast. Abu Sufyan kept by his mule's rump, and when Muhammad turned to see who it was that had come to protect him, said simply, "It is your mother's son." Even the stubborn idolator, Safwan, yelled at a deserter: "God smash your mouth! I'd rather be ruled by a man of Quraysh than a man of Hawazin!"

A Meccan woman had come out, screaming hell at those who fled, very wobbly astride the neck of her husband's great camel on which she kept a stranglehold with one arm while in the other hand she brandished a large knife with which she proposed to rip out the stomachs of the Hawazin. In a compact mass around the Prophet, these staunch ones ushered him through the defile and into the open. And Ali, so quiet in peace but in battle like a demon, lunged viciously about him, fighting to get behind the Hawazin leader's camel and hamstring it, while his comrades took charge of the leader, sending his foot flying through the air with half a shank as well.

Once out of the narrow passage and on the open field, the Muslims, with restored wits and faith in their Prophet, found themselves once more eager to make the acquaintance of their houris who, they knew, were even then warming the silken couchs of many of them in Paradise. Muhammad stood in his stirrups, exulting, "Now the fire is hot!" and his men poured about him while those on both sides who had literary talents collected material for reams of bloodstained verse. The Hawazin could not withstand the Muslim fury. They fled, leaving their women, children, and worldly goods pitiful on the hillside, just as Durayd had predicted. That old man was pulled from his howdah by a young Meccan who thought he was a woman and began to hack away at him inexpertly. Durayd told him, "Feel under my saddle, there! That's my sword—use it, boy! Get me below the head, but above the spine, here, d'you see? And then go home and tell your mother you have killed Durayd ben al-Simma."

So the boy killed him and later told his mother. She said, "God help you! That man set free me and both of your grandmothers!"

Muhammad directed that the spoils be taken to a place called al-Jirana to await distribution, and the sea of women, children, and animals moved off, all stacked high with goods.

With his army almost intact, he did not wish to leave this area without a stiff assault upon at-Taif where the goddess al-Lat still kept her residence. Possibly some personal vindictiveness was mingled with his eagerness to tear that enemy of God from her shrine and from the devotions of her worshipers. And perhaps for that reason God, who always took a stern line with Muhammad, being quick to take him up on his faults, did not favor the siege at at-Taif. The army sat for twenty days and then abandoned it, to the great relief of the men who, with all their minds bent on the Hunayn booty, had no heart for this jihad against al-Lat.

Many details are recorded of the way the Prophet redistributed the riches of the Hawazin and what gifts he gave, either from his own share or from the surplus. They testify not only to Muhammad's great personal generosity, but to the way he wielded spoils as a diplomatic weapon to win clans and tribes to Islam. Most of the Quraysh leaders were given a rich gift of one hundred camels each, and he also gave a hundred camels to his recent enemy General Malik of Hawazin. People like Malik, and others who embraced Islam as a matter of convenience or to save their lives and could therefore be expected to be lukewarm in faith, had a special name in Muhammad's vocabulary. They were "those whose hearts were to be wooed." He believed, correctly, that the best wooing was done with gifts rather than with lectures.

The gifts had to be whisked rather trickily by the Prophet from under the noses of his followers, for of course the spoils belonged not to him but to the victors of battle. To the Hawazin he said, "What is dearest to you? Your sons and wives or your cattle?"

"Are you giving us a choice between our cattle and our honor? Nay, give us back our wives and children, keep the cattle."

"Then do this," said the Prophet. "As soon as I have finished praying the noon prayer, get up and ask for them, and I will make an appeal on your behalf."

The Emigrants and the Helpers complied with his request as he had known they would. What was theirs had been his for years past. More recent converts, however, to whom battle spoils were the wine of life, felt robbed of their rights. It was extremely hard on the eyes of those who had pinned their hopes of worldly gain on this booty to see some thousands of Hawazin women and children, every one of them worth hard cash, marching off, as often as not at the head of a herd of animals. One fine day as Muhammad was riding along on a camel, a group of malcontents surrounded him and forced him back against a tree. They tore his red cloak away and angrily said, "O Muhammad, give us our spoil of camel and herds."

Muhammad cried, "Men, give me back my cloak, for, by God, if I had as many sheep as there were trees, I would divide them among you. Have you ever found me stingy?"

He plucked a hair out of his camel's rump and said, "Men, I have a fifth of the spoils, and that fifth I now promise to give you even to this hair. So give me back my cloak lest you be called thieves on Resurrection Day!"

One man came mocking with a mass of camel's hair in his hand and said, "O Prophet, I stole this hair ball from my camel to make a saddle pad, since she was sore. Am I going to be called a thief on Resurrection Day?"

"I'll tell you what," said the Prophet. "You can have my fifth of that hair ball too."

It was ready wit like this and cool nerve that won him the hearts of rough men as much as gifts, or even the gift of faith. General Malik was so impressed by Muhammad's various transactions that he composed a poem in his honor:

I have never seen or heard a man
Like Muhammad in the world—
True to his word and generous,
And he will even tell your fortune,
if you ask him!

The bounty continued and even increased after the return to Mecca. One Meccan who rode his camel too close to the Prophet and grazed his leg with a rough sandal got a swift cut across the foot with a whip. The next morning he heard that Muhammad was looking for him. "I came out expecting more punishment," he said, "but the Prophet said, 'You hurt my leg yesterday and I struck your foot with my whip. Now I want to pay you back.'"

He gave the man eighty she-camels.

Finally his generosity tried the patience of the long-suffering Helpers who had borne the support of the Emigrants for so long and had been looking forward to the day when their investment would come home to roost. Mingled with chagrin there was jealousy, the fear that now Muhammad was back in the bosom of his tribe, he would never again belong to Aws or Khazraj. Finally one of them burst out with it: "By God, the Prophet is good to his own people!"

Another Helper saw fit to repeat this remark to the Prophet. "Well, where do you stand yourself?" asked Muhammad.

"I stand with my people," replied the Medinan.

"Then call them all here, bring them to me," commanded Muhammad. They came, some Emigrants too. The men Muhammad addressed on that day were a good portion of the men who had shared his struggle from the beginning. He began by addressing the complainers.

"O men of Medina, what is this I hear about you, complaining of me in your hearts? How can you think ill of me? Did I not come to you when you were erring and God guided you? Did I not find you, Aws and Khazraj, divided amongst yourselves and reconciled you? Did I not find you poor and make you rich?"

They examined their dusty feet and mumbled, "Yes—God and His Apostle have been most kind and generous to us."

Muhammad pretended not to hear. "Why don't you answer me, O Helpers?"

They said loudly, "How shall we answer you? Kindness and generosity belong to God and to His Apostle."

Muhammad surveyed them slowly, as if one by one. "Had you so wished, you might have answered otherwise. You might have said to me—and you would have been truthful—'You came to us discredited and we believed in you. You came to us powerless and we supported you. You came to us a refugee, and we took you in. You came to us poor and we shared with you.'

"O my Helpers, are you really disturbed because I have given away a few of the good things of this life, by means of which I want to win over people and make Muslims out of them? To you I have entrusted all Islam!

"Are you so distressed because I have given flocks and herds to some to take away with them? You take with you the Prophet of God!"

He now turned to the old companions of Mecca: "And you Emigrants! But for you what should I be now? I should have had to slink away somewhere by myself, I should have been but an unknown refugee in Medina!"

He raised his voice, "Be sure of this, Helpers! If all men on earth went one way and you another, I'd take your way. God bless you, Helpers, you and your sons' sons!"

By this time he had the flower of Aws and Khazraj weeping until the tears soaked their beards. They said to him in subdued tones, "All we need as our share is the Prophet of God."

And so the Prophet never lived again in his old home. He appointed missionaries to stay in Mecca and teach the new religion.

He returned to Medina to find his two-year-old son Ibrahim dying. His grief when the child died was such that he could not control himself, and he wept without stopping. When others reminded him how in past time he had expressed distaste for excessive displays of grief, he protested, "Ah, it is only for a child! The eye runneth down with tears, the heart swells—but surely I do not offend our Lord by grieving for a child. Ibrahim! O Ibrahim!"

He followed the tiny coffin to the grave, sprinkled it with water, saying to the others, "This eases the afflicted heart. It cannot help the dead, but it comforts the living."

159

Go freely about the earth for four months, and know that you cannot reduce God: but God can reduce the misbelievers . . .
-THE CHAPTER OF REPENTANCE

22

The Pillars of Islam

The Thaqif tribe continued to adore al-Lat for about a year. It was the women, mainly, who were adamantly on the side of the ancient goddess, and they sent their husbands at the beginning of 631 to bargain with the Prophet. They would accept Islam on the condition that they might continue to worship al-Lat for three years more. He said they might not. Then two years? One? One month?

It fell to the ex-idolator, Abu Sufyan, to command the troops that finally marched on the potent shrine with pickaxes to reduce al-Lat to rubble and snatch her jewels from the dust, while outside the women stood and wept. With this, and the destruction of the Manat-shrine nearer Medina, the backbone of the old religion was broken, and when the month of the great pilgrimage rolled round again, Muhammad felt secure enough to issue an ultimatum to the pagan tribes to the area. They had four months to say farewell to the old ways. After that, God had made clear by revelation, He washed His hands of them:

"So when the forbidden months are passed, kill the idolators wherever you find them. Seize them, besiege them, set ambushes—but if they repent, give alms, and keep the hours of prayer, forgive them—for God is forgiving, merciful."

This fierce injunction later traveled with the Muslim armies of Islam as they slashed across the earth, so that for many centuries it was said that Islam converted with a Quran in one hand and a sword in the other. Originally, however, it was a permission given to idol worshipers to walk naked for one last time—631, or A.H. 9—around the empty Kaaba, and then perform their rites no more at the sacred place of qibla. After that, they must be prepared for jihad.

The warning brought into Medina tidal waves of Bedouin from all directions, deputations from far-flung tribes who had so far held perfectly aloof from the turbulent years of Muhammad, but who now became aware that their lives had been touched by a new, electrifying wand of power, and that they could never hope to survive in conflict with it. Nor did they wish to withstand Islam, if only they could capitulate without losing face. The traditions describe for many pages these ticklish encounters between God's Apostle and the children of Ishmael, arrogant and independent, accustomed to being monarchs of all they surveyed, even though it be only a dry wadi or a herd of starved camels. The deputation from the Beni Tamim strode into the mosque and planted themselves before the entrance to Muhammad's inner chambers where he was enjoying an afternoon doze. "Come out, Muhammad!" they bellowed.

When, rather disgruntled, he appeared, they told him they had come to challenge him to a boasting competition. What they insisted upon was an opportunity to brag, in verse, about the glory and greatness of their ancestors. Muhammad, knowing this, hastily sent for his champion poet, Hassan, to counter with verses about the glory and greatness of God. For some time this verbal single combat shook the rafters, after which the Beni Tamim confessed Islam with fairly good grace. God, however, had some afterthoughts about the incident, which He expressed in a Quran:

> *Believers! Do not intrude upon God or His Apostle—for if you do, be sure that God marks it.*
> *Believers! Raise not your voice above the Prophet's voice. Do not shout at him the way you shout among yourselves . . . Those who keep their voices low before the Apostle of God are those whose hearts are fertile ground for piety—they will earn God's forgiveness and great reward.*

To Muhammad directly, God remarked, "Verily, those who shout at you from behind the curtain have no sense. It would be better for them if they waited until you came out—but God is forgiving, merciful."

Such points of etiquette might seem too mundane to deserve comment from the Divine Spirit, and we cannot turn away from the possibility that the Holy Quran contains some of Muhammad's crotchets masquerading as those of God. Yet we have not the smallest ground to suppose that Muhammad purposefully substituted them. In the vast literatures of the traditions, he seems always to be infallibly aware of the distinction between his human opinions and supernatural communication. His own modesty as a man, his awe of the force that possessed

161

him, his total commitment to his mission would have forbidden deliberate char-
latanry. It would not have forbidden hasty work and poor judgment on the part
of his secretaries.

It must also be taken into consideration that any mystic, however "pure," can
only understand the absolute abstractions uncovered in his mind in terms of his
own symbols. This begins, as is well known, with the actual Voice or Vision. The
Jewish rabbis were quite right in being suspicious of Gabriel. One of their own
kind might have seen the Prophet Elijah. A Christian would describe some rec-
ognizably Christian entity, just as in ages past, pagan Greek mystics must have
seen the splendid character they named Hermes.

In the same way, the ideas impinging on limited human understanding are fil-
tered through in the seer's own idiom and in terms of his own experience. The
Voice told Muhammad he was sending everything down in "plain Arabic," under-
standable to any Arab alive in the seventh century. But it was this same wise
Source, not Muhammad, that made the substance of these revelations good for an
eternity of Arabs, and for others too.

Muhammad had perfect recall for every Quran. The written record, consist-
ing of fragments of wood, bone, stone, horn, shell, cloth, as well as paper, was
kept in a box probably belonging to the Prophet's wife Hafsa bint Umar, since
she became the custodian of the precious documents. However, she had no filing
system, and after the Prophet's death, the compilers were faced with jumble that
had to be arranged by wild guesswork. They did what they could, placing together what seemed to belong together, and titling the various chapters with random
catchwords that have all the allure of a magic spell, especially as they do not mean
much. The chief care of the compilers was to include everything.

They made no point of chronology. The account of the first revelation, the
Call, is placed in the back of the Holy Book, while some that loomed larger in the
minds of the compilers because they were more recently revealed and dealt with
some living problem, form the earlier chapters. Thus, the Holy Quran has no
beginning and no end. Some passages can be related to certain events or problems or emotional moods in Muhammad's life, but on the whole it tells no tale
and obeys no scheme. It attacks with energy matters of practical or philosophical
importance, then lets them drop. It jumps ahead, switches about, and doubles
back, and it is written in language obscure, archaic, tangled, and shifting as a
quagmire. Voltaire said it was "an incomprehensible work," and this judgment
must occur to any stranger who picks up the Quran hoping to find a good story,
such as he might read in the Holy Bible.

And yet to Muslims the Quran is luminous, hypnotic, filled with instruction.
This is because in the back of their minds they have a learned pattern that acts as
a mold and a structure for the constant message of the Quran. The structure takes
its shape from the "five pillars of Islam," which in turn were brought into expres-

162

sion by the circumstances of the Prophet's life, his heritage, history, and personality. Even a slight knowledge of that life, such as is related in this book, causes the Quran to light up, just as the tiniest match brings light into a vast room.

Islam, as we know it today, is far beyond the scope of this book to describe, since it comprises thirteen hundred years of development of philosophy, mystical speculation, science, medicine, jurisprudence, social affairs, poetry, music, and art as we see it expressed most magnificently in the architectural monuments which are treasures of the world. It is nothing short of marvelous to reflect that the inner mold of it all was cast in the mind of an unlettered tribesman, born to a semi-primitive culture.

The five pillars of Islam are these: salat, worship, or formal prayer; zakat, almsgiving; sawm, the fast of Ramadan; hajj, the greater pilgrimage; and central to them all, shahadah, the confession of faith.

The first pillar: Shahadah, the Confession of Faith

There is no God but God, and Muhammad is His Prophet. This famous phrase is known to almost everyone as the call of the muezzin from his tower. It was the first formulated thought in Islam, the thought Muhammad brought back from the Cave of Hira, the thought he tried to impress upon his fellow tribesmen throughout the years of struggle. And when victory came, it was the phrase repeated by the tribes capitulating to the King of the Hejaz, and afterward the armies of Islam carried it around the world.

Yet these words do not appear in the Quran. Their origin is not known exactly. Some accounts credit Abu Bekr with having repeated it within days of the Call. To anyone accustomed to the notion of One God, it may seem to be an undramatic statement, but to Muhammad, Khadija, Abu Bekr, and all the idolatrous tribesmen who eventually embraced Islam, it was a stunning thought, a revelation which canopied everything they were asked to do and think as Muslims, no matter how unreasonable, or how contrary to the old laws marked out by the tradition of ages past.

In history it acted like the Ten Commandments, or Buddha's Four Noble Truths. Within half a lifetime it wiped out an era and brought another into being.

The most glorious language in the Quran is written around the theme of the preeminence of God and His relationship to His Creation. The loveliness of such psalms as the so-called Verse of the Throne from the Chapter of the Cow cannot be extinguished by translation into an alien language.

God!
There is no god but God
Now, or ever shall be.

163

Slumber takes Him not, never does He sleep,
His are the heavens, the earth belongs to Him.
Who may intercede with Him, but as He wills?
He knows what is before them and what behind,
And none may know His knowledge, but as He pleases.
His throne spans the heavens and it spans the earth
And it tires Him not to guard them both.
For He is high and splendid.

And again, this passage from the Chapter of Light:

God is the Light of the heavens and the earth
His Light is a niche in which a lamp is set;
And the lamp is in a glass; and the glass looks
to be a shining star,
And it is lit by a mystic tree, an olive tree,
not from the east nor from the west, but its
oil is such that it would blaze though no fire
touched it.
Light upon light!
God gives His Light for guidance to whom He
pleases.
He speaks in riddles to man,
But He knows all things.

This revelation represents no simple sermon pronounced by a loving pastor leaning against a palm trunk. Surely it emerges from the pitch of human experience. God is seen not as the Light itself, light being only an appearance accepted by our senses, but as a mystery, a "niche," a nondescript, shapeless emptiness in which the Light may be seen not by the eyes of the body but of the spirit. The concept is similar to that of the most abstract schools of religious thought—the Jewish Kabala, the Chinese Tao, the speculations of the Vedic sages which dared not define God but only ask questions about Him.

It was a strange idea to emanate from a desert preacher, and alone it shows that he was not only an Arabian tribesman, but a rare, illumined man, whose inspiration moves minds of an entirely different shape from his own, and, threading through art, music, and all of man's capacities, produces civilizations.

The second pillar: Salat, ritual prayer

The formal worship had been taught to Muhammad, it will be remembered,

164

by a vision when, shortly after the Call but before the Cessation of Revelation, Gabriel appeared to him on the hillside above Mecca and showed him how to wash himself ritually and pray. Later, in Medina, he established formal prayer as the first duty of a Muslim and therefore a distinctive feature of Islam. These prayers are still properly performed exactly as he instructed, with no change. They differ from the ordinary prayers of Jews and Christians in that they contain no petition whatsoever, but are intended only to glorify God. They are really a sort of psalm in motion.

The worshiper rises at break of day to the muezzin's comforting cry (which are the words of Muhammad, not God): "Prayer is better than sleep!" He performs the ablutions and then stands, facing the qibla, the direction of which he is certain of, wherever he is. All mosques show a niche which is the direction of the qibla.

He holds his ears between his hands and says, "God is most great!"

He joins his hands at the level of his chest and says, "Glory to Thee, O God, Thine is the Praise, blessed is Thy Name, exalted is Thy Majesty, and there is no God but Thee. I take refuge in God against the Devil, which is made of stone."

He then recites in its entirety the opening chapter of the Quran, the only chapter that has no name being called merely the Fatiha, the "Lord's Prayer" of Islam:

In the name of God the merciful and compassionate,
Praise be to God, the Lord of the worlds, the merciful,
the compassionate, the Ruler of the Day of
Judgment!
We serve Thee, we ask Thine aid.
Guide us in the straight path, the path of those who
please Thee,
Not in the path of those who anger Thee,
Nor of those who go astray.

Next, the Muslim recites any whole chapter of the Quran which he chooses himself. Some of them are not long. When he has finished, he says, "God is most great!" He bows from the waist, placing his hands on his knees, and so bent, he says three times, "Glory to my Lord, the Great One!"

He stands upright and says, "God hears those who praise Him; praise be to God!"

He falls to his knees and bends forward until his forehead touches the ground. He says three times, "Glory to God in the Highest!" He sits back on his heels, bends forward again, stretching until his forehead touches the ground.

He rises to his feet, and starts the second prostration, going through all the

165

motions several times over.

At first Muhammad may have demanded observance of formal worship only three times a day, but by the "Year of Deputations," 631, he had fixed five times as the minimum: dawn, noon, midafteroon, sunset, and two hours after sunset. The Quran also has encouraging words to say to worshipers who train themselves to rise in the middle of the night, as Muhammad did, and perform additional salat. By this heavy punctuation of the day by prayer, Muhammad made it impossible for devout Muslims to expend all their energies on ordinary business, and his demands aroused the opposition of many early converts. The Bedouin protested that they could not possibly conduct raids in conditions like this. He told them to perform salat anyhow. They said they could not perform ablutions in lands where there was no water. He showed them, as Gabriel had shown him, how to perform them with sand.

Not all modern Muslims perform these strenuous prayers as a constant duty but as their conscience prompts them. On the Day of Assembly, which is Friday, they put on clean clothes and attend the mosque where they may hear the imam recite from the Holy Book, as once Muhammad recited standing against his pillar. Friday is not necessarily a day of rest from business, but it is a day of especially studious observation of prayer in the mosque, along with brother Muslims.

The following fragments of the Quran show some of the wishes God first expressed in this matter.

We did create the heavens and the earth and everything between them in six days and no weariness touched us. Do not mind then what they say, but celebrate thy Lord before the rising of the sun and before the setting; and in the early part of the night. And perform the additional prayers.

Believers! When the call to prayer sounds on the Day of Assembly, hasten to leave your daily affairs and remember God. This is good for you, although you may not know it. After your prayer, go your way, asking God's grace. Remember God often: in that way you will prosper.

Believers! When you rise up to pray, wash your faces and your hands as far as the elbows and wipe your heads, and your feet down to the ankles . . . and if you cannot find water, take fine surface sand and wipe your faces and your hands therewith. God does not wish to be a nuisance; but He wishes to purify you and pour His favor on you.

And be faithful in your prayers at both ends of the day and at both ends of the night. Good deeds cancel out evil deeds: that is a reminder to the mindful. Be patient, awaiting your reward, for God will not waste your wages.

O thou under a blanket! Arise and pray, except for a short space, perhaps half the night more or less—and in measured tones chant the Quran . . .

The third pillar: Zakat, legal alms

Muhammad was a generous man, even before the Call. His one extravagance was a tendency to give away his wife's money to the poor. After the Hijra, when the Emigrants desperately needed the financial assistance of the Medinans, it became necessary for God to issue definite instructions on this subject. Charity to the poor had been a feature of Jewish life, and it was a Christian ideal based upon Jesus' remarks about the difficulty the rich encountered in entering the kingdom of Heaven. Muhammad made it an iron-clad obligation to give over surplus wealth to communal needs. One might as well translate zakat as "income tax," since that is what it was. Even in the lifetime of Muhammad it was administered by an internal revenue service employing tax collectors who went about the Hejaz, and far and wide beyond, carrying with them their tax lists, census records, assessments, debits, credits, and all the rest. They were not wanted. They were avoided and rebelled against and circumvented. But they remained in Islam, symbols of God's determination to implant a social conscience in the umma.

As Muhammad's mastery extended, bringing wide areas into the tax fold, the problem arose of what Jews and Christians should be doing when the tax man came around. Muhammad wrote to the princes of Yemen, establishing a poll tax:

> If a Jew or a Christian becomes a Muslim, he has the same rights and obligations as other Muslims. Those who hold fast to their religion, Jews or Christians, should not be obliged to change it, but they must pay the poll tax, one dinar for every adult male or female, slave or free, or its equivalent in goods. He who pays this tax to God and His Apostle has the protection of God and His Apostle. He who fails to pay is an enemy of God and His Apostle.

The word zakat is related to the word for purification. In Muhammad's thought there was the notion that giving away money to the community was a means of purging mind and soul. He therefore urged, in addition to legal zakat, voluntary alms. Still, he was not unreasonable. He understood the human need to maintain standing in the community and feel financially secure against an uncertain future. A man might acquire wealth, spend it on comforts and luxuries in good conscience, and put some aside for future use, but the surplus he should give away.

Generosity allied to purification, or a sense of the corruptive power of great wealth, is a characteristic attitude of Islam.

Proceeds of the income tax, as Muhammad saw it, went principally toward classes of people: to paupers, to ordinary people in temporary need, to tax collectors as their wages, to new converts and such persons whose "hearts are to be wooed," to slaves to buy their freedom, and to wayfarers, or "sons of the road." A final group which could cover almost any Muslim in need of money was designated "those on God's path."

Perhaps it was because the Meccans of Muhammad's youth had become such a greedy tribe of speculators and moneygrubbers that the Quran has so much to say on the subject of alms, of which the following excerpts are only a few:

Pray and pay your zakat: and whatever good you do for your soul's sake, you will find it again in God: for God sees what you do.

You cannot call yourself righteous unless you give in alms something that you want to keep for yourself. God watches the alms you give. He understands them.

They will ask you what they shall bestow in alms: tell them, what they can spare.

Who is the man that will lend to God a goodly loan? He will double it again and again. God can be closefisted; but He can be openhanded too.

They who spend in the cause of God and never follow their money about with reproaches or insults shall have their reward . . . Kind speech and forbearance is better than generosity followed by insult.

Neither hold your hand close to your chest nor yet open it with all openness, lest you strip yourself and sit down in reproach and beggary.

The fourth pillar: Sawm, the fast

The sawm is said to have begun with Muhammad's desire to share with the Jewish community the fast of Yom Kippur. But after the break with the Jews, he turned back to the custom of Arabs, long before Islam, of observing the ninth month of the lunar year, Ramadan, as a time of self-denial. This division of the year came to have additional significance to Muslims, for the Call occurred in that month, and Badr, the first decisive battle, and the march on Mecca, the last decisive action.

Commemorating these events, and also to teach himself patience in facing want or any hardship, the Muslim takes no food or drink during the hours from sunup to sundown during the fast of Ramadan. After sundown he may eat. Since Muhammad did not think of sexual desire in the same terms as gluttony, he permitted sexual intercourse during Ramadan. He thought of man as incomplete without woman, and he could not therefore sanction incompleteness during the holy month.

In Muhammad's time Ramadan occurred at a certain season of the year, which was kept constant by regularly squeezing extra months into the lunar year to take up the slack with the solar year. Curiously, an ancestor of Muhammad is credited with having arranged this fairly efficient calendar. Muhammad, close to the end of his life, undid his ancestor's work by eliminating the extra months, so that Ramadan may now fall in any season, imposing great hardship on the faithful when they are forbidden to drink in daytime during the hottest months. His reason for making this change was that the Arabs had taken to using the extra months, which occurred every few years, for wild celebrations, a sort of nonstop

New Year's Eve. To this pagan habit, Islam put an end.

God's instructions, as given in the Quran, show a certain reasonableness in the matter of the fast of Ramadan:

Believers! Fasting is demanded of you as it was demanded of those before you, that you may turn your thoughts toward God for a prescribed number of days. Should you be ill, or on a journey, you may fast at another time for the same number of days. But if you are able to keep the fast and break it, in expiation you must maintain a poor man.

Eat and drink until you can discern a white thread from a black thread by the break of day: then fast strictly until night and do not approach your wives, but rather pass the time at the mosques. These are disciplines set up by God.

You may on nights of the fast approach your wives: they are your garment, and you are theirs.

God wisheth your ease, not your discomfort: only that you fulfill the days of the fast, glorifying God for his guidance and being thankful to Him.

The fifth pillar: Hajj, the pilgrimage

The hajj firmly places Mecca and the Kaaba as the center of Islam and separates Muslims distinctly from other People of the Book who follow Moses, Christ, or Zoroaster. When the far-scattered Muslim peoples of the present day turn toward Mecca, they turn not only to a point in space, but in time, toward the ordeal of Hagar and Ishmael, to the submission of Abraham, who was ready to sacrifice children, wealth, all he owned to God.

The hajj, the greater pilgrimage, is an obligation of Muslims to visit Mecca in the flesh at least once in a lifetime, and year by year literally millions of them, from all parts of the earth, do so during the month of of Dhu'l-Hijja, the twelfth month, performing their circumambulation of the Kaaba, the touching of the Black Stone, and ritual walks between several other historic sites connected with the life of Muhammad, and other actions congealed by tradition, such as the cutting of hair.

Obviously many Muslims are poor and cannot afford the hajj. Yet all can afford to make some contribution to the expenses of another pilgrim. Poor communities customarily send one of their number as representative of all, and when they hear of his arrival at Beit Allah, they participate in his experience by a "festival of sacrifice."

People who insist on performing hajj personally, though they cannot afford it, are permitted to carry on business during the pilgrimage, but not to distract others by begging. This rule is often abused, as indeed it was in Muhammad's time.

A white seamless robe, such as was worn by the Prophet himself when he visited the Kaaba during the greater pilgrimage, is worn by modern pilgrims at their devotions. The simple uniform serves to eliminate the distinction between rich and poor, to emphasize the brotherhood of Muslims of the many races and

169

degrees of men. While wearing the sacred garments, all luxuries are renounced, all quarreling, all vanities such as perfumes or the cutting of fingernails. Only pious thoughts and good works are permitted.

The Quran enjoining hajj is said to have been revealed about the time that Muhammad, realizing that he was rejected by the rabbis as a true prophet in the line of the Hebrew prophets, turned away from Jerusalem and back to Mecca as the quibla.

O our Lord! Make us Muslims and our posterity a Muslim people! And teach us our holy rites, and turn toward us: for Thou art the One who turns, the merciful One!

Perform the pilgrimage and visit the holy places in honor of God . . . or send whatever offering shall be easiest; but shave not your heads until the offering reach the place of sacrifice.

In [the Kaabal] is the proof: even the place where Abraham stood is there . . . The pilgrimage to the temple is a service due to God from those who are able. And as for him who is able and believeth not—well, God can afford to dispense with all creatures.

All the five pillars of Islam are expressed in one remarkable verse of the Quran given in the Chapter of the Cow. It was part of Muhammad's response to the rabbis, when he changed the direction of his quibla—a statement of faith, pure and simple, such as always holds strong against attack, and is indeed a weapon in itself, since faith moves mountains:

Righteousness is not turning your faces toward the east or west; righteousness is believing in God and the Last Day, in angels and the Book and the prophets. It lives in one who with love gives to his kindred and to orphans, and to the poor and the wayfarer, and to beggars and slaves; and who is faithful in prayer and gives alms; and keeps his given word; and is patient in poverty and suffering and time of war.

The umma

In Medina, where Muhammad and the Spirit that inspired him were faced with the task of constructing a new kind of community, Muhammad's kindly and humane nature may be read in the verses which propound rules of conduct in various areas of human life. Properly compiled and arranged, these instructions have formed the "constitution" or legal code of Muslim societies down to the present day, being interpreted inexhaustibly to feed legal, social, and ethical systems of which Muhammad would never have dreamed.

Many of the concrete laws of Islam bear the stamp of Muhammad's own direct experience. Certainly he must have remembered his own neglected youth when he made such fierce regulations to safeguard the rights of orphans. His regard for women is shown in the laws established to secure their inheritance and dowries.

He prohibited an ancient and inhuman system of divorce whereby a man might end a marriage by saying coldly to his wife, "Be thou to me as my mother's back." He prescribed ethical standards for the treatment of slaves, whom he listed, along with parents and kinsmen, as people to whom kindness must be shown. And he made the buying of freedom for slaves an act of prime virtue. He encouraged abstinence from wine, it is said, because he was tired of seeing Muslims attempting to perform their prostrations while drunk. He hated gambling because this corrupting custom had taken hard hold of the Quraysh, and for the same reason he detested usury. One of the hurts that was dealt him in his relations with the Jews was when he found that, while forbidding usury among themselves, they had no objection to lending money at interest to Muslims. Christians, who also had a prohibition against usury, employed the Jews as moneylenders for this same reason.

His own view was that people ought to be delighted to lend money to one another, and repayment should be at the convenience of the borrower, who was morally responsible for it.

He kept many of the Jewish dietary laws but modified them. His opinion was that the stringent Jewish rules were really a visitation on them by God for their multitude of sins.

The following typical revelations, on these and other subjects, only skim across the surface of the thought that built Islam.

Give freely to your wives their marriage portions; and if they return some of it to you of their own accord, then enjoy it with good appetite. Still, do not leave fools in charge of their property over which God has placed you a guardian. Feed them with it, clothe them with it, give them reasonable explanation about it.

Form good relations with your wives; for if you remain a stranger, perhaps you are a stranger from one in whom God has placed great good.

If a break is at hand between husband and wife, let judges be appointed, one chosen by his family, another by hers. If they really want to agree, God will help them.

When you divorce a wife, either keep her with generosity or put her away with generosity; but keep her not by force.

Men ought to have a part of what their parents and kindred leave, and women a part of what their parents and kindred leave. Whether it be little or much, let them have a stated portion.

Truly those who swallow the substance of orphans shall swallow down fire into their bellies and shall burn in flame.

Give to orphans their property, and substitute not your worthless possessions for their valuable ones, and devour not their property after adding it to your own: for this is a great crime.

Be kind to your parents when they are old and say not Fie! to them or grumble, but speak generously. Lower to them the wing of humility, and compassionately pray, "O my Lord! Have compassion on them, for they cared for me when I was little!"

If you must leave home to earn your living, leave home kindly.

Slay not your children, fearing poverty. God will provide. Beware! The slaying of children is a great sin!

Waste not wastefully, for the wasteful are Satan's own brothers, and Satan is never grateful to his Lord.

Believers! Come not to prayer when you are drunk. Wait until you can understand what you utter!

They will question you about wine and gambling. Say: in both there is sin and advantage; but the sin is greater than the advantage.

Satan sows hatred and strife among you by means of wine and games of chance, and turns you aside from remembrance of God and prayer. So why don't you stop it?

Whoever is forced by hunger, against his will, to eat of forbidden food, to him, verily, God is forgiving and merciful.

And do not say with false tongue: "This is lawful and this is forbidden," falsifying God's word. Verily, those who falsify God's word may enjoy themselves for a minute or two, but then in the end—Oh, grievous woe!

If anyone has trouble repaying a loan, grant a delay until it be easier for him. Still, it would be better if you gave the loan as a gift—if only you knew it.

Whatever you lend with the purpose of increasing it with the substance of others shall have no increase from God. But whatever you give in alms shall be doubled to you.

Obey God, obey the Apostle, and take care: if you fail, remember! The Apostle is here only to deliver a plain warning.

Such were the sayings that were heard by the tribesmen who came to hear Muhammad during the Year of Deputations. Their humanity and workability were appreciated as a basis for practical existence, and however hard it was to love his views on prostrations and taxes, no one could deny that the King of the Hejaz was a patriarch of the old school, with sufficient sound common sense.

There is an area of man's understanding, however, as invisible and intangible as divinity itself, that is less grateful for law than for inspiration. Islam's strength remains with the words that stood behind the aphorisms, the kind of words that came into Muhammad's mind from nowhere when he was a middle-aged, untaught tribesman standing in the fairgrounds near Mecca with his head turned against the jeers and flung sand:

Praise God in the morning, praise Him in the evening;

To Him belong praises in heaven and earth, night and noon.

He brings forth the living from the dead, the dead from the living;

As the earth dies and is quickened, so shall you be brought forth from death.

And among His signs is this: that He created you from dust, that He made you mortal and spread you abroad;

172

And among His signs is this: that He made you wives and set between you love and compassion—think of it! Do you not think this is a sign?

And among His signs is this: that He made light and the world, different languages, different colors;

And a sign is this: that you sleep whether by night or by day; that you crave His grace. Listen! Don't you hear a sign in this?

And a sign is this: He sends you lightning, striking fear in you and hope; He sends you water, bringing to life the dead ground. Surely such signs are seen by anyone with sense!

And a sign is this: that heaven and earth stand only by His will!

For His are the creatures of the world,

To Him all are drawn,

He brings into being,

He wipes away,

It is all easy to Him.

Whatever in heaven or earth is highest, it is only His likeness.

God is mighty, wise.

When the hour of victory is come with God's help, and you see men entering God's religion by swarms, then celebrate His praise; and let the sinner ask forgiveness. Verily, He is forgiving to the repentant.

-THE CHAPTER OF HELP

23

Muhammad and His Flock

He was a great man in Arabia before his life drew to a close, and powerful sheikhs learned to treat him gingerly and lower their voices before him. Some clever fellows started to imitate him, and a rash of inspired prophets sprang up in various parts of the peninsula, some of them women. One such person, Musaylima, acquired a fine following and tried to establish rapport with Muhammad through a letter which commenced, "Musaylima, Messenger of God, to Muhammad, Messenger of God . . ."

Muhammad responded, "Muhammad, Messenger of God, to Musaylima the Liar . . ."

An aura of goodness and holiness surrounded him. People collected his loose hairs and nail clippings and brought their wounds for him to spit upon. They were beginning to remember stories about him, which they would relate forever and which eventually were recorded by the traditionists, together with the names of all the people who had passed the story down.

He was as loved and honored among his innermost circle as among those who only venerated him from the crowd. He was a hero to his servant Anas, who said, "I have served the Prophet for ten years and he has never said 'Uff!' to me for anything I did or failed to do." His friends and close relatives never failed him from beginning to end of his struggle. His wives rewarded his kindness with their affection, especially as they acquired enormous respect among the community, even if their feet did not jangle with wealth when they walked. They were entitled "Mothers of the Faithful," and it was understood by themselves and everyone that they would not remarry when the Prophet died. Some of them became memorable in history for the recollections they passed down or the gossip they disseminated to their relatives and friends, and in the case of Ayesha, for the intrigues she became involved in.

Abdullah ibn Ubayy was won over. The Hypocrite leader who had been such a thorn in Muhammad's side, a magnet for every backslider, malcontent, and misbeliever in Medina, seems to have been himself a person of sense and charm. Once he had insulted Muhammad profoundly when the Prophet had called on him at his home to recite the Quran, hoping to induce him to become an honest Muslim. Ibn Ubayy had let him speak, heard him to the last word. Then he had calmly suggested that Muhammad confine his preaching to his own mosque and not force it on people who were not interested in hearing it.

In 631, the year of Muhammad's triumph, Ibn Ubayy lay dying, and he sent to the Prophet requesting the Quran to be read at his funeral. There was a great fuss among Muhammad's following about this, but Muhammad went off to pray for Ibn Ubayy without any fuss at all.

So numerous are the anecdotes passed down to us about incidents in the Prophet's life that, though they delight a biographer, they are his sorrow too. Whatever traditional account he might select to sketch out the living shape of the man, there are ten others that might have done better.

Yet one point more should be noted. If the Prophet's greatness is told, his jealousy for God, his courage, cruelties, and sufferings, his tenderness, benevolence, shrewdness, and statesmanlike shiftiness, then his sheer magic should have a place. Perhaps we might call it showmanship today, although there was nothing fraudulent about it. He just knew how to put a lesson across.

It was the year after Hunayn, 630. Perhaps the deaths of Zayd and Jafar the year before still pricked him with a need for revenge against the Byzantine Syrians, for in September he resolved to move northward again even over the protests of all but the most loyal companions. It was the season of oppressive heat, when men and fruit prefer to hang in clusters in the shade. But the Prophet said he had sure word that a force of Byzantines were mustering on the northern borders ready to invade Arabia.

Across the fierce landscape Muhammad prepared to move men and beasts, and though his authority was such that men pulled themselves together for his sake and joined him, still there were malingerers in the flock who thought up original excuses. One of them said, "Everyone knows I am strongly addicted to women, and I am afraid that if I see a Byzantine woman I shall not be able to control myself."

Others pointed sensibly to the heat. God said to Muhammad, "Tell them hell's fire is hotter."

The accounts of this expedition to Tabuk in Syria, though fascinating in themselves, leave a puzzle in the mind. We still do not know what impelled Muhammad to move northward, for he met no Byzantines. Khalid ibn al-Walid managed to flush out two Christian princes out hunting. He killed one and brought the other back to camp. This young man was wearing a robe so rich that it made the Medinans exclaim in wonder, but Muhammad told them coolly that heroes in Paradise used far richer stuff for handkerchiefs.

He let the prince go for ransom and brought his weary troops back to Medina. Now excuses, apologies, and regrets began to sprout like weeds in the guilty minds of the faithful who should have gone but had stayed behind. Muhammad forgave them all without reserve.

However, there was another sort of person that presented a different problem. Certain gentlemen of Medina had pretended to follow the army to Tabuk but had not, in fact, gone. There were three of them, and one was Ka'b ibn Malik, who went blind in his old age and told the story to his son who led him about, and so it came to the ears of the grandfather of the man who wrote it down. But it shines like new in the remembered words of the sinner, who begins by assuring us that he was not a coward and had not held back from any previous raid, beginning with Badr.

"But the fact was that when I stayed behind from Tabuk, I had never been more prosperous. Never before had I possessed two camels."

Ordinarily, he tells us, in preparing for a raid, the Prophet was extremely secretive, never telling anyone the exact details for fear of informing the enemy. But in the matter of Tabuk he had been entirely honest.

He planned the raid in violent heat and faced a long journey against a mighty enemy, and he told men exactly what was in store for them so that they could make provision. He even told what direction he intended to take. He did not enroll those who followed him in a written book, therefore it was possible for a few who wanted to stay behind to do so without being found out—that is, unless God sent down a revelation about it.

So the Apostle made ready, and so did the Muslims, and so did I, although I didn't really: I kept telling myself I had plenty of time. But there came a day when the men had gone off with the Apostle and I had done nothing at all. I thought I might catch up with them later, but day after day passed, the expedition had gone far ahead, and though I still thought of overtaking them—and I wish I had done—I did not. Then it was too late. I felt rotten going about town and seeing only Hypocrites or men who had made excuses, because of their helpless women.

Meanwhile Muhammad at Tabuk was inspired one day to look about him and

176

say, "Where is Ka'b ibn Malik? Did he not come with us?" His companions said sarcastically that Ka'b's love of fine clothes and his own image in the looking glass had kept him at home. A better friend said quickly that no one knew anything but good of Ka'b. The Prophet said nothing at all.

"When I heard that the Prophet was on his way back from Tabuk, I was filled with remorse and began to wonder what I could tell and who would support me in it. But as he came nearer, lies flew out of my head. I knew I should have to tell him the truth."

Ka'b went to the mosque the morning Muhammad arrived. After prayers Muhammad sat down to await those who wished to speak to him. Those who had stayed behind, about eighty of them, came with their excuses, for all of whom Muhammad asked divine forgiveness. Last came Ka'b, and Muhammad smiled at him a terrible smile. Ka'b saw at once the pillar of anger he was facing. He said:

O Prophet of God, if I faced anyone but you, I should know how to talk myself out of this because I am clever at talking. But I know that if I tell you a lie now, you may accept it, yet later on God will stir your mind against me. If, on the other hand, I tell you the truth, it will increase your anger, but God may reward me in the end. So I shall tell you: I have no excuse. I was prospering; and that is why I stayed behind.

Muhammad said, "Very well, you have told the truth. Get up until God decides about you."

Ka'b got up, and some of his friends followed him saying, "For goodness' sake, why didn't you make an excuse? The Apostle would have asked pardon for your sin, and that would have been the end of it." Ka'b asked if there were others in the same boat and he learned that two others, honest men of good character, were also confessed pretenders, and had gotten the same response.

Soon the Apostle gave forth judgment. He said that no one was to speak to any of these three men for fifty nights. Fifty nights—about two months. Ka'b found in one second that he had no acquaintances. No one spoke to him at all. "I hated myself," he said, "and the whole world changed for me."

Fifty days and fifty nights: my two companions were so humiliated that they kept to their houses, but I was younger and more defiant and so I used to go out in the town, attend prayers and walk around in the market-place. No one spoke to me. I would go to the Apostle and greet him as he sat after prayers, asking myself if his lips had moved at all. I would try to pray near him, stealing a look. When I performed my prayer, he would look; but when I turned to him, he would turn away.

He lived in a tight agony of silence, crushed with it. God Himself described Ka'b's ordeal in a Quran: "The earth with all its space was too small to hold him,

177

his very soul too narrow for him." Ka'b turned to his best friend, whom he saw walking in his orchard one day, and he climbed over the wall.

I saluted him, and by God he did not return my salaam. I said, "O Abu Qatada, do you not know how I love God and His Apostle?" He answered me not one word. Again I spoke to him and he was silent. Then he said, "God and His Apostle know best!" My eyes filled with tears, I ran back and climbed back over the wall.

Weeks passed in this dismal plight, and a letter came for Ka'b. It was brought from Syria from a chieftain of Bosra, and it read, "We hear that your master is treating you badly. Come to us, we will provide for you."

Ka'b put the letter in the oven. As a matter of fact, he thought it might be a trick.

After forty nights had passed, a message came from the Prophet. Ka'b was to separate from his wife. He went to ask if he was to divorce her. The Prophet let him know that he had not meant that, only that he was not to approach her, and the other condemned men had the same orders. The wife of one of the defectors came to beg the Apostle to let her serve her husband, since he was lost without her in all practical matters such as taking care of himself. She was therefore allowed to remain on condition that their relations remained distant.

Fifty nights passed. Ka'b rose with the muezzin and prayed atop a house at dawn. Then he heard the voice of a crier shouting, "Good news, Ka'b ibn Malik!"

Ka'b fell prostrate on the ground. Then he got up and tore off his clothes to give to the crier as a reward. Then he rushed about in a frenzy, looking for someone who would lend him some clothes. Then, finally, he ran in the direction of the mosque. On his way he met a group of friends come to tell him that Muhammad had announced God's forgiveness at the morning prayers, and in a body they bore him off to see Muhammad.

"When I greeted him, his face shone with joy. He said, 'This is the best day of your life! Good news to you.'"

"From you or from God?" asked Ka'b.

"From God of course!" replied Muhammad.

I told him that as an act of penitence I would give away my property as alms. He told me that I should keep some of it. I said I would keep only my share in the Khaybar booty. I said, "God has saved me through truthfulness, and as part of my penance I shall never speak anything but the truth as long as I live."

And by God [concluded Ka'b when he was an old blind man], I do not know any man whom God favoured more than the Prophet favored me after I told him that. From that day to this, I have never even thought of lying, and I hope God will preserve me from doing so in the time that remains to me.

Another thing Ka'b told us about the living Prophet was this: "When he gave us good news, his face used to shine like the moon. We always could recognize it."

Muhammad was a man God had cracked so that His love might shine through on the world; and people recognized the reflected light.

Muhammad is only an apostle. Apostles have come and gone before him. If he had been killed on the battlefield, would you have turned on your heels? He who turns back on his heels does not harm God at all—but God rewards those who bow to His will.

-THE CHAPTER OF IMRAN'S FAMILY

24

The Death of Muhammad

In March of 632, Muhammad led the greater pilgrimage to Mecca, the hajj. It was the first year that no idolator was present at the shrine. Whatever Muhammad did on that pilgrimage, the rites he performed, the walks he took, became the prescribed ritual for ages to come, and it so happened that he visited once and forever the places that had marked milestones in his life since the Call. It must have been a grand triumph for him: forty thousand men tramping after him and his nine wives in their howdahs; and the Emigrants, the steadfast friends who had shared his years; and Helpers galore; and Hypocrites come round; and converted enemies; and al-Kaswa, the inspired camel.

With everyone watching his every action carefully, committing it to memory, he led them in devotions that would never again be seen by a non-Muslim until Sir Richard Burton, disguised as an Arab, melted into the worshiping crowd in 1853. When all was done, the circumambulations and prayers and some harmless ceremonies like shaving and pebble throwing, which Muhammad allowed to remain from the pagan days, he mounted al-Kaswa and, gathering all his folk together in the valley of Mina, addressed them.

"O men, listen! I do not know that I shall ever meet you again after this year. So this is what I have taught.

"Your lives and your property are your own, to do as you like with until the day you meet God. But He will demand of you an account of what you have done. "You who have pledged your word, return the pledge to him who trusted you. "Usury is abolished. Wrong not, and you shall not be wronged. I am talking about all usury, including that practiced by my uncle Abbas ibn Abd-el-Muttalib. That is abolished too.

"Whatever blood has been shed during the years of idolatry shall be left unavenged.

"You have rights over your wives, and they have rights over you . . . Beat them, but not with severity. Lay injunctions on women kindly, for they are prisoners with you, having no control over their persons. You have them only as a trust from God."

He said much more than this. Men who stood under al-Kaswa so that the foam from her mouth fell on them remembered the scraps and pieces of the last message he gave his followers, enjoining on them the humane treatment of their slaves, their heirs and dependents.

"I have left you," he said, "something which, if you will hold fast to it, will guide you so that you will never fall into error: a plain instruction, the Book of God . . .

"Know that every Muslim is a Muslim's brother, and that Muslims are brethren. It is only lawful to take from a brother what he gives you willingly, so wrong not yourselves.

"O God! Have I not taught you this?"

Soon after the farewell pilgrimage, with his ambition speeding ever northward as if in advance of destiny, Muhammad organized a new expeditionary force to Syria, putting Zayd's son Usama in charge of it—against the advice of some of his generals, since Usama was only twenty. Muhammad told them sharply, "You carp at him as you carped at his father, but he is just as worthy of command as his father was."

He no longer needed to waste time excusing his actions. He placed his standard in Usama's hands and sent him off to the mustering ground, but the argument rankled in his mind all the same.

Usama pitched camp a stage outside Medina and waited for his army to muster. While he was doing this, on an evening in A.H. 11—our year 632—Muhammad went to the cemetery of Medina attended by his freedman Abu Muwayhiba, telling the man that God had commanded him to pray here for the dead through the night. For a while the Prophet meditated. Then he addressed the dead: "Peace be on you, O people of the graves! You are better off by far than we are, for quarrels besiege us like a host of shadows, one blacker than the last!"

He beseeched God's mercy and forgiveness for the dead. Perhaps the holy

181

Voice responded, for afterward he said to the freedman, "I have been given a choice: to live long and enjoy the treasures of the earth before meeting my Lord in Paradise; or to meet Him there at once."

Abu Muwayhiba said, "Choose to stay with us!" But Muhammad said, "I have chosen the other."

He prayed the night through and returned to his home, entering the hut of Ayesha, who had a headache, and upon seeing him she screwed up her face and said, "Oh, my head!"

"No, Ayesha," said the Prophet, "it is oh, my head!" He sat down heavily, his head pounding, pain squeezing his vitals. Presently he said, "Does it distress you to think of yourself dying before me, so that I should have to wrap you in a shroud and bury you?"

He was looking deathly ill, but Ayesha, who believed that he had by no means come to the end of his course of diplomatic marriages, gave him a sour reply: "No. Because I can also think of you coming straight back from the cemetery to spend a bridal night."

The Prophet smiled and soon took his leave. He began to visit in turn the separate apartments of his wives, greeting them for the day. In the hut of Maymuna, his pain overwhelmed him, and he collapsed. He called his wives around him and asked their permission to be nursed in Ayesha's house. They agreed. He lay on Ayesha's mat in a burning fever, and they took turns tending him.

His illness worsened, but he tried valiantly to throw it off for Usama's sake, for as word of Muhammad's sickness spread about, the young man was having a hard time recruiting his troops. Some men who had joined him were returning to Medina, and certainly none were leaving the city. The mosque enclosure was thronging with anxious followers, and Muhammad said to his wives, "Pour seven skins of water over me. I'll go out and speak to them."

Hafsa was the owner of a large tub in which the Prophet sat while the women poured cool water over him until he cried, "Enough, enough!" They wrapped his head in cloth and drenched it, and he went to sit in the pulpit. Without preamble he began to pray for the men who had died fighting him at Uhud, asking God's forgiveness that they had not embraced Islam in time. He then addressed his old comrades the Emigrants who, now that the whole world was wanting Islam, tended to form a sort of aristocracy, drawing a sharp distinction between themselves and tardier Muslims. Muhammad refreshed their memories of the debt they owed to the Helpers, and admonished them, "It is in the nature of things, that while all Islam increases, the Helpers can only grow less. They have been my constant comfort and support. Treat their good men well, and forgive those who are remiss."

He sat down. He was exhausted and said to Abu Bekr sitting next to him, "God has given one of His servants a choice between this world and the one that is with God, and he has chosen the latter."

Abu Bekr began to weep. "Gently, gently," the Prophet soothed him. He turned to those near him, "Go and shut all the doors opening onto the ground of this mosque except the door of Abu Bekr. For he is my friend, the best of all friends to me."

His illness overcame him then, and with feet dragging he was assisted back to Ayesha's hut by Ali and another man. His wives, uncles, and other relatives, his friends, and his friends' wives came pressing about with worried advice, none knowing the cause of the ailment any better than we know it today. It might have been pneumonia caught from praying in the cemetery. Or dysentery. Or poison. Someone started the unlikely but persistent theory that it was all the fault of the Jewess Zaynab who, four years before in Khaybar, had administered the deadly dose. A severe cold, turning to pneumonia, was believed to be the most plausible notion, then and now. Some of the women procured from Abyssinian medicine men a potion said to benefit the lungs, but how to persuade him to take it was a problem. "Give it to me," said Abbas, "I'll force it down him."

"No, we'll do it," said the women, and they did. For a while Muhammad seemed restored, but he was annoyed that he had been given medicine. "Who did this to me?" he asked.

Uncle Abbas tried to justify the deed by waving in the general direction of Africa. "This medicine came all the way from Abyssinia," he said.

"What made you do this to me?" persisted the Prophet.

"We were afraid you would get pleurisy," said Abbas.

"Pleurisy comes from the devil," said Muhammad. "God would never afflict me with it." He was so incensed that he commanded all the women, if they wanted to stay in the sickroom, to take a dose of the same medicine. He let off his Uncle Abbas.

Yet God had mortally afflicted him. He suffered through the night, and in the morning when the voice of Bilal was heard announcing to the faithful that prayer was better than sleep, he knew he had not the strength to preside over the morning worship. He told one of his companions to find someone else to lead the prayers. The man went out looking for Abu Bekr, but he was not to be seen. Of the close companions, only Umar was present in the mosque, and he, on being asked, rose and pronounced the first lines of the Quran in a voice of such boom that the building reverberated, and the sick man exclaimed, "May God and Islam forbid it!"

He then bade Ayesha find her father and tell him to lead the prayers. That sharp young woman, and expert politician, knowing that whatever Abu Bekr did would displease a nervous congregation that had come to hear Muhammad healed and vigorous as usual, said, "You know how my father is. He always begins to cry when he reads the Quran."

183

The Prophet said, "Tell him."

Ayesha said, "He is a delicate man, and his voice is weak."

The Prophet said, "You are worse than Joseph's brothers. Tell him."

Abu Bekr was found. He led the prayers in a quavering voice and wept. Muhammad forced himself to arise and stand outside Ayesha's door where the faithful, seeing him, turned to him with such immense relief that they might have been seduced by joy from their salat, but Muhammad motioned to them with his hand, and they turned back to God. He stood there watching them intently, and as he did the expression on his face became exalted, as if with supernal happiness, and someone observing him said afterward that he had never seen such a noble expression on his face. So profoundly was he transfigured that all signs of his illness were dispelled, and worshipers were convinced he was recovered. Especially since, after the prayers, he advanced a little and spoke to them in a firm voice, "O men, there are fires about, rebellions flare up with somber flame. By God, don't hold them to my account. I have allowed to you what the Quran allows, and I have forbidden to you what the Quran forbids."

Thus he turned back their minds to his testament, his bequest to them, their Book. They departed quietly and hopefully. Abu Bekr got his spirits back and asked permission to go and visit one of his wives, who lived on the edge of town and was having a party. Ali helped Muhammad back to Ayesha's house. Afterward he met Abbas and told him that Muhammad was getting well.

"Ali," said that astute uncle, "I saw death on his face, I swear by God."

The sun blazed up into the morning sky, and Usama came in from his camping ground and watched heavyhearted as Muhammad raised his hand only enough to bless him. He lingered through the morning, lying on a succession of wifely breasts until Ayesha's turn came round again. A man came to visit, holding a new toothpick. Muhammad looked at it so longingly that Ayesha took it and, after chewing it a little so soften the point, put it in his hand. With sudden vigor, Muhammad cleaned his teeth. She had never seen him rub so clean before. Then he dropped the bit of wood, and she felt him heavy against her and saw that his eyes were fixed away from the sights of the world. He said, "Nay, the Exalted Companion of Paradise!"

Ayesha looked at the other wives and said, "Well, he has made his choice, and he hasn't chosen us."

The news of Muhammad's death was brought to Umar outside in the mosque as he was doing his best to preside quietly over the assembly. He slitted his eyes fiercely and, with his voice subdued for once in deadly menace, spoke to his congregation: "There may be some Hypocrites here who will try to tell you that the Prophet is dead, but, by God, he is not dead. He is merely paying a visit to his Lord, just as Moses did once on the mountain, when for forty days he was hidden

184

from his folk and they thought he was dead. But, by God, he was not, and the Prophet is not dead, and he will come back here and cut off the hands and feet of people who say that he is."

In a paralysis of the mind he reiterated such statements, refusing to believe that the Apostle was gone or to hear the laments of the women. In time Abu Bekr was retrieved from the suburbs, and he entered his daughter's house. He lightly lifted the fine Yemeni cloth that covered his friend's face and kissed it, saying, "You are dearer to me than father and mother. Now, by God's will, you have tasted the bitterness of death, but you will never have to taste it more than once."

He covered the Prophet's face again and went out into the mosque where Umar was babbling. He said, "Be still, Umar," but Umar did not heed him. So Abu Bekr went a little apart and raised his thin, cracking voice until some of the faithful turned to hear him. He said, "O men, if anyone has come here to worship Muhammad, Muhammad is dead. If anyone is here to worship God, God is alive and immortal."

Umar had fallen silent as Abu Bekr raised his voice. Now his legs gave way, and the huge man crashed to the ground.

Abu Bekr was elected successor, or caliph. As the political leader of Islam, it fell to him to deal with the first struggles as the quarrels and disaffections that had so troubled Muhammad came to the surface, especially the objections of the tribes to the poor tax. Wisely he seized swift opportunity to siphon off the energies of Arabia by sending an army northward into Palestine and Syria.

The victories came with incredible ease, the mightiest empires crumbling, magnificent thrones toppling against the onslaught of the desert raiders. Within five years the Byzantines had been smashed. Syria was occupied. The Persian army was defeated. By 642, Egypt was brought under Islam.

Ali became caliph in 656 and was obliged to engage in civil war until his assassination in 661 brought victory to his opponents, the descendants of Abu Sufyan, the Umayyads. The great schism in the Muslim world, which remains to this day between the Shia and Sunni sects, stems from these early struggles for power. The Shia believe that Ali's descendants should have been recognized as Muhammad's successors, while the Sunni recognize the legitimacy of the Umayyad succession.

Under this dynasty, Islam spread still farther, laying the groundwork of the earth-girdling civilization that might well have overwhelmed Christian Europe and made Muslims of most of us had not their hordes of heroes met defeat on a battleground between Tours and Poitiers in France. This was 732, just a hundred years after Muhammad's death. Not long afterward, the descendants of Uncle Abbas, known as the Abbasids, succeeded in overthrowing the Umayyads and presided over the luminous explosion of art and profundity of learning and philosophy that characterized Islam at its height.

At the heart of all of it was the genius and endurance of this Quraysh

185

tribesman, Muhammad ben Abdullah ibn al-Muttalib. He was buried as he had wished, like a soldier in battle, in the exact spot where God chose to strike him down—wrapped in Yemeni cloth under the mud floor of Ayesha's wattle-and-daub dwelling.

And there he remains, except that now it is an edifice of splendor.

Appendix

Muhammad's Wives

	Approximate Year of Marriage	Age of Wife
Khadija	595	40
Sawda	620	30(?)
Ayesha	623	9
Hafsa	625	18
Umm Salama	626	29
Zaynab	626	30
Juwayriya	627	20
Zaynab bint Jarsh	627	38
Rayhana (Jewish concubine)	627	?
Maryam the Copt (Christian concubine)	628	?
Umm Habiba	628	35
Safiyya	628	17
Maymuna	629	

Bibliography

Anyone who attempts to re-create the scenes and atmospheres of times gone by, and bring to life men, women, and inspired camels who are long dead, is indebted beyond words to the scholars whose work has made sound and well-considered facts available. My account of Muhammad's life is based mainly on W. Montgomery Watt's *Muhammad at Mecca* and *Muhammad at Medina*, and on John Bagot Glubb's biography of the Prophet. Direct speech is mostly paraphrased—that is, abridged and simplified—from Guillaume's translation of traditionist Ibn Ishaq, except the direct speech of God, which is paraphrased, as little as possible, from Palmer's translation of the Quran. The additional works listed have also been instructive to me.

Ali, Maulana Muhammad, The Holy Quran. Lahore, 1920.

Ali, Syed Ameer, The Spirit of Islam: A History of the Evolution and Ideals of Islam. London, Christopher's, 1955.

Arberry, A. J., The Holy Koran. London, 1953.

Chambers' Encyclopaedia

Glubb, John Bagot (Glubb Pasha), The Life and Times of Muhammad. New York, Stein & Day, 1970.

Guillaume, Alfred, Life of Muhammad, a translation of Ibn Ishaq's Sirat Rasul Allah. Pakistan Branch, Oxford University Press, 1955.

Merchant, Muhammad Valibhai, A Book of Quranic Laws. Lahore, 1947.

Palmer, E. H., trans., The Koran. Oxford University Press, 1900.

Watt, W. Montgomery, Muhammad: Prophet and Statesman. Oxford, Oxford University Press, 1956.

—, Muhammad at Mecca.

—, Muhammad at Medina.

INDEX

A

Abbas, conversation of, 142, And
Abbasids, 144, 185
Abbasid, see Abbas
Abd-el-Muttalib, 6, 10
Abd ulla, death of, 138; prayers of,
44
Abdullah, father of Muhammad, 8
Abdullah ibn Ubayy, as consiliator,
65; death of, 175
Ablutions, ritual, 29
Abraham, Beith Allah and, 5;
Muslim vision of, 4,
Abu Bekr, conversion of, 30;
defense by, 47; as successor, 185
Abu Talib, 31, 40; death of, 52; as
Muhammad's gaurdian, 10;
Abu Jahl, problem of, 34, 46
Abu Jandal, conversion of, 129
Abu Lahat, hostility of, 33, 46, 53
Abu Sufayan of Abd Sams, enmity
of, 34, 95, 116; and Medina raid,
93; raid on caravan of, 84;
reconciliation with, 143
Abyssinia, emigration to, 45
Alcohol, prohibition of, 50
Ali, adoption of, 16, as caliph, 185;
conversion of, 33;marriage of, 70
al-Kaswa, Muhammad's camel, 58,
63
Allah Akbar slogan, 98
al-Lat, destruction of, 160
Alms, legal, 167; custom of, 73
Al Walid, Kaaba and, 18
Al-Zubayr, Kaaba poetry of, 19

Ambitions, Muhammad's, 41
Amina, death, 10;Muhammad's
mother, 8;
Anecdotes about Muhammad, 175
An-Nadir Jews, banishment of,
105; plot of, 104
Ansar, Medianian "Helpers", 64
Appearance, Muhammad's, 17
Aquaba, Pledge of, 55
Arabia, background in, viii;
prohibition of two religions in,
135
Assassination plot, 57
Arabic language, evolution of, 8
Arabs as People of the Book, 142
Ayesha, betrothal to, 54;
description of Muhammad by,
72; escape of, 112; marriage to,
70

B

Backsliding by Muhammad, 41
Badr, Battle of, 81
Battle, of badr, 81; of the ditch,
116; of Hunaya, 153;of muta,
138; of Uhud, 95
Battle corpses, mutilation of, 98
Battles, decisive series of, 81
Bedouins, conflicts with, 124;
forced conversion of, 161; at
Khaybar, 132;Muhammed and,
127, 130; revolt of, 153;wet
nurses, 9
Beit Allah, idol removal from, 147.
See also Kabba.

Bekka, see Mecca.
Bells, revelations through ringing
    of, 72
Bible, knowledge of, 11
Bilal as first muezzin, 74
Birth, 8
Black Stone, 6; Kaaba placement
    of, 18; Muhammad and, 19
Blood price, 36
Bloodshed, Muhammad's path of,
    93
Book, Quran as Muslim, 184
Booty, distribution of, 84, 158, See
    also Spoils.
Boycott of Hashim, 37
"Brothers in God," 73
Buraq, night trip on, 50
Business activities, Muhammad's,
    14, 57; clubs Meccan; Quaraysh
    and, 125

C
Calendar, Muslim, 59
Caliph, Abu Bekr as, 185
Call to prayer, 74
Calls, 25, 31. See also Dreams,
    Messages, Revelations, Vision.
Caravans, in Mecca, 6; raids, 82.
    See also Battles.
Cave retreat on Hira, 23
Chapter of the Cow, 170; of the
    Crow, 163; of Women, 111
Charity, Muhammad's, 15; See also
    Alms.
Childhood, 10
Children, affection for, 71, 108;
    Muhammad's, 16
Christianity, Arab conversions to,
    21
Christians, Muhammad and, 79
Clans, hostility of, 33, 53
Code, of conduct, 73; social, 171

Concubines, disapproval of, 107
Confession of Faith, 163
Constitution of Medina, 63, 67
Converts, early, 29; from Mecca,
    136
Conversion, of Bedouins, forced,
    161; parental consent for, 129;
    tribal, 54
Cruelty, Muhammad's, 89, 123, 146

D
Day of Assembly, Friday as, 166
Day of Atonement, observance of,
    68
Death, Muhammad's, 180, 182,
    184
Deputations, Year of, 166, 172
Dhu'l-Hijja, obligation of, 169
Dietary laws, relaxation of Jewish,
    79
Diplomacy in Arabia,
    Muhammad's, 136
Disputations with Jews, religious,
    76
Divorce, edict on, 171
Donkey meat, prohibition on
    eating, 134
Dreams, 23. See also, Call,
    Messages, Revelations, Visions.

E
Emigrants, relationship with, 158
Emigration to Abyssina, 45, 52
Epilepsy, Muhammad's possible,
    26. See also, Fits.
Executions in Mecca, 146

F
Fatima, marriage to Ali of, 70
Face veiling for women, 111, 148
Fast, Sawn, 168

Feminine characteristics, Muhammad's, 108
Fighting policy, adoption of, 81
Finances, problems of, 52
Fits, theory of Muhammad's 9. See also Epilepsy.

G
Gabriel, revelations by, 25, 72
Gambling, prohibition on, 171
Ghatafan Bedouin and Quraysh, 116
God, continuing instruction by, 103; Jews and, 76; Muhammad and, 20, 29, 39, 41; names of, 49
Grandsons, Muhammad's, 71
Great Pilgrimage, 54. See also Hajj.

H
Habits, Muhammad's personal, 71
Hafas, marriage to, 91
Hajia. See also Emigration.
Hajj, rituals of, 161, 180
Halima, wet nurse, 10
Hamza, conversion of, 48
Hanif, definition of, 78
Harem, enjoyment of, 107
Hasan, grandson, 71
Hashim clan, 6, 33, 43
Hassan ben Thabit, poet, 98
Hatred of opponents, Muhammad's, 38
Hawazin, enmity of, 154
Heaven, vision of, 50
Hell, vision of, 50
Helpers, relationship with, 158
Hind, personality of, 95, 148
Holy war. See also Jihad.
Home in Medina, Muhammad's, 69
Houris in Paradise, promise of, 35
House of Arqam as Islam meeting place, 10

Household, enlargement of, 108
Hubal, 6, 17
Humayn, Battle of, 153
Humor, Muhammad's sense of, 71
Hussein, grandson of Muhammad, 71
Huyayy ben Aktab as Jewish leader, 118
Hypocrites, animosity of, 75, 92, 102

I
Ibn Ubayya, as warrior, 94, 96
Ibraham, Muhammad's son, 137, 159
Idolators, threats against, 16
Ishmael, youth of, 4; Beit Allah and, 5
Income tax, alms as, 167
Inspiration, from Muhammad, 172
Intelligence network, Muhammad's 95
Islam, as Abraham's religion, 78; invitation to join, 33; laws of, 170; Pillars of, 160; spread of, 185

J
Jerusalem, trip to, 49; as early spiritual center, 34; abandonment of centrality of, 80
Jesus, Muhammad on subject of, 77
Jewish, adoption of dietary laws of, 74; dietary laws revisions, 171; Sabbath, observance of, 68; Scriptures of, 77; tribes in Medina, 66. See also Jews, People of the Book.
Jews, Alienation from Muhammad of, vii, 75, 77, 92, 93, 96, 104; and Arabs, relationship of, 66; The Book and, 66; customs of

and Muhammad, 68;
Muhammad's need for, 75;
massacre of, 122, 124; and
Quran, 79. See also Jewish.
Jihad, waging, 117
Jafar, 46, 139
Judaism, Arab conversions to, 21

K

Ka'ab ibn Malik, punishment of,
177
Kaaba, as Mecca center, 30;
rebuilding, 14. See also Beit
Allah.
Ka'b, murder by Muslim of, 92
Kadija, death of, 52; marriage to,
14
Khalid ibn al-Walid, as ally, 99,
139, 153
Khaybar, Jews on oasis of, 124;
warfare against, 131, 133
Kinana ben al-Rabi, execution of,
134
Kinship laws of marriage, 110

L

Language, disdain for lewd, 85
Laws of Islam, 170
League of the Virtuous, 16
Legal code on slander, 115
Lex talionis. See Retaliation, law
of.

M

Male dominance in Arab culture
and Islam, 107
Malik, poet, 158
Marriage, kinship laws of, 110
Marriages of Muhammad,
diplomatic, 109; to Hafsa, 1; to
Khadija, 14; to Maynuma, 142;
to Sawda, 53; to Umm Habiba

137; to Zaynab bint Jursh, 109;
multiple, 106, Quran on multiple,
4
Maryam the Copt, 137
Mecca, executions in, 146; converts
from, 136; as caravan center, 6;
as niche of God, 80; pilgrimage
to, 125; raids on caravans of, 82;
return to, 125, 141
Meccans, hostility of, 47
Medina, clan conflict in, 65; clans
of, 65; emigration to, 55; living
problems in, 70; return to, 159;
welcome in, 63
Messages, multiple, 32. See also
Call, Dreams, Revelations,
Visions.
Messengers, diplomacy of, 137
Messiah, foretelling, 22
Migration, permission for, 57
Missionaries to nomads, 103
Mosque of Omar, 49; in Quba, first,
63
"Mothers of the Faithful," as
Muhammad's wives, 175
Mount Thor, refuge on, 58
Musaylima, as imitator of
Muhammad, 174

N

Nakhlam, raid at, 83
Negus, aid of the, 46
Night Journey, 49
Nomads, missionaries to, 103. See
also Bedouins.

P

Paradise, battle promise of, 150; for
Muslims, 35; sexual pleasures in,
107; vision on Night Journey, 50
Peace of Hudabiya, 141

People of the Book, Arabs as, 142;
Muhammad attraction to Jews as,
47; Muhammad overtures to, 137
Persecution of Muslims, 44, 45
Personality, Muhammad's, 72, 89,
123, 146; ruthlessness as part of,
ix, 92
Pilgrimage. See Hajj.
Pilgrams, abuse of, 16
Pillars of Islam, 160
Pledge, of Aquaba, 55; of Good
Pleasure, 128; Under the Tree,
128; of Women
Poet, Muhammad as, 48
Poetry, Arab lifestyle and, 7; of
Quran, 73, 91
Poll tax on non-Muslims, 167
Prayer, call to, 74; obligatory daily,
74; pleasure in, 108; ritual, 164;
saying, 44
Prisoners, treatment of, 88, 89, 90
Proclamations, final, 182
Prostrations, 29
Pulpit, for mosque, building, 136

Q
Quraysh, armistice with, 128;
attack on, 144; at Battle of Badr,
82; business of, 125; caravan
trade of, 82; enmity of, 46, 116,
118; in Mecca, 6; peace with,
147; practices of, 29; preaching
to, 37; Quran and, 124;
relationship with, 40
Qayla, Muslims in, 59
Qaynuqa, banishment of, 94
Quarash, Jews and, 17
Quba, first mosque in, 63
Qurayza, massacre of the, 116, 122
Quran, compilation of, 35, 162;
ethics in, 73; Jews in, 77, 79;
Muhammad's memory of total,

162; as Muslim "Book," 184;
poetry of, 73, 91; tons of, 73;
written record of, 162; on wives'
behavior, 111
Qurans. See Quran.

R
Rabbis, Muhammad and, 38, 76.
See also Jews.
Ramadan, fast of, 79; observance
of, 168
Ransom, of prisoners, 89
Rayhana as Jewish concubine, 122
Razzia. See Caravan raiding.
Religions in Arabia, prohibition
against any but Islam, 135
Retaliation, law of, 36
Revelations, 35, 72. See also Call,
Dreams, Messages, Visions.
Ruquaya, 34, 91
Ruthlessness, Muhammad's, 92

S
Sa'ad ben Mullah, as emissary to
Jews, 119, judgment on Jews by,
122
Safa, meeting at, 33
Safiyya, marriage to, 136
Safwan, Ayesha escapade with, 113
Salat, ritual prayer, 164
Sallam ibn Abu'l Huquaq,
execution of, 131
Salman, battle tactics of, 117
"Satan," appearance of, 56
Satanic verses, 41
Sawda, alienation from, 91;
marriage to, 53
Sawn, the fast, 168
Schism in Islam, Shia-Sunni, 185
Sexual standards, Muhammad's,
11, 197

INDEX

Shahadah, the Confession of Faith,
163
Shia, Sunni schism, 185
Showmanship, Muhammad's, 175
Slander in legal code, revelation on,
115
Slaves, buying freedom of, 171
Social codes, development of, 54;
revelations on, 171
Spider web, protection of, 58
Spoils, commandment on use of,
84; distribution of, 157. See also
Booty.
Stones, Arab worship of, 20
Suhayl ben Mar, as Quraysh
diplomat, 128
Sunni-Shia schism, 185
Suraqa, conversion of, 59
Syria, caravan to, 124; expedition
to, 176, 181
Syrians, hostility to Byzantine, 175

T
Tabuk, failure at, 176
Tahannuth, as religious exercise, 23
Taxes, alms use for, 167
Teachings of Muhammad, 151
Thaqif, enmity of, 53
Treaty of Hudaybiya, breaking of,
142

U
Ubayda, flag of Islam and, 82
Uhud, Battle of, 95; Muhammad at,
99
Umar, as early Muslim, 48
Umayyah caliphs, 144, 185
Umm Habiba, marriage to, 137
Umm Kyltham, betrothal of, 34
Umm Saloma, 109
Umma, creation of, 103; rules of
conduct and, 170

Usama, Syrian expedition on, 171
Usury, prohibition on, 171
Uthman, and Quraysh, 127

V
Vanity, Muhammad's, 41; views
on, 108
Verse of the Throne, 163
Virginity, ideas on, 107
Visions, onset of, 24. See also Call,
Dreams, Messages, Revelations.

W
Wahshi, actions of, 96
War policy, Muhammad's, 82
Wars, holy, vii
Waraqa, friendship of, 14
Well Zem-Zem, 6
Wives, Muhammad's, as "Mothers
of the Faithful," 175; Quarans
on, 111
Women, attitude toward, 107;
conversions of, 148; face veils
for, 111; rules for and about, 110
Worship of Muhammad, 174

Y
Yathrib, Muhammad and, 54, 55.
See also Medina.
Year of Deputations, 166, 172
Youth, attraction to Islam of, 30

Z
Zakat, legal alms, 166
Zayd ben Haritha, death of, 138; as
Muhammad's slave, 138;
Paradise promise to, 138
Zayhab bint, Jursh, loyalty of, 34;
marriage, 106, 109; problems of,
90

198